A Practitioner's Guide to Powers and Duties of Trustees

A Practitioner's Guide to Powers and Duties of Trustees

Stephen JG Lloyd
A Master of the Bench of the Middle Temple
Barrister

Jill Gibson BA (Bristol)
of Middle Temple and Lincoln's Inn, Barrister

Catherine Finely BA (Cantab)
of Middle Temple, Barrister

Nathan Wells BA (Oxon), LLM (Cantab)
of Lincoln's Inn, Barrister

Tolley
LexisNexis™

Members of the LexisNexis Group worldwide

United Kingdom	LexisNexis Butterworths Tolley, a Division of Reed Elsevier (UK) Ltd, Halsbury House, 35 Chancery Lane, LONDON, WC2A 1EL, and 4 Hill Street, EDINBURGH EH2 3JZ
Argentina	LexisNexis Argentina, BUENOS AIRES
Australia	LexisNexis Butterworths, CHATSWOOD, New South Wales
Austria	LexisNexis Verlag ARD Orac GmbH & Co KG, VIENNA
Canada	LexisNexis Butterworths, MARKHAM, Ontario
Chile	LexisNexis Chile Ltda, SANTIAGO DE CHILE
Czech Republic	Nakladatelství Orac sro, PRAGUE
France	Editions du Juris-Classeur SA, PARIS
Hong Kong	LexisNexis Butterworths, HONG KONG
Hungary	HVG-Orac, BUDAPEST
India	LexisNexis Butterworths, NEW DELHI
Ireland	Butterworths (Ireland) Ltd, DUBLIN
Italy	Giuffrè Editore, MILAN
Malaysia	Malayan Law Journal Sdn Bhd, KUALA LUMPUR
New Zealand	LexisNexis Butterworths, WELLINGTON
Poland	Wydawnictwo Prawnicze LexisNexis, WARSAW
Singapore	LexisNexis Butterworths, SINGAPORE
South Africa	LexisNexis Butterworths, DURBAN
Switzerland	Stämpfli Verlag AG, BERNE
USA	LexisNexis, DAYTON, Ohio

A CIP Catalogue record for this book is available from the British Library.

ISBN 0 75451 489 7

Typeset by Action Publishing Technology Ltd, Gloucester
Printed and Bound by Bookcraft, Midsomer Norton

Visit Butterworths LexisNexis *direct* at www.butterworths.com

Preface

As its title indicates, this book does not set out to be an exhaustive treatise on all aspects of trust law; rather, it concentrates on the day-to-day powers and duties of trustees to manage and, in due course, to distribute the trust funds under their control. The object has been to provide the trustee, whether lay or professional, with a clear statement of the principles to which he must have regard, and to enable the practitioner, called upon to advise a trustee or a beneficiary, to give informed advice. Trust law has over the years generated a substantial body of case law and, in citing authority, we have sought to select either the most recent cases or those that will best facilitate further research. Settled land will remain with us for many years to come, and where appropriate it is specifically dealt with in the text. Matters relevant to charities and pension funds are also noted.

My co-authors and I are grateful to those fellow members of 11 New Square who provided help and advice in the writing of the book. Responsibility for any shortcomings in thc text is, however, that of the authors alone.

We have endeavoured to state the law as at 1 September 2002.

SJGL
11, New Square,
Lincoln's Inn,
London WC2A 3QB

Contents

Table of Cases

Table of Statutes

Chapter 1

Duty to Act Unanimously

Introduction

1.1 In the case of private trusts, the general rule is that where there is more than one trustee they must, in the exercise of their functions, act unanimously. A majority of trustees cannot ordinarily overrule the minority. If absolute deadlock is reached, the intervention of the court on the application of one or other of the trustees or a beneficiary may be the only way to break the deadlock: *Luke v South Kensington Hotel Co (1879) 11 Ch D 121*. The rule is different in the case of personal representatives (save in the case of dealing with land) and the trustees of charities and pension funds – see 1.19 below.

In day-to-day practice, the position is modified by the statutory power to delegate and to appoint agents nominees and custodians (see further CHAPTER 18: POWER TO DELEGATE below). However, decisions relating to delegation by the trustees as a body or to the appointment of an agent, nominee or custodian are decisions on which the trustees must be unanimous and any duty to keep an arrangement under review is a joint obligation.

Rationale

1.2 As regards its general application, the rationale underlying the rule requiring unanimity appears to be that a settlor, in appointing a number of trustees to execute the trusts established by him, is to be taken to have intended the trust to have the benefit of the 'assistance and discretion' of *all* the trustees (*Swale v Swale (1856) 22 Beav 584*). The rule is, however, also a form of protection for the individual trustee whose views cannot be outvoted by a majority. This seems clear from observations in *Re Butlin's Settlement Trusts [1976] Ch 251*. In that case, there was a claim for rectification where the settlor's intention to provide for the trustees to conduct the trust by majority had not been effectively carried into the drafting of the trust instrument. One of the trustees objected to rectification on the basis that she had not known of the settlor's intention so to provide, but giving no other reasoned objection to the rectification. Brightman J ordered rectification but, despite being satisfied that a mistake had been made, did so only 'after considerable hesitation'. Although he did not decide the point, he considered that to 'override the reasonable opposition on the part of a blameless trustee to suit the wishes of the settlor who, or whose advisers, have ex hypothesi, fallen into error might well be thought unjust'.

It is clear that he meant unjust to an opposing trustee who on reasonable grounds favoured a retention of the requirement of unanimity.

A settlor may by express provision in the trust instrument provide that, either generally or in specific circumstances, the decision of a majority of the trustees will prevail.

Consequences of a failure to agree

1.3 There are numerous situations in which trustees might fail to exercise their powers unanimously, but the consequences of such failure may differ according to its nature in any given case.

Real property

Leasehold interests

1.4 Where the trust property comprises or includes a lease or tenancy held by the trustees as joint tenants, all must join in any positive dealing in respect of that joint tenancy. The point in practice arises most commonly in the case of co-owners who, of course, hold the property on trust for themselves as beneficial joint tenants or tenants in common, although the principle is of general application. A single joint tenant cannot:

- exercise a break clause in a lease;
- surrender a term;
- make a disclaimer;
- exercise an option to renew the term or apply for relief from forfeiture.

(See per Lord Bridge in *Hammersmith London Borough Council v Monk [1992] 1 AC 478 at 490 G*).

One of two joint tenants can terminate a periodic tenancy effective at the end of each period (on the basis that both joint tenants must concur in a renewal) but both must be joined in giving notice to terminate during a period (*Hounslow London Borough Council v Pilling [1993] 1 WLR 1242*). Before serving a notice to quit expiring at the end of the term, one joint tenant is not required to consult the other joint tenant pursuant to the

Trusts of Land and Appointment of Trustees Act 1996, s 11 and the failure to do so does not vitiate the validity of the notice to quit (*Notting Hill Housing Trust v Brackley [2001] 3 EGLR 11*).

An application for a new tenancy under *Part II* of the *Landlord and Tenant Act 1954* must be a joint application (*Jacobs v Chaudhuri [1968] 2 QB 470*). Similarly, an application to enfranchise under the *Leasehold Reform Act 1967, s 6*, or to exercise the right of collective enfranchisement or to renew under the *Leasehold Reform, Housing and Urban Development Act 1993*, *s 93A* must be by all the trustees in whom the interest is vested. If the joint tenants comprise only some of the trustees, then as against the lessor or landlord, a right falls to be invoked or exercised by the joint tenants, but their duty is to act in accordance with the unanimous decision of the trustees.

Interests which are let

1.5 Where the trust property includes a freehold or leasehold interest which has been let, then the converse applies and one only of several trustee reversioners can serve a valid notice to quit. The rationale is that the concurrence of all the trustees is required for the continuance of the term (*Hammersmith London Borough Council v Monk [1992] 1 AC 478 at 490H*).

A trustee who unilaterally exercises a right that can be exercised by him alone, or who fails to join in the exercise of a right required to be exercised jointly, may be liable for breach of trust if his act or failure to act is detrimental to the interest of the beneficiaries. The fact that a trustee has power to act alone or by declining to act can veto a course of action, does not mean that it is in any given circumstance justified.

Trust for sale with a power to postpone

1.6 If trustees have power to sell specific property all must concur in a sale (In *Re 90 Thornhill Road, Tolworth, Surrey [1970] Ch 261*). Conversely, if trustees hold land on an express trust for sale, then although they have a power to postpone sale (if not expressly set out in the trust instrument, then under *Trusts of Land and Appointment of Trustees Act 1996, s 4*) they must be unanimous in their agreement to exercise the power to postpone; if they are not unanimous, then the trust for sale takes effect and the land must be sold (*Re Mayo [1943] Ch 302*).

The trustees differ as to detail

1.7 In general, the trustees must agree in detail not just in principle. Thus in *Tempest v Lord Camoys (1882) 21 Ch D 571*, the testator gave his trustees power to sell real property, the proceeds of such sale to be reinvested in real property. Real property having been sold, one trustee wanted to use the proceeds in the purchase of a particular estate, but his co-trustee objected to the suggested purchase. The Court of Appeal held that the dissentient trustee could not be compelled to agree with his co-trustee's choice. The court would interfere if one trustee refused to invest the monies in the purchase of *any* real property (thereby failing to carry out his duty under the terms of the particular trust), but as the trustees together had an absolute discretion as to what real property the monies should be invested in, they had, together, to agree on a suitable estate. The court would not interfere in the exercise of a discretionary power by compelling one trustee to agree with the choice of another.

If, therefore, trustees agree to perform a particular duty, the exact nature of the performance is a matter on which they must agree. The court will not interfere unless the failure to agree on the mechanics of performance is so serious as to lead to a total failure to perform the duty.

The trustees cannot act together amicably

1.8 If one or more trustees obstructs the proper management of the trust, for instance, by simply refusing to join in the performance of the trustees' duties, the remaining trustees can apply to the court to compel the performance of those duties. Where necessary, the court may remove an obstructive trustee (see *Luke v South Kensington Hotel Co (1879) 11 Ch D 121*; and *Tempest v Lord Camoys (1882) 21 Ch D 571*) but if the trustees simply cannot act together amicably and effectively, and the problem cannot be dealt with by the removal of one or more of the trustees, then a receiver may be appointed over the trust property (*Swale v Swale (1856) 22 Beav 584*).

In such circumstances, the costs of the application for the appointment of a receiver (usually brought by an exasperated beneficiary) may have to be met by the trustees, or by those of them whose behaviour is adjudged by the court to have necessitated the application (see *Wilson v Wilson (1838) 2 Keen 249*).

Incapacitated trustee

1.9 Trustees cannot act unanimously where one of their number is rendered incapable of acting through some mental or other disability. In such a case, save where the trustee has granted an enduring power of attorney under the *Trustee Act 1925, s 25* which power of attorney remains in force (see further CHAPTER 18: POWER TO DELEGATE), the proper course is to replace the trustee (see CHAPTER 20: POWERS OF

APPOINTMENT AND RETIREMENT). It is not appropriate to seek an order vesting the trust assets in those trustees who are not incapacitated without removing the incapacitated trustee from his office of trusteeship, even though the court might have jurisdiction to make such an order under the *Trustee Act 1925, s 44* or *s 51* (*Re Harrison's Settlement Trusts [1965] 3 All ER 795*).

Superficial unanimity

1.10 Where a trustee plays no active part in the management of the trust, but permits his fellow trustees to make such decisions as they see fit, he will be liable for loss to the trust fund occasioned by his own inactivity. However, there is a distinction to be drawn between the trustee who passively allows his co-trustee to decide matters which ought to be decided jointly, and the trustee who, reasonably but mistakenly, relies on what he is told, and is deceived into thinking all is well. For example, in *Re Lucking's Will Trusts [1967] 3 All ER 726*, the estate held a substantial holding of shares in a private company. The executor brought in a director to manage the business. A second trustee was appointed. The director improperly withdrew money from the company. The original trustee was held liable for failure properly to supervise the director's drawings but the court held that the second trustee had been entitled to rely on what the original trustee told him about the company affairs as being adequate and accurate. He was, therefore, not liable for the losses.

Another example of superficial unanimity is where a trustee simply does as he is told by his co-trustees, where he 'acts merely for conformity's sake'. Such a trustee will nevertheless be adjudged an active trustee, and may be liable for any default of his co-trustees (see *Trutch v Lamprell (1855) 20 Beav 116*). It is important to note, however, that a trustee will not be adjudged the mere puppet of his co-trustee if he exercises his discretion genuinely, albeit as a result of his having been persuaded by the arguments of that co-trustee. There will be no breach of trust in those circumstances, even if the persuasive trustee has a personal interest in the outcome of the trustees' decision, such as where he is a trustee-beneficiary (*Re Schneider (1906) 22 TLR 223*, per Warrington J).

The deceived trustee

1.11 Where one trustee pursues a course of action resulting in loss to the trust, his co-trustees will not be liable if he kept his actions secret from them. So, in *Re England's Settlement Trusts [1918] 1 Ch 24*, a trustee brought a dilapidations action against the tenants of trust property. He brought the action in the name of himself and his co-trustee but without the knowledge or consent of his co-trustee or the beneficiaries.

In the result, the tenants were ordered to pay £90 to the trustees, but the trustees were ordered to pay costs of around £600. Eve J refused to allow the plaintiff trustee to recover the costs from the trust fund – he was guilty of unreasonable and improper conduct in bringing the dilapidations action without informing or consulting his co-trustee or the beneficiaries, and was therefore personally liable for the costs of that action. Similarly, trustees will not be liable for any fraud perpetrated secretly by a co-trustee without either their knowledge or consent (*Re Lake Bathurst Australasian Gold Mining Co (1862) 3 De GJ & Sm 355*). Where a trustee becomes aware of a co-trustee's default, however, he must where possible seek to prevent it arising, and if necessary apply to the court to compel the co-trustee to perform his duty properly – otherwise, he will become jointly and severally liable for the default (*Gough v Smith [1872] WN 18*).

Subsequent ratification of a trustee's action

1.12 It appears that ratification is effective to legitimate the actions of one or more trustees, albeit that they were not originally performed unanimously, and to prevent any breach of trust arising (*Messeena v Carr (1870) LR 9 Eq 260*).

Payment of trust monies into court

1.13 Where payment into court of money or securities is permissible, but the trustees do not unanimously agree to it, the *Trustee Act 1925, s 63* provides that a majority of trustees can make the payment in and that the receipt or certificate of the proper officer shall be a sufficient discharge for the money or securities so paid in. The practical importance of the exception is limited, in that payments into court of trust funds are now justifiable only in limited circumstances. Old examples, such as where the beneficiary is of unsound mind (*Re Parker's Will (1888) 39 Ch D 303*) or where the beneficiary cannot be traced and it is not known whether he is alive or dead (*Re Elliot's Trusts (1873) LR 15 Eq 194*) would now be better dealt with by invoking the powers of the Court of Protection in the former case or seeking a *Benjamin* order (see CHAPTER 29: POWER TO APPLY TO THE COURT – THE SURRENDER OF DISCRETION TO THE COURT) in the latter. However, circumstances may arise where it would be convenient for trustees to pay monies forming part or all of the trust fund into court, particularly where they cannot get a discharge. For example, where a trustee could otherwise be discharged, but the beneficiaries are fighting over a fund, then a payment into court pending the outcome of the resolution of the dispute may be a convenient way to procure the discharge of the trustees.

The holding of trust property by trustees

1.14 The position at common law is that, in the case of personal property such as money and securities, the property should be held under the control of all the trustees. In the case of money, therefore, it should be held in a bank account in the joint names of the trustees; shares should be registered in the names of all the trustees, and so on. The purpose of the rule is to minimise the risk of one or more fraudulent trustees taking control of the property and applying it improperly - if the property can only be dealt with by the unanimous action of all the trustees, the risk of misappropriation is clearly smaller than if it could be dealt with by a single trustee. The rationale was set out fully by Kay J in *Re Flower and Metropolitan Board of Works (1884) 27 Ch D 592 at 596–7.* Consequently, if a trustee simply hands trust funds to a co-trustee who then misapplies them, both may be held liable for the misapplication (*Trutch v Lamprell (1855) 20 Beav 116*).

Similarly, generally speaking, in the absence of a specific provision to the contrary, trustees have a duty not to allow trust funds to be invested otherwise than in the names of all of them (*Lewis v Nobbs (1878) 8 Ch D 591*). Where the terms of the trust enable investments to be made in the name of a single trustee, however, the other trustees nevertheless remain under a duty to take care that the investments are not misappropriated or otherwise improperly dealt with, and a failure to perform that duty will render them liable for any such improper dealing (*Lewis v Nobbs*). Where a settlor gave particular shares to his trustees which, under the rules of the relevant company, could only be held in the name of a single person, it was lawful for the shares to be held in the name of a single trustee (*Consterdine v Consterdine (1862) 31 Beav 330*).

Where there are proceeds arising from the sale of trust property, it is the duty of the trustees to receive those proceeds together (for example by naming a bank where the monies can be paid to their joint account). The purchaser is not generally bound to pay any agent of the trustees, regardless of whether that agent is himself a trustee, a solicitor or someone with a power of attorney from the trustees; he can instead insist that the trustees together provide a good receipt for the purchase monies (*Re Flower and Metropolitan Board of Works (1884) 27 Ch D 592*).

The common law rule is now modified by statute. The *Trustee Act 2000, ss 16* and *17* enables trustees to appoint nominees and custodians (see further CHAPTER 18: POWER TO DELEGATE). In particular the Law Commission report which preceded the enactment of the *Trustee Act 2000*, envisaged that the appointment of a nominee might, for instance, facilitate dealings with trust funds by a discretionary fund manager or, in the case of registered land subject to a trust, obviate the need for regular changes to the register when trustees of land changed (see Law Com 260, *Trustees' Powers and Duties*, at paragraph 5.3).

Personal representatives

General rule

1.15 At common law one executor may act without the concurrence of his co-executor(s) (*Smith v Everett (1859) 29 LJ Ch 236*). Although there is no decisive authority, a similar rule probably applies to administrators (*Fountain Forestry v Edwards [1975] Ch 1 at 14*). There are, however, exceptions in the case of dealings with real property and stocks and shares (see 1.17 below).

It is commonplace for the same persons to be appointed both executors and trustees. The general rule will apply only to acts done by the executor qua executor. In the case of acts committed as trustee, the rule that all trustees must act unanimously, will apply. In the case of a will or an intestacy under which trusts arise, the position will change once the period of administration ceases and the period of trusteeship begins. Sometimes the change is specifically marked, e.g. by an assent by the personal representatives in favour of themselves as trustees. Other times the change may be a matter of proper inference from the facts (see for example *Attenborough v Solomon [1913] AC 76* –where 14 years had passed since the death, all the debts and legacies had been paid, and the residuary account had been passed a year after death).

The distinction between the power of a personal representative to act unilaterally and the duty of trustees to act unanimously has implications for the person with whom they deal. Thus in *Attenborough v Solomon* one of two persons appointed executors and trustees, without the knowledge of the other, pledged plate, belonging to the estate, with a firm of pawnbrokers who had knowledge that he was not the absolute owner thereof; he then misapplied the money so raised. It was held that by the time of the pledge, the plate was held by them as trustees and, as one trustee had no power to pledge the plate, the current trustees could recover it.

Dealing with real estate

1.16 Where there are two or more personal representatives, a conveyance of land and a contract for the conveyance of land shall not be made without the concurrence therein of all such personal representatives or an order of the court. [*Administration of Estates Act 1925, s 2(2)* (as amended by the *Law of Property (Miscellaneous Provisions) Act 1994*)]. The rule applies to all 'real estate' including chattels real (i.e. leasehold) or any interest in land, real estate held on trust, or by way of mortgage or security but not money secured or charged on land (*section 3*).

Stocks and shares

1.17 Another exception concerns dealings in stocks and shares – where executors are the registered shareholders of shares formerly held by the deceased, *Article 29* of Table A of the *Companies Act 1948* and *Companies Act 1985* provides that the shares can only be transferred by all the personal representatives (in that the deceased's 'personal representatives ... shall be the only persons recognised by the company as having any title to his interest'). Of course, the Articles of Association of any given company incorporated under the 1948 or 1985 Acts may provide otherwise either expressly or by amendment of Table A.

Charitable trusts

1.18 The general rule in the case of charitable and public trusts is the opposite of that for private trusts, and a majority may bind a minority. In *Re Whitely [1910] 1 Ch 600* it was suggested that the rationale is that charitable and public trusts will often have a substantial number of trustees (as to which in the case of charitable or public trusts there is no upper limit) giving rise to the possibility of frequent failure to achieve total agreement and consequential applications to the court. It also guards against the possibility of a trust for the public benefit being obstructed at the whim of a capricious or unreasonable individual or individuals.

This general rule is, of course, subject to the terms of the trust instrument. The settlor may, if he wishes, stipulate the exact number of trustees necessary to form a quorum (*Re Beverley Grammar School (1839) 9 LJ Ch 91*), and there seems no reason in principle why a settlor should not stipulate that his trustees should act unanimously either generally or on specific matters. A majority decision must, of course, be in conformity with the trusts being administered (*Ward v Hipwell (1862) 3 Giff 547 at 555*) but it has been said that the courts will be very slow to interfere with the decision of the majority, even where it is suggested that the decision was capricious or improper (see *Cooper v Gordon (1869) LR 8 Eq 249 at 258*, per Stuart V-C).

The majority cannot, however, arrogate to themselves total control of the trust, to the absolute exclusion of any minority. Where the majority propose to act in a certain way, they must inform the minority of their proposal and listen to any representations which the minority wish to make. The minority may be able to change the views of the majority and in any event a settlor must be taken to have intended the trust to have the benefit of the advice and consideration of all the trustees. Any majority decision taken without such reference to the minority will be invalid (*A-G v Lawson (1866) 36 LJ Ch 130 at 134*). Although, in that case, a decision taken by two trustees only at a time when the third was incapable by age and infirmity from attending to business was held to be valid.

Pension schemes

1.19 The trusts of pension funds are in general governed by the ordinary law of private trusts, subject to any contrary provision in the rules or to other provisions which govern the trust (see Megarry V-C in *Cowan v Scargill [1985] Ch 270 at 292*); so at common law, a majority of trustees of a pension fund cannot prevail over a minority (see *Cowan at page 297*). This common law position has, however, been modified by statute.

The *Pensions Act 1995 (PA 1995), s 32* provides that decisions of the trustees of a trust scheme may, unless the scheme provides otherwise, be taken by agreement of a majority of the trustees. Where decisions of the trustees of a trust scheme may be taken by agreement of a majority of the trustees, the trustees may, unless the scheme provides otherwise, by a determination under *section 32*, specify a quorum to be present when any decision is so taken. Notice of any occasions on which a decision may be taken by a majority must be given to each trustee to whom it is reasonably practicable to give notice. Unless the trustees agree otherwise, the notice is to be a notice specifying the date, time and place of the occasion, and is to be sent to the last known address of the trustee no later than ten business days before the occasion (see *Occupational Pension Schemes (Scheme Administration) Regulations 1996 (SI 1996 No 1715), reg 10*). Notice does not, however, have to be given where it is necessary as a matter of urgency for a decision to be made (*regulation 9*).

The statutory power is subject to other provisions in the *Pensions Act 1995*:

- by *section 8(4)(b)*, where a trustee of a pension scheme is by order appointed under *section 7* by the Occupational Pensions Regulatory Authority, the Authority may provide by the terms of the order that that trustee can act to the exclusion of the other trustees of the scheme;
- by *section 16(3)(b)*, a member-nominated trustee can only be removed by the agreement of *all* the other trustees of the pension scheme;
- by *section 25(2)*, where it has become necessary for an independent trustee to act in relation to the scheme he alone can exercise the powers vested in the scheme trustees (unless there is more than one independent trustee, in which case the powers may be exercised by another trustee, provided he has the consent of at least half of the independent trustees).

Chapter 2

Duty to Consult and to Obtain Consents and Directions

Introduction

2.1 Subject to observing the terms of the trust, their fiduciary duties and, where applicable, the statutory duty of care, trustees are free to run the trusts as they see fit. It is not for the settlor, the beneficiaries, or the court to dictate how powers or discretions should be exercised. However, a prudent trustee will wish to carry the goodwill of the beneficiaries with him and the trust instrument may impose the obligation to obtain consent to a particular course of action. Statute has intervened to impose a duty of consultation or to obtain consents in certain specific circumstances.

In the absence of an express provision to the contrary, a trustee is not under a duty to consult the settlor, or implement the settlor's wishes or to obtain the settlor's consent to a particular course of action. Indeed a trust under which the settlor retained control would be a sham. Trustees must not act for reasons which are irrational, perverse or contrary to any sensible expectation of the settlor (see *Re Manisty's Settlement [1974] Ch 17 at 26*), and there is no reason why the views of the settlor should not be obtained and considered, but a trustee must exercise his independent judgement as to what is in the best interests of the trust and the beneficiaries as a whole even if this means going against the settlor's wishes. It is of course not unusual for a settlor to retain certain rights to himself, e.g. the power to appoint new trustees.

Consultation

The general rule

2.2 The general rule is that trustees are not obliged to consult with the beneficiaries of the trust (*X v A [2000] 1 All ER 490 at 496*, per Arden J). However, it is proper and reasonable for a trustee to take account of the beneficiaries' wishes and opinions and to discuss with the beneficiaries the reasons for and against a particular decision (*Fraser v Murdoch (1881) 6 App Cas 855 at 864*). In the case of a trust of land there is now a statutory duty to consult and so far as consistent with the general interest of the trust to give effect to the wishes of the beneficiaries.

Circumstances where trustee should consult

2.3 There can also be situations in which a trustee may reasonably be expected to consult with one or more of the beneficiaries even though there may be no legal duty on him to do so.

So where a beneficiary has acquired a 'legitimate expectation' of how the trustees will exercise a certain power, the trustees' duty to act fairly and reasonably will usually require them to consult the beneficiary prior to any change in practice that will operate to the beneficiary's disadvantage.

An example was given by Robert Walker J in *Scott v National Trust [1998] 2 All ER 705 at 718*:

> 'if (for instance) trustees (whether of a charity, or a pension fund, or a private family trust) have for the last ten years paid £1,000 per quarter to an elderly, impoverished beneficiary of the trust it seems at least arguable that no reasonable body of trustees would discontinue the payment, without any warning, and without giving the beneficiary the opportunity of trying to persuade the trustees to continue the payment, at least temporarily. The beneficiary has no legal or equitable right to continued payment, but he or she has an expectation'.

Where a trustee has a power of maintenance or advancement in respect of a beneficiary, that beneficiary, if of full age and capacity, might reasonably be expected to be consulted before the power is exercised. Where the beneficiary objected to a power of advancement being exercised to reduce a judgment debt against him by a payment direct to the creditor, the court held that no such payment should be made. However, the court did not rule out the possibility that such a power might, in appropriate circumstances, be exercised despite objections from the beneficiary (*Re Esteem Settlement, Grupo Torras SA v Al-Sabah [2002] WTLR 337*).

A trustee is not, however, a court or an administrative tribunal and is not under a duty to give a hearing to both 'sides' before making a decision (*Scott v National Trust [1998] 2 All ER 705 at 718*).

Duty regarding holdings of private company shares

2.4 Where a trust held the majority of the shares in a private company and the trustees had (quite properly) procured their appointment as sole directors of the company, the beneficiaries, being dissatisfied with the way in which the company was being run, sought a declaration that they were entitled to inspect all documents which came into the possession of the trustees as directors. The Court of Appeal held that the beneficiaries were entitled to be treated as if they were registered shareholders in respect of the trust shares (*Butt v Kelson [1952] Ch 197*). The judgment is difficult to reconcile with cases such as *Re Brockbank [1948] Ch 206* which make clear that the beneficiaries cannot dictate to the trustees how they conduct the trust affairs – see per Upjohn J in *Re George Whichelow Ltd [1954] 1 WLR 5*. However, it does seem that trustees cannot rely on the company structure to deny information to their beneficiaries.

Trusts of land

2.5 In the case of trusts of land, subject to certain specific exceptions, a trustee is required by the *Trusts of Land and Appointment of Trustees Act 1996, s 11* to consult beneficiaries of the trust prior to the exercise of any function relating to the trust land. *Section 11* replaced *section 26(3)* of the *Trustee Act 1925* the wording of which it closely follows.

Section 11(1) provides:

> 'The trustees of land shall in the exercise of any function relating to land subject to the trust—
>
> (*a*) so far as practicable, consult the beneficiaries of full age and beneficially entitled to an interest in possession in the land; and
>
> (*b*) so far as consistent with the general interest of the trust, give effect to the wishes of those beneficiaries, or (in case of dispute) of the majority (according to the value of their combined interests)'.

This statutory duty to consult applies to trusts of land created or arising after commencement of the *Trusts of Land and Appointment of Trustees Act 1996* (1 January 1997). In the case of trusts created or arising before that date, the settlor (or such of the original settlors as are alive and of full capacity) may provide by irrevocable deed that the duty is to apply to the trust created by him. [*Section 11(3), (4)*].

The application of the duty to consult can be excluded or restricted by express provision in the trust instrument or by order of the court. [*Section 11(2)(a)*]. On the application of a trustee, the court may relieve the trustees of their obligation to consult any person in connection with the exercise of any of their functions. [*Section 14(2)(a)*].

Where trustees are holding land for beneficiaries who are of full age and capacity and together entitled to the land absolutely (i.e. they are holding land as bare trustees), they have power under *section 6(2)* of the Act to convey the land to the beneficiaries even though the beneficiaries have not required the trustees to do so. The statutory duty to consult does not apply to any exercise by trustees of that power. [*Section 11(2)(c)*].

Matters on which consultation is required under section 11

2.6 The *Trusts of Land and Appointment of Trustees Act 1996, s 11* requires trustees of land to consult beneficiaries 'in the exercise of any function relating to land subject to the trust'. For this purpose 'function' is a wide term which embraces the exercise by trustees of any of their powers or duties under the trust. However, the service by one joint tenant, who was a trustee-beneficiary of a periodic tenancy, of a notice to quit to terminate the tenancy was not a 'trustee function' and did not require the joint tenant to consult with the other joint tenant. Both joint tenants had to concur in the periodic renewal of the tenancy and the service of the notice to quit was not the exercise of a trustee function but the withholding by one joint tenant of his consent to the continuation of the tenancy into a further period (*Notting Hill Housing Trust v Brackley [2001] 3 EGLR 11*).

Extent of the duty to consult

2.7 The trustee's duty to consult is not an absolute duty, merely a duty to consult 'so far as practicable'. Similarly, whilst the trustees must give effect to the wishes of the beneficiaries or, in the case of dispute, of the majority by value of their combined interests, that duty only extends so far as is consistent with the 'general interest of the trust'.

Failure to consult may be a breach of trust

2.8 Unless the circumstances are such that it is not practicable to consult the beneficiaries, failure to consult is a breach of trust and a beneficiary may be entitled to an injunction to restrain the trustee from acting without consultation (*Waller v Waller [1967] 1 WLR 451*). In that case, a house was bought in the name of the husband alone, although both had contributed to the purchase price; the husband therefore held as trustee upon a resulting trust. The husband had contracted to sell the house without consulting the wife. The court held that this was a breach of the *Law of Property Act 1925, s 26(3)* which imposed on the husband a duty to consult. For that reason (among others) the court restrained the sale, although as contracts had been exchanged, it directed that the purchaser be joined in the proceedings and have liberty to apply to set aside the order.

Applications to the court

2.9 Under the *Trusts of Land and Appointment of Trustees Act 1996, s 14*, any person who is a trustee of land or has an interest in a property subject to a trust of land may make an application to the court. So, for example, if there is a dispute over whether land should be sold, the court may determine that dispute and order accordingly. Save in the case of a transfer by a bare trustee to the beneficial owner of full age and capacity pursuant to *section 6(2)*, the matters to which the court is required to have regard include the circumstances and wishes of any beneficiaries of full age and entitled to an interest in possession in property subject to the trust or (in case of dispute) of the majority according to the value of their combined interests.

Third party protection

2.10 In the case of unregistered land, a purchaser from trustees need not be concerned as to whether or not they have complied with the provisions of the *Trusts of Land and Appointment of Trustees Act 1996, ss 11(1)* and *16(1)*. 'Purchaser' has the same meaning as in *Part I* of *the Law of Property Act 1925*, i.e. a person who acquires an interest in or charge on property for money or money's worth. As to registered land, a purchaser is protected by the *Land Registration Act 1925, s 74.*

Settled land

2.11 Although the *Settled Land Act 1925* does not in terms impose on the tenant for life any positive duty to consult with those interested under the settlement, *section 107(1)* of the Act provides that:

> 'A tenant for life or statutory owner shall, in exercising any power under this Act, have regard to the interests of all parties entitled under the settlement, and shall, in relation to the exercise thereof by him, be deemed to be in the position and to have the duties and liabilities of a trustee for those parties'.

The tenant for life is, therefore, to have regard to the interests of those entitled under the settlement and to the well being of the estate as a whole, including those who worked on the estate and from whom the rents and profits are derived (*Re Marquis of Ailesbury's Settled Estates [1892] 1 Ch 506*, affirmed *[1892] AC 356*). In that case, the tenant for life had squandered his fortune and mortgaged his life interest to a mortgagee who had foreclosed. A purchaser had been found for the estate but the remaindermen, who wished the house and estate to be preserved in the family, opposed the sale. The court sanctioned the sale, the circumstances of the estate being derelict and in the possession of the mortgagee outweighing the wishes of the remaindermen.

Charity trustees

2.12 The trustees of charitable trusts are not subject to any general obligation to consult. However, in individual cases it may sometimes be convenient or necessary to impose some duty of consultation on charity trustees, albeit not necessarily a duty to consult with actual or potential beneficiaries. Thus, in *Brewer's Company v A-G* (unreported, 22 March

2000), a scheme was established under the *Charities Act 1993, s 13* in relation to a substantial surplus of income from the Dame Alice Owen's Schools Foundation. The Brewer's Company was to manage the trust property and to distribute the Foundation's net income, but Lloyd J accepted that the processes regarding the exercise of the trustees' discretion had to be 'opened up' (there having previously been criticism, albeit unjustified, of the Company's failure to apply funds towards general educational purposes in Islington). The scheme was, therefore, to include 'a consultative process', by which the exercise of the trustees' discretion would become more transparent.

Pension trustees

2.13 As in the case of charity trustees, pension trustees are not *per se* subject to any general duty to consult. A pension scheme may, however, make express provision for the trustees to consult particular parties, either generally or in particular circumstances. In addition, some pension schemes will make explicit provision for the trustees to be drawn from amongst the ranks of both the management and the employees – it is likely in such cases that the views of beneficiary employees will be sought and considered, at least by those trustees drawn from amongst their own ranks.

Consents and directions

Consents required by the trust instrument

2.14 The trust instrument may require the consent of a third party to the exercise by the trustees of their powers. To take a common example, the sale of a house may be made subject to the consent of the beneficiary who is permitted to occupy it. In the case of overseas trusts, in order to provide a check on the activities of the trustees, the consent of the protector may be required in respect of the exercise by the trustee of some or all of his powers.

Is a power to grant or withhold consent a fiduciary power?

2.15 If the trust deed confers on a person the power to grant or withhold consent in respect of one or more of the trustee's powers, the question may arise whether that person owes a fiduciary duty to the beneficiaries in respect of the granting or withholding of that consent. If he does, then he must exercise it bona fide in the interests of the beneficiaries as a whole.

If a power is clearly intended to provide protection to the person on whom it is conferred then the power is a personal, not a fiduciary, power. If the power is to protect the trust or the interests of the beneficiaries then the power is a fiduciary power. To take the examples given above, the beneficiary whose consent is required to the sale of the house he or she occupies is given that right to protect his or her personal interest and so it is a personal not a fiduciary right. However, the role of the protector is clearly a fiduciary role and the power to give or withhold consent must be exercised in the interests of the beneficiaries and trust estate as a whole.

The distinction between a private and fiduciary power can have tangible results. Where a settlor had certain powers to appoint members of a committee of protectors (who had power to remove and appoint trustees) and to appoint trustees to fill ad hoc vacancies or additional trustees, it was argued by the Inland Revenue that he was in a position to control the trustees and thereby the application of income of the settlements so as to be assessable to income tax pursuant to the *Income and Corporation Taxes Act 1970, s 478(5)*. The court held that the settlor's powers of appointment were fiduciary powers which could not be properly used by him to ensure that he had trustees who would follow his directions and the matter did not fall within *section 478(5)* (*IRC v Schroder [1983] STC 480*).

Trusts of land

2.16 If a disposition creating a trust of land requires the consent of more than two persons to the exercise by the trustees of any function relating to the land, the consent of any two of them to the exercise of the function is sufficient in favour of a purchaser. [*Trusts of Land and Appointment of Trustees Act 1996, s 10(1)*]. The section replaces *section 26(1)* of the *Law of Property Act 1925*. Although it allows a trustee to confer good title on a purchaser, it does not relieve the trustee of any obligation, vis-à-vis the beneficiaries, to seek to obtain all the requisite consents. Where the person whose consent would otherwise be required is a minor, his consent is not required, but the trustees are required to obtain the consent of a parent or guardian. If the person is mentally incapable of giving consent and is a patient under the Court of Protection, then the court may give consent or authorise a receiver of his property, appointed under the *Mental Health Act 1983*, *s 96(1)(k)* to give the necessary consent.

Section 10 does not apply to personal representatives (*section 18(1)*) or to land held on charitable, ecclesiastical or public trusts (*section 10(2)*).

Partition

2.17 Where trustees propose to exercise their power to partition land between beneficiaries who are all absolutely entitled as tenants in common to land held on trust, the trustees must obtain the consent of each of the beneficiaries. However, the court has power to dispense with the requirement of consent. If a share of land is vested in a minor, the trustees may act on his behalf and retain land or other property representing his share in trust for him. [*Trusts of Land and Appointment of Trustees Act 1996, s 7*].

If, instead of partitioning the land, the trustees decide to convey the land to the beneficiaries as joint tenants or as tenants in common, they can do so under *section 6* of the 1996 Act without obtaining any consents from the beneficiaries.

Both in the case of partition and the transfer to the beneficiaries as co-owners, if the trust instrument makes provision requiring any consent to be obtained to the exercise of any power conferred by *sections 6* or *7*, the power may not be exercised without that consent. [*Trusts of Land and Appointment of Trustees Act 1996, s 8*].

Power of court to dispense with consent

2.18 Under the *Trusts of Land and Appointment of Trustees Act 1996, s 14* the court may, on the application of a trustee or any person who has an interest in property subject to a trust of land, make an order relating to the exercise of the trustees of their functions, including an order relieving them of any obligation to obtain the consent of, or to consult any person in connection with the exercise of any of their functions. If an application is made to the court under *section 14* to dispense with a consent, it is directed by *section 15* to have regard to the intentions of the person creating the trust, the purpose for which the trust property is held and the interests of any secured creditor. In the case of a right to occupy land, the matters to which the court is to have regard include the circumstances and wishes of each of the beneficiaries who is entitled to occupy the land. In the case of partition, the court has regard to other circumstances and the wishes of the adult beneficiaries or, in the case of dispute, the majority of them according to the value of their combined interests.

Statutory powers of investment may be subject to consent

2.19 The trustee's statutory power to invest (*Trustee Act 2000, s 3*) and the statutory power to acquire freehold and leasehold land as an investment or for occupation by a beneficiary or for any other reason (*section 8*) is subject to any restriction or exclusion imposed by the trust instrument or by any enactment or any provision of subordinate legislation. [*Trustee Act 2000, ss 6* and *9*].

Settled land

2.20 Some powers under the *Settled Land Act 1925* may only be exercised by the tenant for life with the consent of the trustees, e.g. the compromise of claims etc, sale of the principal manor house (if, in the case of a post-1925 settlement, the settlement so provides), and cutting timber (if the tenant for life is impeachable for waste in respect of timber). [*Settled Land Act 1925, ss 58, 65* and *66*].

In the case of entailed estates, a tenant in tail cannot bar the entail (and enlarge his interest into a fee simple) with the consent of the life tenant. Entailed estates (which incidentally provided George Eliot with a twist in the plot of her novel, *Felix Holt the Radical*) can no longer be created but existing entails continue. Reference should be made to the specialist works.

Chapter 3

Duty to Exercise Reasonable Care and Skill

Introduction

3.1 In the performance of his duties, a trustee is expected to attain certain standards. It will not avail an incompetent trustee who causes loss to the trust fund or a beneficiary to argue that he has done his honest but incompetent best. If a trustee fails, in his management of the trust, to exercise reasonable skill and care, he will be held to have acted in breach of trust and to be liable for the consequences of that breach. The trustee's fiduciary duty of care imposed by equity has now been supplemented in respect of specific duties by the statutory duty of care introduced by the *Trustee Act 2000, s 1*.

The fiduciary duty of care

The general duty

3.2 The classic statement of the duty of care is that a trustee must, in administering the trust, exercise the same care and skill as an ordinary prudent man of business would exercise in the conduct of his own affairs (*Speight v Gaunt (1883) 9 App Cas 1 at 19*).

In respect of the duty to invest the trust fund, that general statement is subject to the qualification that the duty of a trustee is not to take only such care as a prudent man would take if he had only himself to consider. The duty is rather to take such care as an ordinary prudent man would take if he were minded to make an investment for the benefit of other people for whom he felt morally bound to provide (*Re Whiteley (1886) 33 Ch D 347 at 355*). The effect of this qualification is to reduce the degree of risk which a trustee may properly take in his management of the trust. Businessmen of ordinary prudence may, and frequently do, select investments which are more or less of a speculative character, but such risk taking is not open to the ordinary trustee (*Learoyd v Whiteley (1887) 12 App Cas 727*). A trustee must adopt a relatively cautious approach to his management of the trust. It is not the case that a trustee can take *no* risks in his dealings with trust funds, but he must curb any impulse to risk trust funds in speculative ventures, even where the ventures are of a sort in which the prudent businessman may be prepared to risk his own money. 'The distinction is between a prudent degree of risk on the one hand and hazard on the other' per Brightman J in *Bartlett v Barclays Bank Trust Co [1980] Ch 515 at 531*.

The level of prudence to be observed depends on the economic and financial conditions of the time, not on what judges of the past have held to be the prudent course 50 or 100 years ago (*Nestle v National Westminster Bank plc [1993] 1 WLR 1260 at 1268*). The changing attitude to risk and investment is reflected in the progressive liberalising of investment powers to the point now reached where, unless excluded or modified by the trust instrument, the trustee has all the powers of an absolute owner. However, the fact that a trustee has an unrestricted power of investment in no respect absolves him from the duty to exercise that power in a manner appropriate to the fact that he is managing funds as a fiduciary on behalf of others; on the contrary, it makes it all the more important that the trustee observes the appropriate standard of care.

The professional trustee

3.3 A higher standard is demanded from a professional trustee (i.e. those who hold themselves out as being peculiarly well-qualified or experienced in matters of trust management) than from a lay trustee. Just as, under the law of contract, a professional person possessed of a particular skill is liable for breach of contract if he neglects to use the skill and experience which he professes to have, so a professional trustee is liable for breach of trust if loss is caused to the trust fund because he neglects to exercise the special care and skill which he claimed to have (*Bartlett v Barclays Bank Trust Co [1980] Ch 515 at 534*). Brightman J was there dealing with a trust corporation, but the principle would apply equally to a professional such as a solicitor who was appointed because of his professed expertise in trust matters.

The paid trustee

3.4 A higher standard of care may also be expected of a trustee, whether or not holding himself out as a trust professional, who is remunerated for his services to the trust. A trustee who takes on the task gratuitously usually does so as a family member or friend and is not under any obligation to have more knowledge or skill than that which the testator or settlor knew him to possess when he selected him as his trustee, but where a person is to be remunerated he ought not to accept the employment unless he has competent knowledge and skill in the business he is to transact (see *Speight v Gaunt (1883) 22 Ch D 727*). The duty of care substantially equates the position of a trustee facing a claim for breach of trust with that of a professional man (such as an accountant or solicitor) facing a claim for professional negligence (*Wight v Olswang [2000] WTLR 783*).

When does the duty of care apply?

3.5 Unless excluded or modified by the trust instrument, the duty of care extends to all aspects of the performance of a trustee's duties. The ambit of those duties may, however, vary with the nature of the trust. A trustee holding on a bare trust may be under no duty other than to hold the fund and follow the beneficial owner's instructions. In such a case, although such a trustee must exercise reasonable care in respect of the actions he takes, he may owe no duty to manage the fund actively. A trustee holding for successive interests, or for an infant pending his or her attaining majority, however, is in a very different position. The fiduciary duty of care imposes on him an obligation to ensure that the fund is properly managed for the benefit of the beneficiaries.

Duties may extend the role of the trustee

3.6 If a trust fund includes assets the value of which depends on the performance of others, the duties of a trustee may extend to exercising proper control over those others. The best example is where the trust holds sufficient shares in a company to enable the trustees to assert influence over, or, indeed, control the running of the company. In such a case, the duty of the trustees may be to require the Board to inform and consult them so that, if necessary, the trustees can intervene to safeguard the interests of the trust. It is not sufficient for the trustee merely to rely on information given at an annual general meeting (*Bartlett v Barclays Bank Trust Co [1980] Ch 515*). The trustees should ensure that they have as much information as the directors have (*Re Lucking's Will Trusts [1967] 3 All ER 726*).

Error of judgement

3.7 The fact that a trustee has made an error of judgement is not sufficient to fix him with liability. A trustee is not in the position of an insurer (*Bartlett v Barclays Bank Trust Co [1980] Ch 515*). In considering whether an error of judgement was, or was not, an error which a prudent man of business might have made, all the facts and circumstances will be relevant, including the degree of expertise professed by the trustee, and whether the trustee is being paid or acting gratuitously.

Trustee not to be judged by hindsight

3.8 The conduct of a trustee is to be judged in the light of the knowledge possessed by the trustee, and of the standards and practice obtaining at the relevant time. 'One must be careful not to endow the prudent trustee with prophetic vision or expect him to ignore the received wisdom of his time' per Hoffmann J in *Nestle v National Westminster Bank [2000] WTLR 795 at 802*. Thus the fact that an investment policy had failed to preserve the monetary value of capital was not, in itself, a breach of duty by the trustee.

Taking advice

3.9 If the trustee has taken, and subsequently acted upon, advice from an appropriately qualified adviser in respect of his administrative powers, then he will normally have gone a long way to rebutting a charge of failing to exercise reasonable care. However, taking advice does not guarantee a good defence to a charge of breach of trust. If the advice was obtained on the basis of inadequate instructions, or was obviously wrong, or was challenged by the beneficiaries on reasonable grounds then it may not afford protection to the trustee.

In the case of the distribution of the trust fund, the fact that a trustee has acted on legal advice as to how the fund should be distributed will not provide protection if the advice is wrong and the distribution incorrect (see for example, *National Trust Company of Australasia v General Finance Co of Australasia [1905] AC 373*) but it may justify the trustee being excused from liability pursuant to the *Trustee Act 1925, s 61*. (See *Re Allsop [1914] 1 Ch 1 at 12–13*; *Marsden v Regan [1954] 1 WLR 423*. As to the *Trustee Act 1925, s 61* see CHAPTER 9: LIMITATION OF LIABILITY AND RELIEF FROM LIABILITY.) A trustee who, by following incorrect advice, commits a breach of trust and incurs a liability will prima facie have a right to be indemnified by the adviser.

Good faith not enough

3.10 It is no defence to a charge that a trustee has failed to exercise reasonable skill and care and that the trustee acted in good faith. 'Honesty and sincerity are not the same as prudence and reasonableness' (per Megarry V-C in *Cowan v Scargill [1985] Ch 270 at 289*). His duty to a beneficiary may require a trustee to act in a way a trustee would not choose to conduct his own affairs. For example, if a higher offer is received in respect of trust property for which the trustee has already agreed a sale in principle, the trustee must accept the higher offer even if the practice of 'gazumping' is repugnant to him (*Buttle v Saunders [1950] 2 All ER 193*). Only if the circumstances are such that the adage 'a bird in the hand is worth two in the bush' can be reasonably said to apply, is the trustee justified in rejecting the higher offer. The trustee's duty to his beneficiaries outweighs his moral obligation to the purchaser.

The statutory duty of care

The duty of care

3.11 *Section 1* of the *Trustee Act 2000* sets out the statutory duty of care, which is to be applied in accordance with the terms of *Schedule 1* to the Act.

Section 1(1) provides as follows:

> 'Whenever the duty under this subsection applies to a trustee, he must exercise such care and skill as is reasonable in the circumstances, having regard in particular—
>
> (*a*) to any special knowledge or experience that he has or holds himself out as having, and
>
> (*b*) if he acts as trustee in the course of a business or profession, to any special knowledge or experience that it is reasonable to expect of a person acting in the course of that kind of business or profession.'

Clearly the statutory duty of care extends to persons other than those satisfying the criteria specifically mentioned in paragraphs (*a*) or (*b*) above. Where a trustee has no special knowledge or experience, has not held himself out as having special knowledge or experience, and is not acting as a trustee in the course of a business or profession, then the level of reasonable skill and care to be expected of him will be judged accordingly. The fact that a trustee may be a businessman or a professional does not bring him within (*b*) unless he is acting as a trustee in that capacity. The variety of experience in business and the professions is such that not every businessman or professional is better able to bring a higher standard of trusteeship than a person with no professional or business experience. Even a lawyer may have only a layman's grasp of trusts if he has spent his entire professional life practising in some quite different area of the law. The fact that such a person might be expected to have a hazy recollection of equity and trusts encountered at university ought not to be enough to impose a higher standard of care than would be expected of an intelligent and educated lay trustee. However, if a trustee has held himself out as having special knowledge or experience, he falls to be judged by the expectation he has created, however inaccurate, and if he acts as trustee as part of his profession or business it does not lie in his mouth to deny the special knowledge or experience reasonably to be expected of a person acting in the course of that kind of business or profession.

Paragraphs (*a*) and (*b*) above differ in that paragraph (*a*) imposes a subjective test as to what special knowledge or experience the particular trustee possesses or has held himself out as possessing whereas paragraph (*b*) imposes the objective test of what it is reasonable to expect of a person pursuing a particular business or profession. A similar structure comprising subjective and objective factors is to be found in respect of the degree of care and skill expected of company directors (as to which see *Re D'Jan of London Ltd [1994] 1 BCLC 561*).

Where a person would satisfy the criteria set out in both paragraphs (*a*) and (*b*) above (e.g. a professional man claiming particular expertise in the administration of trusts or estates), it seems clear that the objective standard set out in paragraph (*b*) sets the minimum standard below which the trustee must not fall. Paragraph (*a*) operates only to set a higher standard for those who are, or claim to be, by training or experience, specialists. That certainly was the intention of the Law Commission, whose report (Law Com 260, *Trustees' Powers and Duties*) led to the enactment of the 2000 Act.

The statutory duty and the fiduciary duty would appear to be, for all practical purposes, the same in respect of the standard imposed and the criteria by which that standard is set.

When does the statutory duty apply?

3.12 The statutory duty of care will apply to a trustee in the circumstances set out in *Schedule 1* to the *Trustee Act 2000* (see *section 1(2)*) unless and to the extent that the trust instrument provides otherwise. In the absence of any contrary provision, therefore, the statutory duty of care will apply to a trustee in the following circumstances:

(i) when exercising a power of investment (whether the general power conferred by *section 3* of the Act, or any other power of investment however conferred) or carrying out the duties with regard to the standard investment criteria, reviewing investments, and taking advice with regard to investment or the variation of investments (i.e. the powers in *sections 4* and *5* of the Act);

(ii) when exercising a power to acquire land for the trust (whether under *section 8* of the Act or under any other power, however conferred) and when exercising any power in relation to land so acquired;

(iii) when entering into arrangements under which a person is authorised to exercise functions as an agent or appointed to act as a nominee or custodian (whether under the powers conferred by the Act or under any other power, however conferred) or carrying out the duties of review of such agent nominee or custodian;

(iv) when exercising the powers of compounding liabilities etc granted by the *Trustee Act 1925, s 15* or any corresponding power, however conferred;

(v) when exercising the power to insure trust property granted by the *Trustee Act 1925, s 19* or any corresponding power, however conferred;

(vi) when exercising the powers with regard to reversionary interests and valuation etc conferred by the *Trustee Act 1925, s 22(1)* or *22(3)*; or any corresponding power, however conferred;

(vii) (in relation to trustees of land) when exercising their general powers or their powers of delegation under the *Trusts of Land and Appointment of Trustees Act 1996, s 9.*

[*Trustee Act 2000, Sch 1* and *Trusts of Land and Appointment of Trustees Act 1996* (as amended), *ss 6(9)* and *9A(1)*].

In respect of the power to insure, the wording of paragraph (v) of the *Schedule* is such that the duty appears to apply only to the exercise of the power to insure and not to the decision whether or not to insure at all. Whether the provision will be given such a limited construction remains to be seen, but there is no reason in principle why the fiduciary duty of care should not apply where the statutory duty does not. As to insurance see CHAPTER 7: DUTY TO GET IN AND SAFEGUARD TRUST PROPERTY.

Exclusion of the fiduciary or statutory duties of care

3.13 Both the fiduciary duty and the statutory duty can be excluded by an appropriate provision in the trust instrument. However, words excluding liability for breaches of trust or negligence by a trustee must be clear and unambiguous (*Wight v Olswang [2000] WTLR 783*). The liability of a trustee for breaches of the duty of honesty, good faith or recklessness cannot be excluded. For limitation of liability see CHAPTER 9: LIMITATION OF LIABILITY AND RELIEF FROM LIABILITY.

Consequences of failure to exercise reasonable skill and care

3.14 A trustee who commits a breach of trust comes under an immediate duty to remedy such breach. Whilst the trust is current, the primary remedy for breach of trust is to require the defaulting trustee to restore the trust fund to the position it would have been in had the breach of trust not occurred although once the trust has come to an end and the fund is held for those entitled absolutely then their remedy is in damages. Because the remedy is restitutionary, the common law rules of remoteness of damage and causation do not apply, although there must be some causal connection between the breach of trust and the loss to the trust estate for which compensation is recoverable. The quantum of loss is fixed at the date of the judgment, not at the date of the breach of trust, so if, following the breach, all or part of the loss has been recouped, the amount of compensation is reduced. However, where the value of property had fallen and the trustees' breach of trust had prevented the property being sold at the peak of the market, the loss was calculated by reference to the highest value (*Jaffray v Marshall [1993] 1 WLR 1285*).

In a commercial situation, if the commercial objective is achieved then there will be no compensatable loss even if a breach of trust occurred in the course of achieving it. The principles relating to remedies for breach of trust are considered in *Target Holdings Ltd v Redferns [1996] AC 421 at 433–440.*

In an action by a beneficiary claiming damages on his or her own behalf (as opposed to on behalf of the trust fund), the burden of proving damage lies on the beneficiary, and if that burden is not discharged the action will fail (*Nestle v National Westminster Bank plc [1993] 1 WLR 1260*).

Where a breach of trust results in a profit, the profit belongs to the trust. Generally speaking a trustee is not entitled to set off the profits from one breach of trust against the losses from another, but must account in full for the profits and reinstate the losses. An exception is where the breaches of trust stem from the same transaction or are part of the same policy that comprised the breach of trust complained of (*Bartlett v Barclays Bank Trust Co [1980] Ch 515* (where a series of speculative developments led to a loss on the main project and a profit on a minor project; the trustee was liable for the net loss)).

Interest payable by a trustee in breach of trust should have regard to the prevailing rates of interest. If necessary, to compensate the trust fund or the beneficiary, it may be compounded on yearly or half yearly rests (see *El Ajou v Dollar Land Holdings plc (No 2) [1995] 2 All ER 213 at 224*). In a period of high inflation when interest rates reflect and compensate for the erosion in the value of money, the interest may have to be adjusted between life tenant and remainderman with some of the interest payable being apportioned to capital to help restore the corpus of the trust fund (*Bartlett v Barclays Bank Trust Co [1980] Ch 515 at 547*; see also *Jaffray v Marshall [1993] 1 WLR 1285 at 1294*).

A trustee may be ordered to pay the costs of a successful action against him for breach of trust on the indemnity as opposed to the standard basis.

Chapter 4

Duty to Act Honestly

Introduction

4.1 The trustee's duty to perform the trusts honestly and in good faith for the benefit of the beneficiaries is fundamental to the very concept of the trust – if a trustee is not obliged to act honestly for the benefit of his beneficiaries, there is simply no substance to the trust. The principle applies to trusts of all kinds including trusts of land, trusts of personalty, settled land, charitable trusts and pension funds. In the case of settled land the duty is imposed on the life tenant as well as the trustees.

The meaning of dishonesty

4.2 Dishonesty in this context is not confined to deceit. A trustee acts dishonestly if he pursues a particular course of action, either knowing that it is contrary to the interests of the beneficiaries or being recklessly indifferent whether it is contrary to their interests or not (*Armitage v Nurse [1998] Ch 241*).

Honesty, and its counterpart dishonesty, has a strong subjective element in that it is a description of a type of conduct assessed in the light of what a person actually knew at the time. Dishonest conduct is usually advertent, not inadvertent: negligence or carelessness is not dishonesty unless it is so gross as to amount to recklessness. However, individuals are not free to set their own standards of honesty in particular circumstances and, ultimately, the test of honesty is an objective one (*Royal Brunei Airlines v Tan [1995] 2 AC 378 at 389*). The honesty or dishonesty of conduct can be tested by looking at the circumstances and seeing whether they were such that the person must have known that what he did was, by the standards of ordinary decent people, dishonest (*Abbey National plc v Solicitors Indemnity Fund [1997] PNLR 306* approved in *Twinsectra Ltd v Yardley [2002] 2 WLR 802 at 812*).

Despite what was said in *Royal Brunei Airlines v Tan* about the test being objective, the test of honesty may vary from case to case, depending on, among other things:

- the role and calling of the trustee;

- his experience;
- the nature of his conduct; and
- the role of any other trustees.

For example, a solicitor-trustee would be dishonest where, although he genuinely believed that his actions were not contrary to the beneficiaries' interests, that belief was so unreasonable that no reasonable solicitor-trustee could have held it (*Walker v Stones [2001] 2 WLR 623 at 657*).

Personal benefit not relevant

4.3 The presence or absence of any personal benefit to the defaulting trustee is irrelevant to the question of dishonesty (see, for instance, *Armitage v Nurse [1998] Ch 241 at 251* and *Walker v Stones [2001] 2 WLR 623 at 662*).

Moral justification not relevant

4.4 Also irrelevant is a belief by the trustee that he was morally justified in doing what he did (*Twinsectra Ltd v Yardley [2002] 2 WLR 802 at 812*).

Dishonestly assisting the misappropriation of trust property

4.5 A trustee who misappropriates trust property obviously acts dishonestly. Less obvious may be cases where a third party dishonestly assists a trustee or where a trustee dishonestly assists a third party to misappropriate trust property.

In *Royal Brunei Airlines v Tan [1995] 2 AC 378,* the airline engaged a company as its agent, of which the defendant was the managing director and principle shareholder. The contract provided that money collected by the agent was the property of the airline and was held by the agent as trustee. Monies were not, however, put into a separate account but were paid into the agent's own bank account and used for its own business purposes. The agent became insolvent. The defendant was held to have acted dishonestly. He had caused or permitted the agent to commit a breach of trust by using in the conduct of its business money held in trust for the airline when he knew that the company was not authorised to do so by the terms of the trust and was, therefore, liable to the airline for the amount owed to it by the company.

A more controversial result on the facts was reached in *Twinsectra Ltd v Yardley [2002] 2 WLR 802*. A solicitor 'A' was acting for a client in connection with the purchase of land for which the client needed to borrow £1m. A lender was found but was only willing to lend if secured by a personal undertaking by A that the monies would be applied in the acquisition of the property. A was not willing to give that undertaking. The client retained a second solicitor 'B' who was willing to, and did, give the undertaking. B received the monies and on instructions of the client passed the monies onto A who then paid out the monies on the instructions of the client without taking any steps to ensure that they were applied in the acquisition of the property. A took the view that he was bound to follow the instructions of the client and that the undertaking was a matter for B, not for him. A substantial part of the money was used by the client for other purposes. B (who was clearly liable for breach of his undertaking) went bankrupt and the loan was not repaid. The lender commenced proceedings against A on the basis that A had dishonestly assisted in B's breach of trust. It was held that the terms of the undertaking made it clear that the money was not at the free disposal of the client and that B had held the money on trust even though the lender had not intended to create a trust. However, A had honestly believed that the terms of the undertaking were not his concern and that, therefore, he had not acted dishonestly.

The House of Lords held that the Court of Appeal had been wrong to substitute (as it had) a finding that A had been dishonest when the trial judge had reached the opposite conclusion on the facts. Dissenting, Lord Millett found that although A believed honestly that B's obligation to the lender was in contract only rather than in trust, knowing as he did the terms of the undertaking, he knew that he was assisting B to breach his undertaking to the lender and this was sufficient to make A liable to repay the money improperly applied; Lord Millett did not think it necessary to consider whether A realised that honest people would consider his conduct as dishonest.

In *Abbey National plc v Solicitors Indemnity Fund [1997] PNLR 306*, the claimant agreed to make an advance to enable the purchaser to buy a leasehold property. The claimant believed that the lease had 125 years to run; in fact, the lease had 47 years to run, but the lessor had agreed, for the payment of a small premium, to extend the term by the grant of a new lease. The loan was negotiated on the basis that the price payable was the amount payable to the vendors for the existing lease plus the premium payable to the lessor for the new lease. The solicitor released the bulk of the advance on completion of the purchase of the existing lease and certified to the claimant that the transaction had been completed according to its instructions. That certification was not correct – no new lease had been, or was thereafter, granted. The issue was whether the solicitor was guilty of any 'dishonest or fraudulent act or omission' so as to place the claim outside the scope of his insurance cover. It was held that the solicitor had plainly acted dishonestly both in releasing the money when he knew this was contrary to the claimant's instructions and in subsequently certifying to the claimant that its instructions had been carried out when they had not.

Bribery

4.6 Where a trustee receives what amounts to a bribe (however described) to perform his duties in a certain way, he will be held to have acted dishonestly. In *Re Smith [1896] 1 Ch 71*, one of two trustees received a £300 commission for investing a portion of the trust estate in certain debentures. The court held that the other trustee (himself a tenant for life of two-thirds of the residue) had agreed to the investment in the bona fide belief that it was a good one, but that, as regards the trustee who received the commission, '... the fact that he took a bribe is conclusive against him. Honesty seems to be out of the question after that; and I must hold that he is liable to make good the loss occasioned by the investment'. In addition to making good any loss to the trust estate, the trustee who received the £300 bribe or commission was liable to account to the estate for it.

Consequences of a finding of dishonesty

4.7 A number of important consequences can flow from a finding that a breach of trust was dishonest. First, there can be no question of a trustee being granted relief from the consequences of the breach under the *Trustee Act 1925, s 61* (see further CHAPTER 9: LIMITATION OF LIABILITY AND RELIEF FROM LIABILITY) for that section, in terms, applies only where a trustee has 'acted honestly and reasonably'.

Second, whereas the period of limitation for damages for breach of trust is six years from which the right of action accrued, no period of limitation prescribed by the *Limitation Act 1980, s 21* applies to an action by a beneficiary under a trust in respect of any fraud or fraudulent breach of trust to which the trustee was a party or privy: fraud or fraudulent breach of trust means conduct involving dishonesty (*Armitage v Nurse [1998] Ch 241 at 260*). Further, where a person who is both trustee and beneficiary has received more than his proper share, his obligation to make restoration is limited to the excess over his proper share where he has acted honestly and reasonably; if he has been dishonest his liability is not so limited. [*Limitation Act 1980, s 21(3)*].

Third, in the case of a professional trustee, the loss may fall outside the cover of the trustees' professional indemnity insurance – see for example *Solicitors Indemnity Insurance Rules 2001, rule 6.9* which provides that the exclusion may exclude liability to indemnify the person committing or condoning the dishonest act or omission giving rise to the civil liability, but any other insured must be covered.

Fourth, in the case of a bankrupt trustee, his discharge from bankruptcy will not release him from any bankruptcy debt which he incurred in respect of, or forbearance in respect of which was secured by means of, any fraud or fraudulent breach of trust to which he was a party. [*Insolvency Act 1986, s 281(3)*]. Again, fraud or fraudulent breach of trust means conduct involving dishonesty (*Woodland-Ferrari v UCL Group Retirement Benefits Scheme [2002] 3 All ER 670* per Ferris J).

Trustee's liability for the dishonesty of co-trustee

4.8 In principle, a trustee is not liable for the dishonesty or wrongdoing of a co-trustee, unless the trustee has facilitated that dishonesty by his own neglect of duty, in which event he will be liable for the loss occasioned by his own, albeit honest, default. A trustee who is himself dishonest in facilitating a breach of trust by a co-trustee is of course liable as a dishonest trustee.

Until its repeal, the principle was, in part at least, spelt out in the *Trustee Act 1925, s 30*. That section provided that a trustee should be chargeable only for money and securities actually received by him (notwithstanding his signing any receipt for the sake of conformity) and should be answerable and accountable only for his own acts, receipts, neglects or defaults, and not for those of any other trustee, nor for any banker, broker, or other person with whom any trust money or securities may be deposited, nor for the insufficiency or deficiency of any securities, nor for any other loss, unless the same happened through his own wilful default. In *Re Vickery [1931] 1 Ch 572*, Maugham J had given a restrictive interpretation of 'wilful default' with the result that a trustee (at least in those cases subject to the subsection) would not be held liable for the wrongdoing of others unless he was himself guilty of a conscious breach of duty or a reckless performance of duty.

Section 30 was repealed by the *Trustee Act 2000* which did not provide a replacement for it. The position is now governed by the common law. If the dishonesty of one trustee is facilitated by the negligence of another or, where the statutory duty of care applies, a breach of that duty, then the honest trustee will find himself liable by virtue of his own shortcomings. If a trustee discovers the dishonesty of a co-trustee but fails to take steps to expose it or procure redress then he may be held liable for his own breach of trust occasioned by that failure. Similarly, if an honest trustee knows of an intention by a co-trustee to commit a breach of trust then he may be held liable if he fails to take reasonable steps to prevent it.

Failing to join in the taking of possession of trust property

4.9 Both the *Trustee Act 1925, s 30*, and the common law before, absolved a trustee from responsibility where he joined in giving a receipt for trust property but did not, himself, take possession of the property.

Where it is reasonable for him to do so, the trustee will not incur liability by so doing. So where the executors included the deceased's stockbroker of many years standing and his co-executors, having no reason to distrust him, placed certain bonds in his hands for sale, those co-executors were not liable for the loss to the estate when he misappropriated part of the proceeds and absconded (*Re Gasquoine [1894] 1 Ch 470*). Had the co-executors had reason to distrust him then different considerations might have applied. The court also found that there had been no undue delay in calling the stockbroker to account.

The duty to supervise actions of co-trustees

4.10 It is no defence for a trustee to say, following some misappropriation or other wrongdoing by his co-trustee, that he was merely a sleeping trustee or that he considered that the circumstances justified him in leaving the management of the trust entirely to a co-trustee. All trustees are under a duty actively to supervise the actions of their co-trustees and properly to satisfy themselves that their co-trustees are acting in accordance with the duties of their office.

There is, however, a distinction to be drawn between a trustee who simply lets his co-trustee decide matters which ought to be the subject of a joint discretion and a trustee who reasonably relies on what he is told by his co-trustee and is deceived (see *Re Lucking's Will Trusts [1967] 3 All ER 726 at 733*). In that case, the trust fund included the majority of shares in a private company. Initially the trust had one trustee who brought in a director to run the company. The director made unauthorised drawings from the company which were discovered by the trustee, who took no effective safeguards. In due course, a second trustee was appointed, but the original trustee failed to give him complete and accurate information about the director's defalcations. The original trustee was held liable for the loss to the trust fund, however, the second trustee was not held liable because he was entitled to rely on what he was told as being accurate and adequate unless and until he had positive reason to think the contrary.

Actual or threatened breach by co-trustee – duty to act

4.11 A trustee will be held liable for the defalcations of his co-trustee where he has learnt of the breach of trust and has chosen to conceal it (see *Boardman v Mosman (1779) 1 Bro CC 68*). Where a trustee becomes aware that his co-trustee is intending to commit a breach of trust, he should seek to prevent it. If the breach has actually been committed by the time it comes to the trustee's attention, he should seek to prevent further breaches and, if necessary, he must bring an action against the defaulting co-trustee or risk being held jointly liable (see *Gough v Smith [1872] WN 18*).

Liability for dishonesty of agents, nominees and custodians

4.12 By virtue of the *Trustee Act 2000, ss 11–22*, trustees are given power to appoint agents, nominees and custodians, to assist in the performance of the trust. By *section 22* of the Act, trustees who have made such an appointment are obliged, while the agent, nominee or custodian continues to act, to keep under review the arrangements under which the agent, nominee or custodian acts and how those arrangements are being put into effect. This includes an obligation, where necessary, to terminate the appointment or to give appropriate directions to the appointee.

The statutory duty of care (as defined in the *Trustee Act 2000, s 1*) applies to a trustee when appointing an agent, nominee or custodian (whether that appointment is made under the relevant statutory power or under a power specifically granted by the trust instrument) and when keeping any such appointment under review (see *Trustee Act 2000, Sch 1, para 3*). Provided that a trustee complies with the statutory duty of care when making the appointment and keeping the arrangements under review, the trustee will not be liable for any default of the appointee. [*Trustee Act 2000, s 23(2)*].

Exclusion clauses

4.13 A trustee cannot be absolved from the duty to perform the trusts honestly and in good faith, for these are the irreducible core of obligations owed by trustees to the beneficiaries and enforceable by them, which is fundamental to the concept of a trust (*Armitage v Nurse [1998] Ch 241 at 253*). An exemption clause will also not protect a trustee against liability for a reckless breach of trust (see *Armitage v Nurse [1998] Ch 241 at 254*). However, with the exception of fraud, bad faith or wilful default, the liability of a trustee can be excluded by clear words (*Midland Bank Trustee (Jersey) Ltd v Federated Pension Services Ltd [1996] PLR 179 (Court of Appeal Jersey)*). For limitation of liability see CHAPTER 9: LIMITATION OF LIABILITY AND RELIEF FROM LIABILITY.

Settled land

4.14 The *Settled Land Act, s 96* which (like the *Trustee Act 1925, s 30*) limited the liability of trustees to his own acts, receipts and defaults only has been repealed by the *Trustee Act 2000* and not replaced. The common law position thus obtains in respect of liability for the dishonesty of co-trustees.

Chapter 5

Duty not to Benefit Personally

Introduction

5.1 A trustee is not allowed to make a profit from his position of trust, nor must he place himself in a position where his interest and duty conflict. The rule is strictly applied. It is the basis for the rule (now modified by the *Trustee Act 2000*) that even a professional trustee could not charge without the express authority of the trust instrument, the consent of the beneficiaries or an order of the court.

Keech v Sandford

5.2 The leading case is *Keech v Sandford (1726) Sel Cas Ch 61*. That was a case where the trustee took advantage of an opportunity to acquire property with which the trust was associated. A trustee held a lease of a market on trust for a child. Before the expiry of the lease he applied to the lessor for a renewal for the benefit of the child. This was refused, so the trustee himself took a lease for his personal benefit. It was held that the trustee was obliged to assign the lease to the child and account for the profits. The Lord Chancellor remarked that if a trustee on a refusal to renew could have the lease himself, few leases would be renewed in favour of beneficiaries. The case is notable because the trustee had attempted to secure the leasehold for the trust but without success - nevertheless, he was not entitled to keep the benefit for himself.

A more recent example is *Protheroe v Protheroe [1968] 1 WLR 519* where the husband, a joint owner with his wife of a leasehold property, purchased the freehold reversion; it was held that because he was a trustee the freehold reversion became subject of the trust although the husband was entitled to recoup the expense of the purchase.

Pre-existing rights

5.3 If a trustee acquires a personal right before, and not in anticipation of, the inception of the fiduciary relationship, then he is not prevented from enforcing it. For example, where a testator had granted to a bank an option to purchase certain premises at a specified price and thereafter appointed the bank and his widow to be his executors and trustees, the bank was entitled to exercise the option despite having proved the will following the testator's death and thereby taken on the role with the widow of personal representative (*Re Mulholland's Will Trusts [1949] 1 All ER 460*). In that case the price had been determined before the bank took on its fiduciary duties but the more difficult situation is where the nature of the right is such that terms remain to be worked out. For example, if the right had been a right of pre-emption under which the price had to be agreed with the trustees. Presumably the trustee would have to take steps to avoid the conflict of interest by leaving the determining of the price to his co-trustees or having it fixed by the court.

Purchasing trust property

5.4 The true rule is not that a trustee may not purchase trust property (although often expressed in those terms) but that a purchase by a trustee of trust property is voidable within a reasonable time at the instance of a beneficiary (per Danckwerts LJ, *Holder v Holder [1968] Ch 353 at 398D*). The sale may be avoided even if fair and honest and made at a public auction. However, the rule does not apply if:

(*a*) the trust instrument provides otherwise;

(*b*) the beneficiaries are all of full age and capacity and consent; or

(*c*) the sale is authorised by the court.

In the case of settled land, the *Settled Land Act 1925* makes special provision to enable the tenant for life to buy settled land (see 5.20 below).

Appropriation

5.5 The rule applies to the exercise by a person who is both trustee and beneficiary of the power of appropriation (as to which see CHAPTER 17: POWER TO APPROPRIATE AND POWER TO PARTITION).

Thus, in *Kane v Radley-Kane [1999] Ch 274*, a widow took a grant of letters of administration to the estate of her late husband. The estate included a number of shares in a private company. The shares were valued for the purpose of the grant at £50,000 so that the estate was within the statutory widow's legacy and the widow treated herself as being absolutely entitled to all the assets of the estate, including the shares, and took them in specie. Within two years of the death, the widow had sold the shares for a sum in excess of £1.1m. One of the sons of the deceased by a previous marriage successfully applied to have the appropriation set aside, the court holding that the proceeds of sale of the shares formed part of the estate, for which the widow was accountable.

A specific example of appropriation is the statutory right of the surviving spouse of a person dying intestate to have the matrimonial home appropriated on account of his or her interest in the estate (see CHAPTER 17: POWER TO APPROPRIATE AND POWER TO PARTITION). The *Intestates' Estates Act 1952, Sch 2, para 5* provides that where the surviving husband or wife is one of two or more personal representatives, the rule that a trustee may not be a purchaser of trust property shall not prevent the surviving husband or wife from purchasing out of the estate of the intestate an interest in a dwelling house in which the surviving husband or wife was resident at the time of the intestate's death. If the surviving husband or wife is the sole personal representative then he or she should seek the written approval of the beneficiaries or an order of the court.

Non-proving executor

5.6 Where a person named as one of several executors in the will had renounced probate, and subsequently bid at auction for the freehold of a farm (of which he was the tenant) which was an asset of the estate, the Court of Appeal held that he was not debarred from purchasing the property. The court found that the acts of administration were minimal, that any knowledge he acquired in respect of the farm had been as a result of being the tenant not an executor, and in respect of the sale he had acted only as purchaser not as vendor (*Holder v Holder [1968] Ch 353*). The issue in the case was complicated by the fact that the purchaser had taken some steps in the administration (i.e. intermeddled) before renouncing his right to probate, thereby raising the question whether, by renouncing probate, he could escape the normal operation of the rule that a purchase by him could be set aside as of right. However, if a person named as executor renounces before intermeddling, there is no reason, in principle, why the rule should apply to him at all.

Application of the rule to a retired trustee

5.7 An executor or trustee who has acted as such cannot avoid the operation of the rule by renouncing or retiring in order to purchase trust property (*Wright v Morgan [1926] AC 788*). However, if a trustee had been retired for a sufficient period of time, that it cannot be said that he retains any advantage as a result of his former trusteeship, the rule will not apply. In *Re Boles and British Land Co's Contract [1902] 1 Ch 244* the rule was not applied to a trustee who had been retired for over 12 years and there had been no idea of a sale at the time of his retirement. That was a clear case given the length of time that had elapsed. It may well be that a much shorter time would suffice particularly if the proposal to sell has arisen only after the retirement.

Sale to the spouse, relative or other associate of a trustee

5.8 In Scotland it has been held that a sale to a spouse of a trustee is not within the rule but liable to be set aside if at an undervalue (*Burrell v*

Burrell's Trustees 1915 52 SLR 312). In *Tito v Waddell (No 2) [1977] Ch 106 at 240* it was observed that:

> '... there are wives and wives. In one case the trustee may have sold privately to his wife with whom he was living in perfect amity; in another the property may have been knocked down at auction to the trustee's wife from whom he has been living separate and in enmity for a dozen years'.

It is important to note that in that passage a distinction is drawn not only between connubial bliss on the one hand and estrangement on the other but sale by private treaty and public auction. However, any sale, particularly a sale by private treaty, to a spouse or other close relative or associate would be highly suspect and is not a transaction that would be undertaken by a prudent trustee without the informed consent of the beneficiaries or the sanction of the court. The court will apply safeguards similar to those it would apply in the case of a sale to the trustee himself (*Re McNally [1967] NZLR 521*).

In *Re Thompson's Settlements [1986] Ch 99* it was held that the self-dealing rule would apply to a sale of certain trust assets to a firm of which one trustee was a partner and of other trust assets to a company of which another trustee was a shareholder and he and his wife directors. In that case, Vinelott J held that the self-dealing rule, that a trustee's sale of trust property to himself was voidable, was an application of a wider principle that a man must not put himself into a situation where his duty and interest conflicted and it was not confined to the sale of property by trustees to themselves.

Custodian trustees

5.9 The rule also applies to a custodian trustee. In *Re Brooke Bond & Co Ltd's Trust Deed [1963] Ch 357* the trustees of a company pension fund appointed an insurance company custodian trustee of a pension fund. The question arose whether an insurance policy could be taken out by the trustees with the custodian trustee to secure the payment of benefits. It was held that while the chance of conflict might be less in the case of custodian trustees, the possibility of conflict was still there, and the custodian trustee could not lawfully enter into the contract with the trustees of the fund without the authority of the court.

Transaction authorised by the trust instrument

5.10 The trust instrument itself may authorise trustees to do acts which might otherwise infringe the rule against self-dealing. In *Sargeant v National Westminster Bank plc (1990) 61 P & CR 518* the testator's will contained an express power for a trustee to purchase trust property. Two of the trustees were entitled to one-third each of the proceeds of sale and were tenants of farms on the trust property under leases granted by the testator. The owner of the remaining one-third claimed that the trustees were not entitled to sell the farms to themselves so long as their tenancies subsisted, as the purchase price would be depressed. It was held that the rule that the trustees must not put themselves in a position where their interest and duty conflicted did not apply. They had not put themselves in that position, but had been put there mainly by the testator's grant of tenancies to them and by the provisions of his will. They were, therefore, entitled to purchase the trust property.

A clause in a will or settlement permitting self-dealing may have important consequences in the event of bankruptcy or liquidation. Property held in trust does not vest in the trustee in bankruptcy or liquidator. In *Space Investments Ltd v Canadian Imperial Bank of Commerce Trust Co (Bahamas) Ltd [1986] 1 WLR 1072* a bank trustee deposited monies with itself as banker having been expressly authorised by the trust instrument to open and maintain savings accounts with any bank including itself, and to deposit trust money to the credit of such account. The bank went into liquidation and the question arose whether the monies deposited with the bank remained trust monies amenable to the tracing remedy. It was held that as the trust instrument permitted the bank to deposit trust monies with itself as banker, the trust monies became the property of the bank and could be used for its own purposes subject to its obligation (as banker) to pay out an equivalent amount in the manner required in the settlement or by law. The beneficiaries were, therefore, only entitled to claim as unsecured creditors in the same manner as any other customer.

Extent of authority given by the trust instrument

5.11 The fact that the trust instrument authorises one trustee to buy a trust asset does not mean that any other trustee is similarly so licensed. In *Wright v Morgan [1926] AC 788* an option to purchase was given to a trustee under a will. The trustee assigned the benefit of the option to another of the trustees who exercised it. It was held that the sale to the assignee must be set aside as a conflict of duty and interest arose. It was accepted that:

(*a*) the trustee beneficiary was entitled to deal with the option as he wished; and

(*b*) had *he* exercised the option and assigned the property the transaction would have been unimpeachable.

The case was a severe application of the rule as the will regulated the terms of the sale including the appointment of valuers so that there was no question of negotiating the price (or, as the case puts it, 'higgling of the market'), but the court considered that nevertheless a conflict of duty might arise.

Acquiescence by a beneficiary

5.12 A beneficiary may fail to have a sale set aside if he or she has acquiesced in the transaction. So, in *Holder v Holder [1968] Ch 353* the court would also have declined to set aside the transaction on the ground that the beneficiary complainant had known of the sale but had not objected to it. The charge of acquiescence in that case was very strong as the beneficiary had (unsuccessfully) pressed the proving executors as vendors to forfeit the purchaser's deposit when he failed to complete on time; that was, of course, an option open to the vendors only by virtue of the contract of sale. It was argued for the beneficiary that he could not be taken to have acquiesced unless and until he knew his legal rights (i.e. to avoid the sale) but the court held that the whole of the circumstances had to be looked at to see if it was just that the complaining beneficiary should succeed against the trustee.

Repurchase by trustee from a third party

5.13 If trust property has been the subject of a bona fide sale to a third party, there is no reason, in principle, why a trustee should not purchase it from that third party, the trust's interest in it having ceased on the first sale. However, if the first sale is not bona fide or is on terms that it will or might be resold to the trustee then it is liable to be set aside. If the sale and repurchase are in quick succession then the bona fides of the sale may be called in question. If, pending completion of the sale, a trustee purports to purchase (so as to acquire a right to the property by way of subsale) then the transaction is liable to be set aside (*Delves v Grey [1902] 2 Ch 606*).

Dealings with beneficiaries

5.14 Different considerations apply where the trustee purchases the interest of a beneficiary who is of full age and capacity. In this situation there is no conflict of interest as the beneficiary is able to look to his own interest and make whatever bargain he sees fit. However, the trustee is in a fiduciary relationship with the beneficiary and, therefore, must deal fairly.

> 'The transaction may be set aside by the beneficiary unless the trustee can show that he has taken no advantage of his position and has made full disclosure to the beneficiary and that the transaction is fair and honest' (per Megarry V-C, *Tito v Waddell (No 2) [1977] Ch 106 at 241*).

So where a trustee had in his possession a valuation of the trust estate which he did not disclose to the beneficiary, and which demonstrated that he stood to make a profit, the sale by the beneficiary was set aside (*Dougan v Macpherson [1902] AC 197*).

A trustee who contends that what appears to be a purchase of a trust asset is, in truth, a purchase from the beneficiaries, must prove the same by clear affirmative evidence (*Williams v Scott [1900] AC 499*).

Consent by a beneficiary and sanction of the court

5.15 If the beneficiaries are of full age and capacity they can, of course, agree to a purchase of trust property by a trustee. If there are infant or unborn beneficiaries, their consent cannot be obtained. The court has jurisdiction to sanction a purchase of trust property by a trustee in a situation where the consent of all the beneficiaries cannot be obtained. There seems no reason in principle why the court should not sanction a transaction, even in the face of objection by a beneficiary if the transaction is in the interest of the beneficiaries as a whole and there is no substance to the objection. If the property is being sold by auction it is a matter for the discretion of the court whether or not to give a trustee leave to bid (*Holder v Holder [1968] Ch 353*).

An application for consent of the court is by application under CPR Pt 8 and all relevant beneficiaries should be parties. The co-trustees should make a witness statement exhibiting the instructions given to the valuer and giving their views on the benefit of the sale to any infant and unborn beneficiaries.

Remedy of beneficiary

5.16 Where a sale is set aside for breach of the self-dealing rule, the complainant beneficiary is entitled to have it sold again or, if all the beneficiaries consent, to have it reconveyed to the trust (see *Holder v Holder [1968] Ch 353 at 370*). Cross J at first instance had held that the transaction had breached the self-dealing rule. This finding was reversed on appeal, but the first instance decision remains of interest in that it sets out his directions consequent on his finding that the sale to the trustee should be set aside and so provides a useful guide for other cases.

The judge held that the property should be put up for resale but that if it failed to show a profit for the trust the trustee should be held to his original bargain. He directed that the reserve on the resale should not be less that the figure which the trustee would be entitled to receive out of a resale. That sum was repayment of the original purchase price to be refunded to him or his mortgagees, and an allowance for improvements made by him which enhanced its value. The trustee would be entitled to interest on the purchase but debited with the profits of the property.

Cross J had held that he could not authorise the trustee to bid on the resale if any of the beneficiaries objected but, in the Court of Appeal, Sachs LJ (*page 402*) held that the court had a discretion, even in the face of objection, to allow a trustee to bid in appropriate circumstances. As an alternative to resale the beneficiaries could elect to have the property reconveyed to the trust but one beneficiary could not so insist against the wishes of his co-beneficiaries (*page 370*).

Cross J would have reserved the matter of the costs of the resale, indicating that if the property sold for more than the trustee had originally paid, the cost of resale would come out of the trust fund, but that if the reserve was not reached or not exceeded by sufficient to cover the costs, there would be a 'strong argument for ordering the plaintiff (i.e. the beneficiary) to pay the costs or some of them ...' (*page 375*). Cross J also indicated that a beneficiary seeking a resale might be ordered to put up security for the costs if the court thought that it was a case of an impecunious beneficiary insisting on a resale in order to spite the trustee or to put himself in a strong bargaining position. However, if the evidence is that a resale is likely to yield a profit for the trust the court will be unwilling to prevent an impecunious beneficiary from getting his share of that profit.

It would, therefore, appear from the judgment of Cross J that although the rule against self-dealing is a right a beneficiary is entitled to invoke, exercising that right is not without risk of being penalised in costs if a resale fails to better the price paid by the trustee.

Incidental profits

5.17 A trustee is not entitled to make an incidental profit from his position of trust, and if he does so he must account for it, although in respect of pension schemes special provisions apply (see 5.20 below). A common and important application of this rule is where a trustee becomes a director of a company the shares of which are trust assets. If he owes his position as director to the votes attached to the trust shares then, unless the matter falls within one or other of the following situations he must account to the trust for any remuneration paid to him. The situations where he may retain the remuneration are:

(*a*) where the trust instrument expressly so permits;

(*b*) if he was a director before becoming a trustee and is not dependent on the votes of the trust share to retain that position; or

(*c*) if he obtained the position independently of his position as trustee, e.g. by the votes of shares owned by him personally or of the shares of other shareholders.

Competition with the trust

5.18 A trustee must not put himself into a conflict between his duty and his personal interest by carrying on a business in competition with the trust. It follows that a trustee may not set himself up in business in competition with the trust business. So in *Re Thompson [1930] 1 Ch 203* it was held that an executor was not entitled to set up in business as a yacht broker in competition with the deceased's business which was being carried on by his co-executors in the course of administration.

Settled land

Dealings between the tenant for life and the estate

5.19 The *Settled Land Act 1925, s 68* makes specific provision to enable a tenant for life to purchase or otherwise acquire an interest in the settled land. The interests of the other beneficiaries under the settlement are protected by the trustees, who for this purpose, are given the powers that would otherwise be vested in the tenant for life.

Section 68 provides that:

(*a*) the sale, grant, lease, mortgage, charge or other disposition of settled land, or of any easement, right, or privilege, over the same may be made to the tenant for life; or

(*b*) capital money may be advanced on mortgage to him; or

(*c*) a purchase may be made from him of land to be made subject to the limitations of the settlement; or

(*d*) an exchange may be made with him of settled land for other land; and

(*e*) any such disposition, advance, purchase, or exchange, as aforesaid, may be made to, from, or with any persons of whom the tenant for life is one.

In every such case the trustees of the settlement, in addition to their powers as trustees, have all the powers of a tenant for life in reference to negotiating and completing the transaction and power to enforce any covenants by the tenant for life. Where the tenant for life is himself one of the trustees, then the powers are vested in the other trustee or trustees. The powers of the tenant for life are exercised by the trustees of the settlement in the name and on behalf of the tenant for life.

Section 68 applies notwithstanding that the tenant for life is one of the trustees of the settlement, or an order has been made authorising the trustees to act on his behalf, or that he is suffering from a mental disorder, but it does not apply to dealings with any body of persons which includes a trustee of the settlement, not being the tenant for life, unless the transaction is either previously or subsequently approved by the court.

Pension schemes

5.20 A trustee who is also a member of a pension scheme is in a special position. The *Pensions Act 1995, s 39* provides that the rule that a trustee must not exercise his powers so as to give rise to a conflict between his personal interest and the interests of the beneficiaries shall not apply to a trustee of a trust scheme, who is also a member of the scheme, merely because the exercise of his powers may benefit him as a member of the scheme.

Chapter 6

Duty to Act Impartially

Introduction

6.1 It is the duty of trustees to act impartially as between the different beneficiaries under the trust and to administer the trust in as fair and detached a manner as possible. Traditionally expressed, the duty is to hold the scales evenly between different beneficiaries or classes of beneficiaries. However, in the context of a power of investment, Hoffmann J preferred to say that trustees 'must act fairly in making investment decisions which may have different consequences for different classes of beneficiaries'; he did so because investments carry expectations about their future income yield and capital appreciation which may or may not be realised and 'the image of scales suggests a more mechanistic process than I believe the law requires' (*Nestle v National Westminster Bank Plc [2000] WTLR 795 at 803*).

Partisanship

6.2 The trustee cannot act as a partisan on behalf of one beneficiary. This is a fairly obvious application of the rule. An example is *Ellis v Barker (1871) 7 Ch App 104*. In that case the testator intended that his nephew should replace him as tenant of his farm (assuming that the landlord would accept him), and bequeathed him the farm stock and two freehold properties. If these bequests were satisfied, there would not have been enough left in the estate to pay the various legacies and annuities which were also provided for in the will (these were to go to the nephew's parents, sisters and other persons, including the trustees). The trustees concluded that the testator must have made the will under a mistake as to the amount of his assets. They consulted the farm landlord, who left it to their decision whether or not the nephew should be accepted as tenant, and, purportedly acting in pursuit of a morally sound aim, they refused to let the nephew be accepted as tenant unless he executed a deed making over the freehold properties, which were to be used to pay the legacies and annuities. The Lords Justices held that this constituted a clear breach of trust:

> '... their duty was to carry out [the testamentary] trusts into effect impartially; they had no right to use the power given to them by their

position as trustees, or any other power which they had, as a means of making a new will for the testator' (per James LJ *at 108*).

Partisanship may lead to the removal of a trustee, although it will not invariably do so (as where, for instance, his partisan behaviour results from an innocent misinterpretation of the trusts – see *Simpson v Bathurst (1869) 5 Ch App 193*).

Assisting or accommodating a beneficiary

6.3 Trustees must not jeopardise the trust fund by assisting or 'accommodating' one of a number of beneficiaries. In *Knox v Mackinnon (1888) 13 App Cas 753*, trustees sold trade premises (the property of the trust) to one of seven beneficiaries. The purchaser was unable to pay the £12,000 purchase price, but the trustees permitted him to retain the property, taking as security for the purchase price certain real property (which was already heavily mortgaged) and the personal guarantees of the purchaser and his father in law, both of whom subsequently became bankrupt. As a result of the failure of these securities, the trust lost some £10,000. The entire transaction was condemned as 'an accommodation to William Miller [the purchaser beneficiary] and not a bona fide investment of the trust funds' (*at 763*, per Lord Halsbury LC) and the trustees were held personally liable for the loss.

Not every accommodation will be a breach of trust. In *Ward v Ward (1843) 2 HL Cas 777n*, a debt was owed by the beneficiary and to enforce immediate payment would have ruined the beneficiary and his children who were also beneficiaries. The trustees were held to have acted reasonably in making an arrangement for payment by instalments even though, in the event, the debtor went bankrupt and the trust fund suffered a loss.

Involvement in disputes between beneficiaries

6.4 It is not the role of a trustee to take sides in disputes between beneficiaries and they should refrain from doing so. In the event that the beneficiaries disagree over a matter concerning the trust which impacts on its administration and cannot be resolved by agreement, the trustees may, and should, take the directions of the court.

In litigation commenced by a beneficiary in respect of the trust, the trustees will be proper parties, but should confine themselves to placing information before the court and assisting the court in a non-partisan way. The one exception to this rule is when trustees are called upon to represent interests that are not otherwise represented, for example unborns. CPR r 48.4 expressly provides that a trustee, who is entitled to be paid costs of proceedings in which he has been a party in the capacity of trustee or personal representative, is entitled to be paid the costs of the proceedings, in so far as they are not recovered from or paid by the other person, out of the relevant trust fund or estate. However, the rule applies only to costs which the trustee or personal representative is entitled to be paid and will not apply to costs which the trustee incurs improperly or costs which the trustee is ordered to bear personally.

It is not the rule that the trustee is under a duty to defend the trust fund; the trustee should either remain neutral leaving it to the rival claimants to fight it out or, in a proper case, take the directions of the court on a Beddoe summons as to whether or not to commence or defend the proceedings (*Alsop Wilkinson v Neary [1995] 1 All ER 431*).

Impartiality and the exercise of a discretion

6.5 In considering the duty to act impartially in relation to the exercise of a discretion, there is a clear distinction to be drawn between the exercise of an administrative power and the exercise of a dispositive power. In the case of the latter, it is of the essence of the power that the trustees do prefer some beneficiaries over others.

Administrative powers

6.6 The obligation to strike a balance between beneficiaries, or classes of beneficiaries, applies in respect of the exercise of administrative powers. To take the simplest example, the power of investment, a life tenant will want the maximum income whereas the remaindermen will benefit most from capital growth; an investment policy must endeavour to strike a balance between these two, apparently competing, requirements. In practice, of course, a balanced investment policy will, in the long run, often produce benefits for both classes of beneficiary.

The investment policy of a professional trustee came under attack in *Nestle v National Westminster Bank [1993] 1 WLR 1260 (CA)* (the first instance judgment of Hoffmann J is reported in *[2000] WTLR 795*). The deceased left a portfolio of investments. Under his will his widow was entitled to an annuity, subject to that there were further dispositions in favour of his two sons and their children which, in the event, resulted in the fund passing to his surviving grandchild. During the life of the widow the bank invested for income to fund the annuity. After her death it pursued a restricted investment policy, apparently under a misapprehension of its powers under an express investment clause. It also seems that one of the sons had encouraged the bank to invest his fund in fixed interest stocks to maximize income, whilst he invested his personal fortune in equities thereby getting the best of both worlds. On the death of the surviving son in 1986 the fund was worth £269,203. The grandchild contended that had proper investment policies been followed by the bank, the fund would have been worth over £1m.

In the event the action failed because the grandchild could not prove that she had suffered loss, but a number of aspects touching on the duty of the bank as trustee in regard to investment were considered both at first instance and on appeal and, in respect of the duty of impartiality, it was made clear that striking a balance is not simply a dry mathematical calculation. A trustee is entitled to take into account a matter such as a gross disparity in the wealth of two beneficiaries. As Staughton LJ puts it (*page 1279*):

> 'If the life tenant is living in penury and the remainderman already has ample wealth, common sense suggests that a trustee should be able to take that into account, not necessarily by seeking the highest possible income at the expense of capital but by inclining in that direction'.

However, if the trustee is going to take into account relative wealth as a factor he should make proper inquiry to satisfy himself of the position. A trustee may also pay some regard to the relationships between the various beneficiaries and the settlor. So, for example, a trustee might incline towards income needed for the settlor's widow as opposed to capital which is destined to pass to a more distant relative or to a person who stands to take only in default. However, as Hoffmann J pointed out at first instance these are factors for a trustee to bear in mind, not overriding considerations in the management of the trust.

Leaseholds – rent-free periods

6.7 If trustees, when letting business premises comprised in the trust, employ the not uncommon practice of granting a rent-free period, or concessionary rent as an inducement to the incoming tenant, the question arises whether there should be any adjustment in the event that a life interest terminates during the relevant period.

The relevant period would be from commencement to the first rent review after the cessation of the concessionary period. Current accountancy practice (UITF 28) is to spread the rent over the relevant period and this is the basis upon which the rent is taxed (IM356d). There seems no reason in principle why trustees should not similarly apportion the income over the relevant period so that a life tenant becomes entitled to a proportionate share of the rent payable even though receipt of income is postponed; the tenant's obligation to pay the rent arises on the grant of the lease. If the life tenant survives the relevant period then the issue does not arise.

In respect of other inducements (e.g. if the trust bears fitting out costs) two issues may arise: (i) whether any part of the cost should be borne by capital; this will normally be determined by the nature of the expense and whether it makes a permanent or transitory improvement to the property;

and (ii) whether, like a rent-free period, the cost should be set off against rents received over a period. If there is disagreement between beneficiaries and the amount involved justifies the cost, the trustees should seek the directions of the court.

Undistributable funds

6.8 The duty to balance the differing interests in a trust fund continues after the end of the trust in respect of any trust monies which cannot be distributed. In *X v A [2000] 1 All ER 490* the trustees were entitled to continue to hold part of the trust fund by virtue of a lien in respect of potential liabilities which might arise under the *Environmental Protection Act 1990* (contaminated land). In respect of their management of the retained funds they were not required to disregard their own position and interest by virtue of the lien but were required to act fairly as between the beneficiaries and themselves, taking into account the different rights and interests of the parties in the trust assets.

Appropriation of assets

6.9 A duty to act impartially may arise in connection with the trustees' power to appropriate assets. Thus, trustees who appropriated assets without determining their respective values, with the result that one family was given worthless mortgages and the other took assets of value, committed a breach of trust and were liable in damages (*Re Brookes [1914] 1 Ch 558*).

The duty to act impartially may make it inappropriate to exercise a power, such as a power to appropriate. Where an appropriation to a beneficiary of part of a holding of shares in a private company, equivalent to that beneficiary's share in residue, would have broken up the estate's controlling interest and given the transferee markedly more than the pro rata value of the shares, the court ordered that the holding be sold as a block, not appropriated. An appropriation favouring, as it would, one beneficiary against the others would have offended the principle that one beneficiary should not be favoured over another (*Lloyds Bank v Duker [1987] 1 WLR 1324*).

Where the personal representative is also a beneficiary, the rule against self dealing applies in respect of the power of appropriation (see CHAPTER 17: POWER TO APPROPRIATE AND POWER TO PARTITION). So where a widow appropriated to herself, on account of her interest under intestacy, shares which had been valued for probate at £50,000 and which, within two years, were sold for a sum in excess of £1m, the appropriation was set aside at the suit of another beneficiary (*Kane v Radley-Kane [1999] Ch 274*).

Duty to realise assets

6.10 The duty to act impartially may require trustees to realise assets which favour income at the expense of capital or vice versa. In the case of will trusts, the rules of equitable apportionment may apply if not expressly excluded (see 6.20 below).

Where the duty to act impartially requires trust property to be sold and the proceeds reinvested, the court will not interfere with the discretion which the trustees possessed as to the particular time or manner of sale, so long as their conduct is bona fide and they act fairly between the beneficiaries (*Re Burrage (1890) 62 LT 752*).

Dispositive powers

6.11 A dispositive power differs from an administrative power in that it does confer on a trustee the power to prefer one beneficiary over another; that is the essence of the power conferred. However, a trustee does not enjoy complete freedom. When exercising a discretionary power to choose, a trustee must not take into account irrelevant, irrational or improper factors, but providing he avoids doing so he is entitled to choose and to prefer some beneficiaries over others. In *Edge v Pensions Ombudsman [2000] Ch 602 at 627*, Chadwick LJ described the duty to act impartially as the ordinary duty imposed on a person entrusted with the exercise of a discretionary power, to exercise the power for the purpose for which it is given, giving proper consideration to the matters which are relevant and excluding from consideration matters which are irrelevant.

The court will not interfere with the exercise of a trustee's discretion simply because it would have exercised it differently. If trustees take into account irrelevant or improper or irrational factors, their exercise of discretion may well be flawed, but it is not flawed simply because someone else regards their partiality as 'undue'. The discretion is for the trustees to exercise as they see fit and, except in a case in which the discretion has been surrendered to the court, it is not for a judge to exercise the discretion (*Edge v Pensions Ombudsman [1998] Ch 512 at 534*).

Settled land

6.12 As regards the *trustees* of settled land, the duty of impartiality applies just as it applies to the trustees of any other private trust and that includes a duty to hold an even hand as between the interests of life tenant and remaindermen (*Re Hotchkin's Settled Estates (1887) 35 Ch D 41*).

The tenant for life of settled land occupies a dual capacity as beneficiary and as a trustee of the powers vested in him. The *Settled Land Act 1925, s 107(1)* provides that:

> 'A tenant for life or statutory owner shall, in exercising any power under this Act, have regard to the interests of all parties entitled under the settlement, and shall, in relation to the exercise thereof by him, be deemed to be in the position and to have the duties and liabilities of a trustee for those parties'.

In exercising his statutory powers, therefore, a tenant for life is at one and the same time entitled to consider his own interests and bound to consider the interests of the remainderman (*Re Sutherland Settlement Trusts [1953] Ch 792*).

The *Settled Land Act 1925, s 106* entrenches the right of the tenant for life to require the settled land to be vested in him and to exercise any power conferred on him under the Act, including the power to sell the land. In *Thomas v Williams (1883) 24 Ch D 558 at 556* the court made clear that in deciding whether or not to sell, the tenant for life was entitled to look to his own interest, but having decided to sell, the tenant for life is bound to act bona fide and get the best price. Thus, where a tenant for life whose right to occupy a certain house would come to an end on remarriage, proposed, in purported exercise of her *Settled Land Act* powers, to lease the property to her intended husband, she was restrained from so doing on the ground that it was not a bona fide exercise of her *Settled Land Act* powers as tenant for life (*Middlemas v Stevens [1901] 1 Ch 574*).

Personal representatives

6.13 The duty of an executor is generally expressed as a duty to have regard to the interests of the estate as a whole, rather than as a duty to hold the balance evenly between the beneficiaries. An executor or administrator has to wind up the affairs of the deceased and, therefore, owes duties to persons other than the beneficiaries (in particular the deceased's creditors). The functions of a personal representative are:

- to get in the testator's estate;
- preserve its properties;
- discharge its liabilities; and
- distribute the resulting net assets.

During the administration of an estate, no legatee, devisee or next-of-kin has any beneficial interest in the assets being administered. The position of a personal representative is, therefore, quite different from that of a trustee who holds property of which the beneficiaries are the beneficial owners (*Re Hayes [1971] 1 WLR 758 at 764*). Once the administration has been completed and the personal representatives have assented to the vesting of any property to be held in trust in the trustees (who may, or may not, be the same persons) then the usual trust rule will apply.

In *Re Hayes* the deceased by his will provided that the trustees were to have power to sell certain real property to his son at probate value. His daughter contended that it was, therefore, incumbent on the executors to agree a probate value at the highest price it *might* fetch on the open market but the court held that the executors were not under a duty to agree it at the highest price, as opposed to the more usual mean price lying between the highest and lowest in the range estimated by a valuer.

In *Re Charteris [1917] 2 Ch 379* the executors had to raise a legacy from the testatrix's investments and to pay the income therefrom to her son for life. They had power to appropriate and to postpone sale or appropriation and the will directed that until the legacy was invested the life tenant was to be paid interest at 3½%. The war had occasioned a depression in the value of all securities making it an unfavourable time to realise securities and the executors postponed realisation or appropriation. It was held that the executors were entitled to take that course and the son's entitlement in the meantime was limited to 3½%. Warrington LJ observed that the duty was not to have regard to the interests of one person or of another interested in the estate, but to have regard to the interests of the estate as a whole which in such a case meant exercising their discretion in the way that would, in their opinion, tend to produce ultimately the largest amount of money for distribution amongst the several persons interested. It was observed that the exercise of a power to postpone conversion necessarily affected some of the persons interested in the testator's estate prejudicially and others advantageously.

Apportionment

6.14 The duty to treat all beneficiaries impartially gives rise to the issue of apportionment. If a life interest falls in shortly before a dividend or interest is due to be paid, is it fair that the next interest takes the benefit? If the realisation of a non-income producing asset is delayed should the life tenant receive some compensation? The nineteenth century provided the three principal authorities – *Howe v Lord Dartmouth (1802) 7 Ves 137*; *Re Earl of Chesterfield's Trusts (1883) 24 Ch D 643* and *Allhusen v Whittell (1867) LR 4 Eq 295* – and the *Apportionment Act 1870*. In practice, save where large sums are involved, the time and cost of apportionment is disproportionate and it is commonplace to exclude the duty to apportion.

The Apportionment Act 1870

6.15 The *Apportionment Act 1870, s* 2 provides that all rents, annuities, dividends and other periodical payments in the nature of income shall, like interest on money lent, be considered as accruing from day to day and shall be apportioned in respect of time accordingly. The Act does not apply if it is expressly stated that no apportionment is to take place (*Re Lysaght [1898] 1 Ch 115*).

An income payment made for a period partly before and partly after death has to be apportioned according to the Act. If the payment relates to a period occurring wholly before the relevant date for apportionment then the whole sum is due to whoever was then entitled to income (*Re Muirhead [1916] 2 Ch 181*; *Re Winder's Will Trusts [1951] 2 All ER 362*). The *Apportionment Act 1870* is not to be applied to any unauthorised investments (*Re Fawcett [1940] Ch 402*).

Howe v Lord Dartmouth

6.16 There are two rules in *Howe v Dartmouth* (see 6.14 above). The first requires the trustees to realise wasting or future or reversionary assets unless the will reveals a contrary intention. The second operates to adjust the income received by the life tenant to what would have been received had the property been converted, the balance of income being treated as capital.

First rule

6.17 The first rule applies only in the case of residuary personalty settled by will. The rationale of the rule is that if a testator leaves residue in successive interests, then it must be put into a state so each successive interest can enjoy it. It gives way to a contrary intention. It does not apply to settlements *inter vivos* (*Re Van Straubenzee, Boustead v Cooper [1901] 2 Ch 779*) or to property specifically given by will, for in each case the settlor or testator knows the nature of the asset of which he is disposing. Nor does it apply to realty. In *Re Gough [1957] Ch 323* it was held that the rule no longer applied to long leaseholds over 60 years as they had become authorised investments by the *Settled Land Act 1925* and the *Law of Property Act 1925*. By the same reasoning it should follow that leaseholds of less than 60 years (which since 1997 trustees are authorised to hold and purchase) are no longer subject to the rule.

Second rule

6.18 The second rule in *Howe v Lord Dartmouth* is that where personal property (not just reversionary personal property) which is held for persons in succession ought to have been sold, then for the period it remains unsold the tenant for life is entitled to interest rather than the actual income on the basis that this is what the life tenant would have received had the asset been realised. The amount of interest allowed to the tenant for life was originally 4%, later reduced to 3% but then raised again to 4% in *Re Beech [1920] 1 Ch 40*. The rule may be excluded by providing that the tenant for life is to have all the income of an asset before conversion.

So where a residuary estate, which was held on trust for sale for the testator's wife for life and thereafter to his daughters, included a hotel business which was not an authorised investment but was carried on by his personal representatives pending a sale, the widow was entitled to 4% interest on the proceeds of sale rather than the actual profits. The testator had expressly excluded in his will the provisions of the *Apportionment Act 1870*, but this was not sufficient to cover profits from the business of a sole trader nor profits from a partnership as the Act did not apply to these (*Re Berry deceased [1962] Ch 97*).

The relevant date for apportionment is the end of the executor's year (i.e. the first anniversary of the testator's death) unless the will contains an express power to postpone. In that event, as there is no duty on the trustees to sell at any particular time, the rational date for valuation to preserve the balance of the successive interests is the date of the testator's death (*Re Parry [1947] Ch 23*).

The 4% interest falls to be paid out of the actual income received from the unauthorised investments (to be treated en bloc if more than one). If the income received is more than enough to pay the 4% any balance is added to capital. If it is not sufficient, the tenant for life is not entitled to immediate recoupment out of capital but to be paid the deficit at 4% simple interest less tax when the unauthorised investments are sold (*Re Fawcett [1940] Ch 402*).

Re Earl of Chesterfield

6.19 The rule in *Re Earl of Chesterfield's Trusts (1883) 24 Ch D 643* applies a similar approach to reversionary interests of personalty in wills. If residuary personalty is, pursuant to a power to postpone, left outstanding for the benefit of the estate it should be apportioned between capital and income when it falls in. The method used in *Re Earl of Chesterfield* was to ascertain the sum which, put out at interest at 4% per annum and accumulating at compound interest with yearly rests and deducting income tax, would, with the accumulation of interest, have produced the amount actually received; the sum so ascertained was treated as capital, going to the remaindermen, and the balance as income due to the tenant for life.

These seemingly archaic rules can have relevant modern application. In *Chance's Will Trusts [1962] 1 WLR 409* it was held that the rule applied to compensation, paid after the testator's death, under the *Town and Country Planning Act 1954*. In that case, the tenant for life argued that the rule only applied to non-income producing assets, and that it did not apply where the asset ultimately came in, bringing with it accrued interest. If the rule did not apply the tenant for life would have been entitled to seven years statutory interest. The remaindermen however argued in favour of the rule, since it would result in part of the income being apportioned to capital. Wilberforce J saw no reason in principle why the rule should not apply to something that did not produce anything pending realisation of the estate. The broad purpose of the rule was to secure the tenant for life's interest in respect of the period up to the time when the debt was paid, and also to secure interest at a reasonable rate, and was just as applicable where there was interest involved in the payment as where it was only capital.

Exclusion of the rules

6.20 Where a clause gives the tenant for life the whole income of the residuary estate whether unconverted or not, it excludes the rules in *Howe v Lord Dartmouth (1802) 7 Ves 137* and *Re the Earl of Chesterfield's Trusts*. However, notwithstanding such a clause, if the trustees have not, in fact, exercised their discretion to retain property in its unconverted state or to sell, the rule of equitable apportionment in *Re the Earl of Chesterfield's Trusts* still applies until the discretion is actually exercised (*Re Guinness's Settlement [1966] 1 WLR 1355*). So when the court found that it never crossed the trustees' minds to consider whether a reversionary interest should be converted, but that, if they had thought about it, they could not properly have refused to sell it (despite an express power to postpone) the proceeds had to be apportioned on the principles laid down in *Re the Earl of Chesterfield's Trusts* (*Re Rowlls [1900] 2 Ch 107*).

In *Bartlett v Barclays Bank Trust Co (No 2) [1980] Ch 515*, the court had found that the trustees had committed a breach of trust by allowing a company, of which the trust held 99.8% of the shares, to pursue a speculative property development. Brightman J awarded damages in respect of the loss to the trust fund and interest on those damages at the rate allowed on the courts' short-term investment account. As it was a period of high inflation and the high interest rates were, in part, a reflection of the erosion in the value of money, he suggested (without deciding the point) that there should be an adjustment between life tenant and remainderman.

Apportionment of losses

6.21 Provision has to be made between life tenants and remaindermen for losses as well as gains. In *Re Atkinson [1904] 2 Ch 160* a mortgage proved to be insufficient to pay off principal and interest in full – the sum realised on the security had to be apportioned between the tenant for life and the remaindermen. The apportionment was the proportion which the amount due for arrears of interest bore to the amount due in respect of the capital debt. In the case of unauthorised securities the rights of the parties have to be adjusted as at the time the investment was made.

The rule in Allhusen v Whittell

6.22 The rule in *Allhusen v Whittell (1867) LR 4 Eq 295* relates to the determination of residue settled in succession and the treatment of income arising during the 'executor's year' or such other period (longer or shorter) during which debts or other expenses remain unpaid. The underlying concept is that a life tenant is entitled to the income on 'residue', which by definition comprises only that part of the estate left after such payments, and so is not entitled to income on the monies used to make such payments. There is no prescribed method of adjustment which must be used in each case, the object is to produce a fair result as between the tenant for life and remainderman (*Re McEuen [1913] 2 Ch 704*). It is, in practice, important only if the debts are substantial or payment delayed. If the debts carry interest which is charged against income, then that would fall to be taken into account and if the interest would equal or exceed the income earned by the money pending payment, the rule would seemingly not apply at all.

The rule in *Allhusen v Whittell* was applied to annuities in *Re Perkins [1907] 2 Ch 596*.

In *Re Shee [1934] Ch 345* the estate included two houses held on onerous leases. The executors paid the rent for nine months and then succeeded in assigning the leases, paying the assignees out of the capital of the estate to take them on. It was held firstly that the remaindermen were not entitled to have the whole of the capital payments recouped out of the income, even though the payment had relieved the tenant for life from liability to pay the rent and, secondly, that the obligation to pay the rent ought not to be wholly borne by the tenant for life as he was not entitled to any income until residue had been ascertained upon the freeing of the estate from the leasehold liabilities. Accordingly, the sums ought to be apportioned between income and capital on the basis of the rule in *Allhusen v Whittell*. A sum was to be ascertained which, when added to the interest on it, at the rate for the time being produced by the estate for the period from the death until the expenditure, amounted to the sum expended; the sum so ascertained was to be borne by capital and the balance by income.

Charitable trusts

6.23 The duty to act impartially applies in the case of charitable trusts. The Charity Commissioners, in their leaflet CC 3, *Responsibilities of Charity Trustees*, state at paragraph 8 that:

> 'Trustees must act reasonably and prudently in all matters relating to the charity and must always bear in mind the interests of the charity. They should not let their personal views or prejudices affect their conduct as trustees … The property of the charity must be applied for the purposes set out in the governing instrument and with complete fairness between persons who are properly qualified to benefit from it'.

Pension trusts

6.24 The general principles applicable to private trusts apply equally to pension schemes. In *Edge v Pensions Ombudsman [1998] Ch 512* the point was made that, just as it was not for the court to interfere with the exercise of a discretion by the trustees simply because it would have exercised that discretion differently, so it was not for the Pensions Ombudsman to set aside a discretion of the trustees or to substitute his own opinion.

Chapter 7

Duty to Get in and Safeguard Trust Property

Introduction

7.1 Trustees are under a duty to take control of the trust assets and thereafter take all proper steps to safeguard the same. If they replace other trustees and are aware that their predecessors have failed in their duty to get in and protect trust assets, they must take reasonable steps to make good the shortcomings or, if that is no longer possible, to consider proceedings against the former trustees who were at fault, in order to make good any loss to the trust fund. The duty to get in assets thought to belong to the trust, however, is not an absolute one, and in the case of dispute over the trust's entitlement to a particular asset, or if the cost of getting in the asset might outweigh the value of the same, the trustees are entitled to, and should, use their discretion acting as prudent men of business. This is reflected in the provisions of the *Trustee Act 1925, s 15*.

Debts and other things in action

7.2 It is the duty of trustees to press for payment of monies due to the trust and if they are not paid within a reasonable time to enforce payment by legal proceedings (*Re Brogden (1888) 38 Ch D 546*). However, where the debt was owed by a beneficiary, and enforcing immediate payment of the whole would have ruined the beneficiary and his children, who were also beneficiaries, the trustees were held to have acted reasonably in making an arrangement for instalments – although in the event the debtor went bankrupt and the trust fund suffered a loss (*Ward v Ward (1843) 2 HL Cas 777n at 786*).

In the case of difficulty the power conferred on a trustee by the *Trustee Act 1925, s 15* includes the power:

(*a*) to accept any composition or security, real or personal, for any debt real or personal;

(*b*) to allow any time for the payment of any debt;

(*c*) to compromise, compound, abandon, submit to arbitration, or otherwise settle any debt account claim or thing whatever relating to the trust or estate;

and for any of those purposes a trustee may enter into, give, execute and do such agreements, instrument, instruments of composition or arrangement releases and other things as to him or them seem expedient without being responsible for any loss occasioned by any act or thing so done by him or them if he has or they have discharged the duty of care set out in *section 1(1) of the Trustee Act 2000* (*TA 2000*).

The reference to the duty of care is, of course, a reference to the statutory duty of care (see 3.11 above). The section originally required the trustee to act in good faith. A trustee who fails to act in good faith does not discharge the duty of care so the modification extended the scope of the proviso. *Section 15* gives the trustees a wide discretion in exercising their duties (*Re Earl of Strafford dec'd [1980] Ch 28* – where a compromise involved the surrender of certain beneficial interests in the trust).

Section 15 also expressly allows the trustees to accept any property, real or personal, before the time at which it is made transferable or payable.

Reversionary interests and wasting assets

7.3 In the case of residuary personal estate settled by will, assets comprising future or reversionary interests or assets of a wasting nature or unauthorised investments should be realised and the proceeds invested in authorised investments. This is known as the rule in *Howe v Lord Dartmouth (1802) 7 Ves 137* (see 6.14 *et seq*). An example of a future or reversionary interest would be an interest under some other trust or estate postponed by a current life interest; an example of a wasting asset might be a short leasehold. The rule is a reflection of the trustee's duty to balance the interest of those entitled to income and those entitled to capital for a life tenant may get no benefit from a future interest and a remainderman may get no benefit from a wasting asset. It can be, and usually is, excluded.

Where the trust property includes any share or interest in property not vested in the trustees, or the proceeds of the sale of any such property, or any other thing in action, the trustees, on the same falling into possession, or becoming payable or transferable, may:

(*a*) agree or ascertain the amount or value thereof or any part thereof in such manner as they think fit,

(*b*) accept in or towards the satisfaction thereof, at the market or current value, or upon any valuation or estimate of value which they may think fit, any authorised investments, (*c*) allow any deductions for duties, costs, charges and expenses which they may think proper or reasonable,

(*d*) execute any release in respect of the premises so as effectually to discharge all accounting parties from all liability in respect of any matters coming within the scope of such release,

without being responsible in such case for any loss occasioned by any act or thing done by them if they have discharged the duty of care set out in *TA 2000, s 1(1)* (the statutory duty of care). [*Trustee Act 1925, s 22(1)*].

If the trust assets include an interest under some other trust, it is the duty of trustees to get in that interest promptly once it falls into possession (*Re Brogden (1888) 38 Ch D 546*). Until a share or an interest or other thing in action falls into possession, a trustee is not under an obligation to take steps to protect relevant securities or other property or to take any proceedings on account of any act, default, or neglect on the part of the persons in whom such securities or other property is or has been vested, unless and until the trustee has been required in writing so to do by some person or the guardian of some person beneficially interested under the trust, and unless due provision is made for the payment of the costs of any proceedings required to be taken. [*Trustee Act 1925, s 22(2)*].

Chattels

7.4 Where trust assets include chattels of value, trustees must consider what arrangements can and should be made for their safe custody. In the case of chattels settled to devolve with settled land the custody of the chattels will be with the tenant for life.

The *TA 2000, s 17* gives trustees statutory powers to appoint a person to act as custodian in relation to such of the assets of the trust as they may determine. A person is a custodian in relation to assets if he undertakes the safe custody of the assets or of any documents or records concerning the assets. Accordingly, one answer to the question how chattels should be safeguarded is for a custodian to be appointed. A custodian must be one of:

(*a*) a person who carries on a business which consists of or includes acting as a nominee or custodian;

(*b*) a body corporate controlled by the trustees;

(*c*) a body corporate recognised under the *Administration of Justice Act 1985, s 9*.

The appointment must be in, or evidenced in, writing. It does not apply to any trust having a custodian trustee or in relation to any asset vested in the Official Custodian for Charities. For appointment of custodian trustees and nominees see CHAPTER 18: POWER TO DELEGATE.

Trustees should, of course, make an inventory of chattels subject of the trust. As to insurance, the statutory duty of care applies to a trustee exercising a power to insure but is not expressly applied to the taking of a decision whether or not to insure. However, the trustee's duty to act as a prudent man of business surely requires a trustee to take all proper and reasonable steps to ensure that chattels of value are sufficiently insured, particularly if chattels are to be enjoyed in specie by a beneficiary.

In the case of National Heritage items, which are favourably treated for the purpose of inheritance tax and capital gains tax, arrangements will have to accommodate the requirement for the maintenance and preservation of the character of the item and for securing reasonable access to the public (see *Inheritance Tax Act 1984, s 30* and *Taxation of Chargeable Gains Act 1992, s 258*).

One solution to the safeguarding of valuable and important chattels or documents (whether or not National Heritage items) may be to loan the same to a local or national institution for public display or for study or research (see for example the provisions of the *National Heritage Act 1983* which gives certain institutions powers including power to borrow objects. The *National Heritage Act 1980, s 16* authorises the Secretary of State to indemnify against loss or damage to any object on loan to institutions specified in the section).

Bearer securities

7.5 If trustees retain or invest in bearer securities then they must appoint a person to act as a custodian of the securities unless expressly permitted by the trust instrument or by any enactment or subordinate legislation to invest without doing so. The appointment must be in, or evidenced in, writing. It does not apply to any trust having a custodian trustee or in relation to any asset vested in the Official Custodian for Charities (see generally *TA 2000, s 18*). The duty also does not apply to a sole trustee which is a trust corporation (*section 25(2)*). For appointment of custodian trustees and nominees see CHAPTER 18: POWER TO DELEGATE.

Documents of title etc

7.6 The power given under *TA 2000, s 17* to appoint a custodian of assets of the trust extends to the custody of any documents or records concerning the assets.

Land

7.7 In the case of land, other than settled land, the *Trusts of Land and Appointment of Trustees Act 1996, s 6* provides that for the purposes of exercising their functions as trustees, the trustees of land have in relation to the land all the powers of an absolute owner. Trustees of land, therefore, have the power to maintain and repair the trust property in order to preserve it in good condition. *Section 11* of the Act requires the trustees to consult the beneficiaries of full age and capacity and beneficially entitled to an interest in the land and, as far as consistent with the general interest of the trust, to give effect to those wishes or the wishes of the majority (by value).

The cost of periodic maintenance should be paid from income. However, major works (e.g. eradication of dry rot or damp or dealing with subsidence) can give rise to difficult questions whether the same constitutes a repair the cost of which is to be borne by income, or an improvement the cost of which should be borne by capital. When it arises, the question can have two aspects:

(*a*) how is the cost to be funded in the first place; and

(*b*) where should the final incidence lie.

Prior to 1997, the *Law of Property Act 1925, s 28* conferred on the trustees the powers of the *Settled Land Act* tenant for life, including the power to apply capital money in respect of improvements, as defined under the *Settled Land Act 1925* which incorporated detailed provisions as to both the funding and incidence of the cost of improvements (see 7.8 below). However, *section 28* has now been repealed and so no longer provides a guide as to what is an income expense and what is a capital expense. In many cases, major works of repair will be a consequence of an insured risk and the problem will not arise providing the level of cover is adequate to meet the total cost. In other cases, trustees should check to see if the trust instrument makes specific provision for funding or incidence. If difficulties arise which cannot be resolved by agreement with the beneficiaries, the trustees should take the directions of the court under the *Trustee Act 1925, s 57.*

Practical difficulties may arise if the only asset of the trust is a house occupied by the immediate beneficiary. In this case, there will be no ready cash with which to fund repairs and nor will there be an income from the trust property to support a mortgage to fund the works. In the case of serious disrepair there may be no alternative to seeking possession in order that the property can be sold. In particular, it should not be overlooked that if a property becomes a hazard the local authority may compel the trustee, as the owner of the property, to take action (e.g. under the *Building Act 1984, s 77* relating to dangerous structures). In any event, the prudent trustee will discuss the problem with the beneficiaries well in advance to see if some practical solution can be found and, if necessary, apply to the court for directions.

Where property is let otherwise than on a full repairing lease, there seems no reason in principle why trustees should not retain a reasonable sum to build up a fund for periodic repairs, particularly if the terms of the lease are producing a higher rent than if the letting had imposed repairing obligations on the tenant. If a property is let on terms throwing the obligation to repair on to the tenant, the tenant's covenant is an asset of the trust and the trustees should take all proper steps to enforce it. If legal proceedings are necessary, a prudent trustee should first secure the authority of the beneficiaries or the sanction of the court on a Beddoe summons (see CHAPTER 16: POWER TO COMPROMISE AND POWER TO LITIGATE).

Settled land

7.8 Land which remains settled land is vested in the tenant for life. However, a tenant for life is not liable for damage to the settled land resulting from a failure to keep it in repair (this damage being called 'permissive waste') unless the trust instrument imposes an obligation upon him. Conversely, a tenant for life will be responsible for 'voluntary waste' or 'equitable waste', both of which involve deliberate damage (equitable waste being the more severe) unless the trust instrument otherwise provides.

Closely allied to the matter of repairs is the issue of improvements. The *Settled Land Act 1925, ss 83, 84* and *Sch 3* set out a comprehensive scheme relating to improvements. The underlying scheme of the provisions in the Act is that the cost of any authorised improvements is borne in the first instance by capital but, in the case of certain improvements, capital is recouped out of income by instalments. *Schedule 3* is divided into three parts.

- Listed in *Part I* are those improvements the cost of which are not liable to be replaced by instalments and include major works of construction and improvement.
- Listed in *Part II* are improvements the cost of which the trustees or the court may require to be replaced by instalments.
- Listed in *Part III* are improvements the cost of which the trustees of the settlement or the court must require to be replaced by instalments.

Instalments are, by *section 84*, required to be not more than 50 half-yearly instalments and by *section 85* the tenant for life is authorised to create a rent charge. Where the court authorises improvements other than an improvement authorised by *Part I,* it may as a condition of making the order, require the capital to be repaid out of income by instalments and in the case of an improvement listed in *Part III* it must do so. *Part III* extends also to farm machinery.

In the case of agricultural land, the *Agricultural Holdings Act 1986, s 89, Sch 7* expands the list in *Part I* and incorporates repairs (not just improvement) to fixed equipment which would include such items as Dutch barns (*Re Lord Brougham and Vaux [1954] Ch 24*). Reference should also be made to *section 73* (application of capital monies). In applying capital money the trustees should, as far as practicable, consult the tenant for life and, so far as consistent with general interest of the settlement, give effect to his wishes (*section 75(4)*). The lists in the *Settled Land Act 1925, Sch 3* have an antiquarian ring about them reflecting, as they do, the needs of the late 19th and early 20th century and the large estates for which the provisions of the *Settled Land Act* were intended. If there is doubt whether or not work is authorised and whether or not the cost should be recouped by instalments and that doubt cannot be resolved by agreement with the beneficiaries, application may be made to the court for directions and, if necessary, for authority under the *Settled Land Act, s 64.*

The tenant for life and his successors in title are charged by the *Settled Land Act, s 88* to maintain and repair at his own expense every improvement carried out under the Act (i.e. the section imposes a liability for permissive waste) and, if he fails to do so, *section 88(5)* specifically makes the estate of the tenant for life liable in damages to the person having under the trust instrument an interest or estate in the settled land.

In summary, therefore, a tenant for life of settled land may allow the settled land and building thereon in its original state to fall into disrepair; however, if capital monies are spent on improvements (whether or not recouped from income) the tenant for life or his estate may be held liable in damages to the person or persons beneficially next entitled if the improvements are not maintained and kept in repair.

Insurance

7.9 Insurance is now commonplace, particularly in respect of buildings and valuable chattels. Although it was uncertain whether, at common law, a trustee had power to insure at the expense of the trust without an express provision to that effect, or the consent of the beneficiaries against whose interest the premiums were to be charged, a statutory power to insure has long been available. The current power is the *TA 2000, s 19* (see CHAPTER 14: POWER TO INSURE TRUST PROPERTY).

Chapter 8

Provision of Information and Disclosure of Trust Documents

Introduction

8.1 In considering who has the right to information as regards the trust fund and who has a right to inspect trust documents, a distinction must be drawn between those who are beneficiaries and those who are merely potential objects of a discretionary power. A discretionary object is not a beneficiary unless and until the discretionary power has been exercised in his favour and, until then, he does not have the rights of a beneficiary. In the context of who has a right to inspect trust documents, a distinction must also be drawn between documents relating to the administration of the trust assets and documents relating to the exercise of a discretion by the trustees. Generally speaking, trustees are not obliged to disclose the reasons for the exercise of a discretion, even to a beneficiary whose interest is directly affected by it, or documents relating thereto.

Existence of a trust

8.2 A trustee of an *inter vivos* trust is under a duty to inform a beneficiary of the existence of the trust and his rights under it. In the case of a will the rule is different and an executor does not have such a duty. In *Hawkesley v May [1956] 1 QB 304* the distinction was rationalised on the basis that a trust deed is a private document whereas a will is a public document. In practice an executor invariably does inform all beneficiaries that can be traced, at least in so far as their interests are vested in possession. The point, however, is not unimportant. For example, in *Cancer Research Campaign v Ernest Brown & Co [1997] STC 1425* an allegation of negligence against an executor for failing to inform legatees of their interests under the will of the deceased until after the time for making a deed of variation under the *Inheritance Tax Act 1984, s 142* failed, the executor being under no duty to give such information to the legatees.

Production and inspection of a trust document

8.3 The basis of a beneficiary's right to information and production and inspection of a trust document is his proprietary interest in the trust assets (*O'Rourke v Darbishire [1920] AC 581*). It is important to distinguish his right to production and inspection as an incident of his beneficial interest under the trust from his right of disclosure in connection with litigation. A right of disclosure is a right to see documents the property of another; the right of a beneficiary is a right to see documents which are (to the extent of his beneficial interest) in his beneficial ownership. Therefore, if the bona fides of the trustee is called in question and a beneficiary commences legal proceedings against a trustee, then the rules of disclosure come into operation (see CPR Pt 31). In the case of bona fide proceedings a trustee may be required to produce documents which are disclosable as a matter of litigation even though, litigation apart, he would have been under no duty to reveal them.

Information

8.4 The general principles as to what information a beneficiary is or, conversely, is not entitled to, were considered in *Re Londonderry's Settlement [1965] Ch 918*.

Information to which a beneficiary is entitled

8.5 A beneficiary is entitled to a written summary of the state of the trust fund and to sight of the documents of title. Subject to what follows, a beneficiary is generally entitled to sight of correspondence passing between the trustees and solicitors acting for the trustees in respect of the affairs of the trust and to sight of the opinion of counsel and, therefore, presumably the instructions pursuant to which the opinion was written.

Information to which a beneficiary is not entitled

8.6 A trustee is not bound to disclose to the beneficiaries his reasons for exercising a discretionary power and is, therefore, not bound to disclose the agenda or other documents prepared for any meeting of the trustees or the minutes of such meetings. Nor is a beneficiary entitled to copies of correspondence between the trustees or between a trustee and another beneficiary. These are regarded as confidential matters and the trustees' duty and the administration of the trust might be made impossible if the trustees were under a duty to make disclosure to any beneficiary. However, if the bona fides of the trustees is called in question, and litigation ensues, different considerations may apply.

Information relating to a company

8.7 If the trust assets include all, or substantially all, the shares in a private company of which a trustee is a director, and holds office by virtue of the trust holding, then a beneficiary is entitled, in a proper case, to see company documents in the hands of the trustee as director, not merely documents in the hands of the trustee as trustee or shareholder (*Butt v Kelson [1952] Ch 197*), notwithstanding a provision to the contrary in the articles of the company (a provision to the contrary in the trust deed would be a different matter).

The reasoning in the judgment in *Butt v Kelson* is, in some respects, difficult to reconcile with the principle that a beneficiary (other than in the case of a bare trust) cannot dictate how a trustee carries out his powers and duties (see per Upjohn J in *Re George Whichelow Ltd [1954] 1 WLR 5*) but the proposition that a trustee cannot rely on the company structure to deny information to a beneficiary seems unexceptional.

The beneficiary must specify the documents that he wishes to see and make out a proper case for seeing them; there must be no valid objection by the other beneficiaries, or by the directors from the point of view of the company. A request from a beneficiary to see commercially sensitive information might well fail on one or other of these grounds, save in exceptional circumstances or where the legitimate concerns of the company could be met. In the case of doubt, the trustee should seek the directions of the court. If the trust holding of shares does not comprise all or substantially all of the shares in the company, then the balance between the interest of the beneficiary and the interest of the company will shift against disclosure.

The reasoning in *Butt v Kelson* was that the trustee could be compelled to use his voting power to make the company disclose the documents. On that basis, the principle would, in any event, apply only to holdings which are sufficient to give the trustee the necessary voting power including, if necessary, the power to abrogate a contrary provision in the articles. If documents come into the hands of a trustee, in his capacity as trustee then the trustee's duty of disclosure is the same as in respect of any other trust document.

Duty to keep accounts

8.8 A trustee is under a duty to keep proper accounts. Since 1926 a trustee has not been obliged to do so personally but has been authorised to employ an agent (e.g. an accountant) to do so on his behalf (see now *Trustee Act 2000, s 11*). In the case of a solicitor trustee, provisions of the Solicitors Accounts Rules 1998 may apply particularly if the solicitor is either a sole trustee or a co-trustee only with a partner or employee in which event trust monies are 'controlled trust monies' for the purpose of the rules. Rule 32 of the Solicitors Account Rules 1998 provides that a solicitor must at all times keep accounting records properly written up to show the solicitor's dealings with controlled trust monies received, held or paid by the solicitor.

Auditing of trust accounts

8.9 Trustees are not obliged to have their accounts audited. Under the *Trustee Act 1925, s 22(4)* trustees may have the accounts of the trust property examined or audited by an independent accountant at the expense of the trust. It is a matter for their absolute discretion whether or not they do so. Such an examination or audit must not be occasioned more than once in every three years, unless the nature of the trust or any special dealing with the trust property make a more frequent exercise of the power reasonable.

For the purpose of the examination or audit, the trustees must produce such vouchers and give such information as the accountant may require. The costs are payable out of capital or income or both as the trustees in their absolute discretion think fit, but in default of direction by the trustees, costs attributable to capital are to be paid out of capital, and those attributable to income by income.

Production of accounts to a beneficiary

8.10 A beneficiary with a vested or contingent interest under a trust, whether in possession or reversion, is entitled to inspect the accounts and vouchers and other documents relating to the trust. If the trustee fails to do so then the court will order him to produce an account and he may be liable to pay the legal costs incurred through his failure. A trustee is not obliged to supply copies of documents otherwise than at the beneficiary's expense.

The object of a discretionary power

8.11 The position of the object of a discretionary power is different from that of a beneficiary with a contingent or vested interest under a trust. The only right of an object of a discretion (before the discretion is exercised) is to require the trustee to consider the exercise of their power of appointment from time to time (*Re Manisty's Settlement [1974] Ch 17*). The object of a discretionary power is entitled to communicate to the trustees his circumstances and claims to be considered as a potential beneficiary. He is, therefore, prima facie entitled to know the names and addresses of the trustees; however, an application for an order against a third party to disclose such names and addresses will be balanced against any cost inconvenience or other problems which might be caused to the third party from compliance with such an order (*Re Murphy's Settlement, Murphy v Murphy [1999] 1 WLR 282*).

In the Irish case of *Chaine-Nickson v Bank of Ireland [1976] IR 393* it was held that an object does have the right to ask the trustees for information as to the nature and value of the trust property, the trust income and how the trustees have been investing and distributing it. That was accepted as correct in *Re Murphy's Settlement, Murphy v Murphy* (*at page 290*). However, a different decision has been reached in the High Court of the Isle of Man following an extensive review of authorities from a number of jurisdictions (*Re Angora Trust; Rosewood Trust v Schmidt [2001] WTLR 1081*).

In the *Angora* case, a company in the Isle of Man was a trustee of two settlements under which the objects of a discretion were certain Russian businessmen one of whom had died; in default of appointment the trust property was held for charitable purposes. Distributions had from time to time been made either directly to the businessmen or to their nominee companies. The deceased's son, as administrator of his father's estate, was endeavouring to trace his father's assets and sought accounts and 'full details of all trust assets and all transactions relating to trusts assets'. The High Court held that the status of the deceased was not sufficient to entitle him (or his son as administrator of his estate) to the information. It held that:

> '... only the person or entity to whom the trust results in default of the exercise of such power had the power to object to any wrongful exercise of the power and to obtain an account of the trustee's stewardship of the trust assets' (see *page 1106C-E*).

The decision in the *Angora* case is not binding, but as the decision in *Murphy* was based on a concession (albeit a concession with which the judge concurred) and was not preceded by any English authority, the position as regards the law of England and Wales must be regarded as uncertain. Furthermore, even if *Murphy* is in future followed in preference to *Angora* the position of a discretionary object will not necessarily be on a par with a beneficiary with a vested or contingent interest. A beneficiary has an absolute right to the information, however, it is possible that a court, if minded to find that a discretionary object had any right at all, could find that it was no more than a right to ask the court to exercise a discretion whether or not to order the disclosure of information. If that is the case, the court could, and no doubt would, refuse to order disclosure if the object had only a remote interest or there were no obvious reasons for believing that an account is required (see observations in *Angora* at *page 1106*). In *Angora,* had the court considered that the claimant had the locus standi to seek the information, they would have ordered its disclosure (*at page 1107*).

In *Angora* the terms of the trust gave an absolute discretion to the trustees and provided for a gift over to charitable purposes in default of the exercise of the power. Had the trust been an onshore trust, the Attorney-General would have had the locus standi to call the trustees to account even if the charitable purposes had not been defined. If the trust had been a trust power (i.e. where the discretion had to be exercised among a class of objects with no gift over) then different considerations might well have applied, particularly if the application had been made by all, or substantially all, the members of the class.

Charities

8.12 The trustees of a charity required to be registered, and not excepted from registration, are required by the *Charities Act 1993, s 3(7)* to provide to the Commissioners copies of its trusts and such other documents and information as may be prescribed by regulation or as the Commissioners may require for the purpose of registration, and to notify any changes in the trusts or particulars in the Charities register. Save in so far as the Commissioners otherwise determine in respect of any particular information contained on the register, the register is open to public inspection. Exempt charities are specified in *Schedule 2* to the *Charities Act 1993* (for example certain universities and museums) and charities which have neither permanent endowment nor the use and occupation of any land and whose income does not exceed £1,000 a year are not required to be registered.

Right of the Commissioners to documents and information

8.13 The Commissioners may by order require any person to furnish them with information in his possession and (save in the case of an exempt charity) to furnish copies of any document (or the document itself) which relates to charity or is relevant to the discharge of their functions or the functions of the official custodian. [*Charities Act 1993, s 9*]. *Section 10* authorises certain public bodies or persons discharging functions of a public nature to disclose information to the Commissioners.

Section 11 provides that any person who knowingly or recklessly provides the Commissioners with information which is false or misleading in a material particular, or who wilfully alters, suppresses, conceals or destroys any document which he is liable under the Act to produce to the Commissioners is guilty of an offence.

Accounts

8.14 Charity trustees are required to keep accounting records sufficient to show and explain all the charity's transactions and retain them for at least six years. [*Charities Act 1993, s 41*]. The records must:

(*a*) disclose at any time, with reasonable accuracy, the financial position of the charity at that time; and

(*b*) enable the trustees to ensure that, where any statements of accounts are prepared by them under *section 42(1)* of the Act, those statements of accounts comply with requirements of the regulations under that provision.

The accounting records must in particular contain:

(i) entries showing from day to day all sums of money received and expended by the charity, and the matters in respect of which the receipt and expenditure takes place; and

(ii) a record of the assets and liabilities of the charity.

The *Statement of Recommended Practice* issued by the Charity Commissioners (Revised Version October 2000) gives general guidance.

Section 42 of the 1993 Act requires charity trustees (except where the charity is a company) to prepare in respect of each financial year of the charity a statement of account in accordance with regulations made by the Secretary of State. Where a charity's gross income in any financial year does not exceed £100,000, the charity trustees may elect to produce instead of a statement of accounts:

- a receipts and payments account, and
- a statement of assets and liabilities.

A statement of account or the more abbreviated alternative must be preserved for at least six years from the end of the financial year to which it relates.

Audit

8.15 *Charities Act 1993, s 43* provides for the auditing of charity accounts where the charity's gross income in the relevant year, or in either of the two financial years of the charity immediately preceding the relevant year exceeds £250,000. In the case of smaller charities, the trustees may either elect an audit, or an examination by an independent person who is reasonably believed by the trustees to have the requisite ability and practical experience to carry out a competent examination of the accounts. Where it appears to the Commissioners that this obligation has not been complied with within ten months of the end of the financial year, or it would be desirable for the accounts of the charity to be audited, the Commissioners may by order require the accounts of the charity to be audited at the expense of the trustees. The section does not apply to a charity which is a company (which will be subject to the requirements of the *Companies Acts 1948* and *1985*).

Annual report

8.16 Charity trustees are also required by the *Charities Act 1993, s 45* to prepare an annual report containing:

(*a*) such a report by the trustees on the activities of the charity during that year; and

(*b*) such other information relating to the charity or to its trustees or officers,

as may be prescribed by regulations made by the Secretary of State.

The regulations are contained in the *Charities (Accounts and Reports) Regulations 2000 (SI 2000 No 2068)*. The annual report has to be sent to the Commissioners by the trustees within ten months from the end of the relevant financial year, or such longer period as the Commissioners may for any special reason allow. The annual report has to have attached to it the statement of account, or, where applicable, the account and statement.

Any annual report kept by the Commissioners is open to public inspection, and where charity trustees are requested in writing to provide a copy of the charity's most recent accounts, and are paid such reasonable fee (if any) as they may require in respect of the cost of compliance, they must comply with the request within two months. [*Charities Act 1993, s 47*].

Annual return

8.17 Registered charities are required by the *Charities Act 1993, s 48* to prepare and submit to the Commissioners an annual return, in such form as the Commissioners prescribe by regulations, unless the Commissioners in any particular case dispense with the requirement.

Exemptions

8.18 Exempt charities specified in *Schedule 2* to the *Charities Act 1993* (for example certain universities and museums) are not subject to the requirements of *sections 41–45* of the Act. The trustees are, however, required to keep proper books of accounts by *section 46*, and where not required by any other enactment to prepare periodical statements of account, they must prepare consecutive statements of account consisting of income and expenditure accounts relating to a period of not more than 15 months and a balance sheet relating to the end of that period.

Charities which have no permanent endowment nor the use and occupation of any land and whose income does not exceed £1,000 a year are not required to be registered. If not registered they only have to keep accounting records and prepare annual statements of account. They do not have to carry out an audit or examination, or prepare an annual report.

By virtue of the *Deregulation and Contracting Out Act 1994* charities whose gross income or expenditure in a financial year is less than £10,000 are exempted from the duty to audit, to have their accounts examined, to submit an annual report, and to make an annual return.

Penalties

8.19 Persistent failure by any person without reasonable excuse to send the annual report to the Commissioners, provide a copy of the accounts on request, or make an annual return is a criminal offence punishable by a fine. [*Charities Act 1993, s 49*].

Companies

8.20 Charities that are companies are subject to company law rules on accounts. By *section 69* of the *Charities Act 1993* the Commissioners may require the accounts of a charity which is a company to be investigated and audited at the Commissioners' expense by an auditor appointed by the Commissioners.

The statute gives the auditor the statutory authority to have access to all books, accounts and documents in the possession or control of the charity trustees or to which the charity trustees have access, to require information from any of the charity trustees past or present or any past or present officer or employee of the charity.

At the conclusion or during the progress of the audit, the auditor reports to the Commissioners and must send a copy of the report to the charity trustees. If any person fails to afford to the auditor the facilities to which he is entitled, then the Commissioners may give that person or the charity trustees such direction as they think appropriate for securing that the default is made good. Disobedience to an order of the Commissioners may be dealt with on the application of the Commissioners as disobedience to an order of the High Court. [*Charities Act 1993, s 88*].

Pension schemes

8.21 The *Occupational Pension Schemes (Disclosure of Information) Regulations 1996 (SI 1996 No 1655)*, made under the *Pensions Act 1995, s 41* provides for disclosure by the trustees to members and prospective members of the scheme and their spouses, the beneficiaries and independent trade unions, recognised to any extent for the purpose of collective bargaining in relation to members and prospective members of the scheme. By *Regulation 3* the trustees must disclose the contents of the trust deed, or, if no trust deed, the documents constituting the scheme and the rules if separate, and must make provision for inspection and the supply of copies.

Regulation 5 of *SI 1996 No 1655* deals with the furnishing of individual details set out in *Schedule 2*, and *Regulation 6* with the annual report, which must include the audited accounts and a copy of the latest actuarial statement. *Regulation 7* provides for the availability of the actuarial valuations, schedule of contributions, payment schedule and statement of investment principles. If any person fails without reasonable excuse to comply with the regulations, the Regulatory Authority may impose a monetary penalty.

Chapter 9

Limitation of Liability and Relief from Liability

Introduction

9.1 The prudent trustee avoids committing a breach of trust but however diligent a trustee may be, breaches of trust do occur. A breach of trust may be a result of indolence or incompetence but other common causes are inadvertence, poor advice or succumbing to the blandishments of a beneficiary. A breach of trust may be committed for the very best of reasons – hence the classic remark attributed to Selwyn LJ in *Perrins v Bellamy [1899] 1 Ch 797 at 798*, 'the main duty of a trustee is to commit judicious breaches of trust' (although the words 'main duty' are undoubtedly an overstatement and the word 'judicious' of the essence) and if no loss is occasioned no problems ensue. However, the risk of liability can be a serious disincentive to accepting the task of trusteeship particularly for the lay trustee who takes on the responsibility unpaid. Accordingly, it is commonplace to find in a well-drawn trust document a clause excluding or limiting the liability of the trustees. The *Trustee Act 1925, s 61* also empowers the court to relieve a trustee of liability in whole or in part and *section 62* empowers the court to order that the trustee be recouped from the interest of a beneficiary who has instigated, requested or consented in writing to the breach of trust.

Limitation of liability

Trustee exemption clauses

9.2 The law was comprehensively reviewed in *Armitage v Nurse [1998] Ch 241*. In that case it was held that there is an irreducible core of obligations owed by a trustee to the beneficiaries and enforceable by them which is fundamental to the concept of a trust. The duty of a trustee to perform the trusts honestly and in good faith for the benefit of the beneficiaries is the minimum necessary to give substance to the trust. However, duties of skill and care, prudence and diligence are not core obligations. It follows that liability for the latter can be excluded by an appropriately worded clause but liability for the former cannot. There is no reason why liability for 'gross negligence' cannot be excluded in just the same way as negligence of any other description but liability for fraud, bad faith and wilful misconduct cannot be excluded.

Millett LJ in *Armitage v Nurse* also considered what would constitute fraudulent conduct. It does not matter whether the trustee stands or thinks he stands to gain personally from his actions. If he acts in a way which he does not honestly believe to be in the interest of the beneficiaries, then he is acting dishonestly. Reckless indifference whether a transaction was contrary to the interests of the beneficiaries would constitute dishonesty.

Millett LJ also held (*page 251*) that the conduct of a trustee who commits a deliberate breach of trust but does so in the honest belief that he is acting in the interest of the beneficiaries is not fraudulent. However, in *Walker v Stones [2000] WTLR 975* this proposition was qualified at least in respect of 'solicitor trustees' to cases where the 'honest belief' was, on an objective view, reasonable. The qualification was necessary to take account of the case where the honest belief, though actually held, was so unreasonable that, by any objective standard, no reasonable solicitor trustee could have thought that what he did or agreed to do was for the benefit of the beneficiaries. In giving the judgment Sir Christopher Slade said that he was limiting his observations to solicitor-trustees because, on the facts of the case, the court was dealing with a solicitor trustee and the test of honesty may vary from case to case '... depending on, among other things, the role and calling of trustees'. In principle, however, the qualification would appear apt to apply to any trustee, given that the objective standard will vary according to whether the trustee is a lay or professional trustee and the level of expertise reasonably to be expected of the particular trustee.

If an exemption clause confines liability to loss or damage caused by a trustee's *actual* fraud, then liability is excluded for constructive fraud or equitable fraud, that is to say 'breach of the sort of obligation which is enforced by a court (i.e. a Court of Equity) that from the beginning regarded itself as a court of conscience' (*Nocton v Lord Ashburton [1914] AC 932 at 954*). Examples of constructive fraud or equitable fraud would be a fraud on a power, or the purchase by a trustee of a trust asset either of which could result in liability on the trustee but neither of which necessarily involves actual fraud in the common law sense.

Independent advice not required

9.3 A solicitor, who includes an exemption clause (at least in a form commonly found in precedent books) when drafting a will or settlement of which he expects to be a trustee, is not obliged to advise his client to take independent advice in the same way that he would be expected to do if he included a substantial benefit for himself. An exemption clause does not confer a benefit, it defines the extent of the trustee's potential liability and there is no conflict between the interest of the solicitor and of the client (*Bogg v Raper (1998/9) ITELR 267*).

Conflicting clauses

9.4 Where a trust document included more than one exemption clause, one of which was a general exemption and another of which expressly did not apply to paid trustees, then the paid trustees could not rely on the general exemption clause (*Wight v Olswang (No 2) [2001] WTLR 291*). In that case clause 11 exempted the trustees from loss caused by investments, mistakes and omissions made in good faith or caused by anything other than wilful fraud or wrongdoing of the trustee sought to be made liable. It drew no distinction between paid and unpaid trustees. Clause 18(A) exempted trustees from loss accruing from exercising or failing to exercise any discretion or power. Clause 18(B) exempted trustees (other than those charging remuneration for so acting) from liability for any error of judgement, mistake of law or other mistake, and anything else except wilful misconduct. It was held that the conflict between clause 11 and clause 18(B) was too great to be ignored and the clauses could not take effect cumulatively and a paid trustee could not rely on clause 11. Clause 18(A), however, did not overlap in the same way and could be reconciled with 18(B) so a paid trustee could rely on 18(A).

The statutory duty of care

9.5 The statutory duty of care set out in the *Trustee Act 2000, s 1* does not apply if, or in so far as, it appears from the trust instrument that the duty is not meant to apply. [*Sch 1, para 7*]. It is, therefore, clear that the statutory duty can be excluded or modified either by express words or necessary implication.

Pension funds

9.6 The *Pensions Act 1995, s 33* provides that liability for breach of an obligation under any rule of law to take care or exercise skill in the performance of any investment functions, where the function is exercisable by a trustee of a trust scheme, or by a person to whom the function has been delegated, cannot be excluded or restricted by any instrument or agreement. Excluding or restricting liability includes:

(*a*) making the liability or its enforcement subject to restrictive or onerous conditions;

(*b*) excluding or restricting any right or remedy in respect of the liability or subjecting a person to any prejudice in consequence of his pursuing any such right or remedy; or

(*c*) excluding or restricting rules of evidence or procedure.

By *section 34*, this section does not prevent the exclusion or restriction of any liability of trustees of a trust scheme for the acts or defaults of a fund manager to whom a discretion has been delegated, where the trustees have taken all such steps as are reasonable to satisfy themselves, or the person who made the delegation on their behalf has taken all such steps as are reasonable to satisfy himself:

(i) that the fund manager has the appropriate knowledge and experience for managing the investments of the scheme; and

(ii) that he is carrying out his work competently and complying with *section 36* (investment principles).

Charity trustees

9.7 The *Charities Act 1993, s 29* provides that the Charity Commissioners may, on the written application of any charity trustee, give him their opinion or advice on any matter affecting the performance of his duties as such. A charity trustee who acts in accordance with that advice is deemed to have acted in accordance with his trust unless, when he does so, either:

(*a*) he knows or has reasonable cause to suspect that the opinion or advice was given in ignorance of material facts; or

(*b*) the decision of the court has been obtained on the matter or proceedings are pending to obtain one.

The Commissioners also have power to authorise dealings with charity property under *section 26* of the Act whether or not it would otherwise be within the powers of the charity trustees.

The Charity Commissioners will authorise charity trustees to maintain indemnity insurance at the cost of the expendable funds of the charity (see *Report of the Charity Commissioners*, 1995 para 20). The insurance may cover personal liability for acts properly undertaken in the administration of the charity or undertaken in breach of trust but under an honest mistake but must not cover an act or omission which the trustee knew to be a breach of trust or committed by the trustee in reckless disregard of whether or not it was a breach of trust or duty, and the insurance must contain an exclusion to that effect.

Relief from liability

Trustee Act 1925, s 61

9.8 The court may relieve trustees in whole or part from the personal consequences of breaches of trust if they have acted honestly and reasonably, and ought fairly to be excused for the breach of trust and for failing to seek the court's directions. *Trustee Act 1925, s 61* is not confined to situations where the trustee has committed some executive or administrative blunder, but extends to a case where, as a consequence of a wrong construction, money is paid to a person who is not entitled to it.

The fact that a trustee has acted honestly does not mean that he has acted reasonably. In *Re Pauling's Settlement Trusts [1964] Ch 303* a bank acting as trustee made improper advances to the beneficiaries. It was held to have acted honestly but in respect of a number of the advancements not to have acted reasonably and as to those it was not entitled to relief under *section 61*. Relief was refused in *Bartlett v Barclays Bank Trust Co [1980] Ch 515 at 538* where the bank embarked on a speculative development which resulted in loss to the trust fund; it was held to have acted honestly but not reasonably. *Section 61* applies equally to a paid professional trustee and an unpaid lay trustee but, in practice, a paid professional may have greater difficulty in satisfying a court that conduct which constitutes a breach of trust has been reasonable.

The fact that the trustee has acted under legal advice will not automatically result in relief being granted; it is important to have regard to the nature of the estate, the circumstances of the defendant, and his or her actions in the light of the advice received. In *Re Pauling* relief was refused in respect of certain advances even though the majority of the Court of Appeal found that they had been 'ill-advised by their own solicitors' (*page 358*).

However, the court will have regard to practical realities. In *Re Evans [1999] 2 All ER 777* the administrator of a small estate took out a missing beneficiary policy in respect of a beneficiary who had not been heard of for more than thirty years; the cost of doing so was much less that the cost of seeking the direction of the court (a *Benjamin* order – see further CHAPTER 29: POWER TO APPLY TO THE COURT – THE SURRENDER OF DISCRETION TO THE COURT). The beneficiary turned up and sued for the cost of the policy and the shortfall between the policy proceeds and the full amount of the interest. The court held that taking out a policy had in all the circumstances been a practical course and relieved the administrator from liability, save to the extent that the administrator (who was also a beneficiary) still held property derived from the deceased's estate.

In *Re Allsop, Whittaker v Bamford [1914] 1 Ch 1*, where a trustee had relied on the advice of a solicitor, which advice turned out to be wrong, one of the matters taken into account by the court which granted relief, was the fact that the trust fund was small. If a trustee wrongly ignores legal advice he is unlikely to be held to have acted reasonably.

Section 61 cannot be used to relieve a trustee from a prospective breach of trust (*Re Rosenthal [1972] 3 All ER 552*).

Acquiescence by a beneficiary

9.9 A beneficiary who is of full age and capacity and who requests or consents to a breach of trust by a trustee cannot sue for loss to himself (*Fletcher v Collis [1905] 2 Ch 24*). A person under a legal disability such as incapacity or infancy cannot make a request or give consent such as would protect a trustee. A consent or request which would otherwise protect a trustee may be vitiated by matters such as undue influence, so a trustee should always act with caution particularly in respect of vulnerable beneficiaries such as children recently of age (*Re Pauling's Settlement Trusts [1964] Ch 303*).

Indemnity by beneficiary

9.10 Where a trustee commits a breach of trust at the instigation or request or with the consent in writing of a beneficiary, the court has a discretionary power under the *Trustee Act 1925, s 62* to make an order impounding all or any part of the interest of the beneficiary in the trust estate by way of indemnity to the trustee for the loss to the trust estate. The interest of the beneficiary may be impounded even though the beneficiary derived no benefit from the breach of trust.

Time limits

9.11 Originally there was no time limit for bringing an action for breach of trust. This was modified by the *Trustee Act 1888* and the modern law is now set out in the *Limitation Act 1980*.

The *Limitation Act 1980, s 21* provides that no period of limitation prescribed by the Act shall apply to an action brought by a beneficiary under a trust being an action:

(*a*) in respect of any fraud or fraudulent breach of trust to which the trustee was a party or privy; or

(*b*) to recover from the trustee trust property or the proceeds of trust property in the possession of the trustee, or previously received by the trustee and converted to his use.

Subject to the above, an action by a beneficiary to recover trust property or in respect of a breach of trust, not being an action for which a period of limitation is prescribed elsewhere in the Act, must not be brought after the expiration of six years from the date on which the right of action accrued.

The right of action accrues when the breach of trust occurs, not when there is loss to the beneficiary (*Re Somerset [1894] 1 Ch 231*). However, where a beneficiary has a future interest, a right of action does not accrue until the interest falls into possession (*section 21(3)*). An invalid advance of capital does not constitute a future interest falling into possession (*Re Pauling [1962] 1 WLR 86 at 115*). Limitation may be postponed in the case of concealment or mistake under the *Limitation Act, s 32*.

Fraud means dishonesty, so liability for breach of trust is statute barred after six years but liability for a dishonest breach of trust endures without limitation of time (*Armitage v Nurse [1998] Ch 241*). However, where a trustee is in possession of trust property or the proceeds of trust property or has received trust property and converted it to his own use, an action to recover the same is without limit as to time even if there has been no dishonesty. In the situation where a trustee, who was also a beneficiary, received a share of a distribution which was subsequently challenged as wrongful, it was formerly the case that where the other beneficiaries would be protected by limitation if more than six years had passed, the trustee would be liable to the disappointed beneficiary up to the total amount of his interest, not just the amount of the wrongful distribution to him. However, the *Limitation Act 1980, s 21* now provides that in those circumstances, after the period of limitation has expired, a trustee who has acted honestly and reasonably in making the distribution is only liable in an action to recover trust property to the amount of the excess over his proper share.

A beneficiary against whom there would be a good defence under the Act is not entitled to derive any greater or other benefit from a judgment or order obtained by any other beneficiary than he could have obtained if he had brought the action and the Act had been pleaded in defence (*section 21(4)*). The *Limitation Act 1980, s 23* provides that an action for an account shall not be brought after the expiration of any time limit under the Act, which is applicable to the claim which is the basis of the duty to account.

By *section 28*, where the person for whom the right of action has accrued is under a disability, the limitation period is six years from the date when he ceased to be under a disability or had died, whichever first occurs. The period of limitation is also postponed by *section 32* where:

(i) the action is based upon the fraud of the defendant; or

(ii) any fact relevant to the claimant's right of action has been deliberately concealed from him by the defendant; or

(iii) the action is for relief from the consequences of a mistake.

In those circumstances, the period of limitation does not begin to run until the claimant has discovered the fraud, concealment or mistake (as the case may be) or could with reasonable diligence have discovered it.

Deliberate concealment includes a deliberate breach of duty either concealed or undisclosed and committed in circumstances such that it was unlikely to be discovered for some time and also the taking of active steps to conceal a breach of duty after becoming aware of it; but it does not include failure to disclose a negligent breach of duty that the person in breach was not aware of committing (*Cave v Robinson Jarvis and Rolf (a firm) [2002] 2 WLR 1107*).

Chapter 10

Power to Charge Remuneration

Introduction

10.1 Historically, a trustee gave his services free. A trustee was not permitted to profit from his office as trustee. He was entitled to be reimbursed for any expenses properly incurred in the performance of his duties as trustee but was not entitled to be paid profit costs unless expressly authorised so to do by the trust instrument. Such was the strictness of the rule that even an express authority to a professional man acting as trustee to charge for professional services did not authorise him to charge for work which a lay trustee could have been expected to perform without professional assistance. The one exception to the general rule was that a solicitor-trustee was entitled to his profit costs for acting as solicitor for himself and a co-trustee (though not for acting for himself alone) in any action or other legal proceedings except so far as the costs had been increased by his being one of the parties (*Cradock v Piper (1850) 1 Mac & G 664*).

Express charging clauses became commonplace; a charging clause in a will took effect as a legacy. In the case of the Public Trustee, judicial trustees and trust corporations appointed to act as trustee, statute either provided for them to charge or for the court to authorise them to charge. The court also has an inherent jurisdiction to authorise a trustee to charge for past or future work.

In the case of a trust corporation or a professional trustee the position has been modified by *Part V* of the *Trustee Act 2000* (*TA 2000*) in respect of services provided after the relevant provisions of the Act came into force (1 February 2001). However, in the case of a lay trustee the position remains unchanged; he has no right to charge for his services in the absence of express authority in the trust instrument.

TA 2000 has also modified the rule that a charging clause in a will takes effect as a legacy. [*TA 2000, s 28(4)*].

Express charging clause

Extent of charging clause

10.2 Where a trust instrument contains an express authority to charge, the extent to which the trustee is permitted to charge is determined by the terms of the charging clause. A right to charge the trust will not, in the absence of express provision, entitle a professional trustee to retain director's fees and other benefits received by him for acting as a director of a company, shares of which are held by the trust, if he owes his position to his trusteeship, notwithstanding that he has taken that position the better to perform his duties as a trustee (*Re Gee [1948] Ch 284 at 295*). A charging clause authorising a 'professional person' to charge for his time will not authorise a trust corporation to charge remuneration (*Re Cooper (1939) 160 LT 453*).

In the absence of an express provision so permitting, a trustee (whether a trust corporation or otherwise) may not charge scale fees as opposed to making a reasonable charge for work actually done. The size of a trust fund (and hence the degree of responsibility) may be a matter to take into account in determining what is a reasonable rate to charge for time expended, but a right to charge *ad valorem* fees must be expressly authorised.

In the case of services provided after 1 February 2001 (and regardless of when the trust was created) *section 33(1)* of the *Trustee Act 2000* has reversed the rule that, in the absence of an express provision, a professional trustee cannot charge for work which a lay trustee could have done. Save to the extent (if any) that the trust instrument makes inconsistent provision, if there is a provision in the trust instrument entitling the trustee to receive payment out of trust funds in respect of services provided by him to, or on behalf of, the trust, and the trustee is a trust corporation or is acting in a professional capacity, the trustee is to be treated as entitled under the trust instrument to receive payment in respect of services, even if they are services which are capable of being provided by a lay trustee. [*TA 2000, s 28*].

In the case of a trustee of a charitable trust, the foregoing provision applies only to a trustee who is not a trust corporation only if he is not a sole trustee, and to the extent that a majority of the other trustees have agreed that it should apply to him. [*TA 2000, s 28*].

Charging clause in will is not a legacy

10.3 In respect of a trust corporation or a trustee acting in a professional capacity, the *TA 2000, s 28* has also modified the rule that a charging clause contained in a will takes effect as a legacy. The rule had unfortunate consequences. If such person (e.g. a solicitor named as executor) attested the will the charging clause was void by virtue of the *Wills Act 1837, s 15* (*Re*

Pooley (1888) 40 Ch D 1). The charges abated with other gifts if the estate was insufficient to pay all legacies in full. [*Administration of Estates Act 1925, s 34(3), Sch 1, Pt II*]. In the case of any person dying after the commencement of the *Trustee Act 2000*, any payments to which a trustee is entitled in respect of services are to be treated as remuneration for services and not as a gift for the purpose of the *Wills Act 1837, s 15* and the *Administration of Estates Act 1925, s 34(3)*.

Save as provided in *section 35*, the *Trustee Act 2000* applies to personal representatives administering an estate according to law as it applies to a trustee carrying out a trust for beneficiaries. In the case of a person dying after the Act came into force (1 February 2001), remuneration to which a personal representative is entitled under *sections 28* or *29* of the Act (i.e. under the will or under the Act) are treated as administration expenses for the purpose of the *Administration of Estates Act 1925, s 34(3)* (order in which estate is to be paid out) and any provision giving reasonable administration expenses priority over the preferential debts listed in the *Insolvency Act 1986, Sch 6*.

Professional capacity

10.4 A trustee acts in a professional capacity if he acts in the course of a profession or business, which consists of, or includes, the provision of services in connection with the management or administration of trusts generally, or a particular kind of trust; or any particular aspect of the management or administration of trusts generally, or a particular kind of trust, and the services he provides to or on behalf of the trust fall within that description. [*TA 2000, s 28(5)*]. A person acts as a lay trustee if he is not a trust corporation and does not act in a professional capacity [*TA 2000, s 28(6)*].

Statutory right to remuneration

10.5 Under *TA 2000, ss 29, 30*, trust corporations and trustees acting in a professional capacity are in certain circumstances given a statutory right to charge where there is no charging clause in the trust instrument and no other statutory right to charge. The modifications differ as regards trust corporations and professional trustees and as between private trusts and charitable trusts.

Private trust

Trust corporation

10.6 By *TA 2000, s 29(1)* a trustee who is a trust corporation is entitled to receive reasonable remuneration out of the trust funds for any services which the trust corporation provides to or on behalf of the trust.

Trustees acting in a professional capacity

10.7 By *TA 2000, s 29(2)* a trustee who acts in a professional capacity other than a sole trustee is entitled to receive reasonable remuneration out of the trust fund for any services that he provides to or on behalf of the trust if each other trustee has agreed in writing that he may be remunerated for the services.

Exclusion by express provision etc

10.8 A trustee is not entitled to remuneration under *TA 2000, s 29* if provision about his entitlement to remuneration has been made by the trust instrument or by any enactment or any provision of subordinate legislation. Accordingly, if a trust instrument includes a charging clause *section 29* is excluded even if the charging clause is in some respect unsatisfactory. Whether the right to remuneration under *section 29* can be excluded may have to be judicially determined, but there seems no reason in principle why an express provision that the trustee should act without remuneration should not be a 'provision about his entitlement to remuneration'.

Meaning of reasonable remuneration

10.9 In either case, reasonable remuneration means in relation to the provision of services by a trustee, such remuneration as is reasonable in the circumstances for the provision of those services to or on behalf of that trust by that trustee and includes, in relation to the provision of services by a trustee who is an authorised institution under the *Banking Act 1987*, and provides the services in that capacity, the institution's reasonable charges for the provision of such services. [*TA 2000, s 29(3)*]. The definition of reasonable remuneration would not appear to permit charging of *ad valorem* fees even if that is the basis upon which, say, a trust corporation habitually offers its services. A trustee is entitled to remuneration under *section 29* even if the services in question are capable of being provided by a lay trustee.

Trustees acting as agents, nominees or custodians

10.10 The provision for remuneration under *TA 2000, s 29* applies as much to a trustee who has been authorised under a power conferred by *Part IV* of the Act or the trust instrument to exercise functions as an agent of the trustees or to act as a nominee or custodian as it applies to any other trustee.

Charitable trusts

10.11 By *TA 2000, s 30* in respect of the remuneration of trustees of charitable trusts, the Secretary of State may by regulations make provision for remuneration of trustees by charitable trusts who are trust corporations or act in a professional capacity. No regulations have yet been made.

Trustees' expenses

10.12 By *TA 2000, s 31* a trustee (whether of a private or charitable trust) is entitled to be reimbursed from trust funds, or may pay out of trust funds, expenses properly incurred by him when acting on behalf of the trust. The section applies to a trustee who has been authorised to exercise functions as an agent of the trustees or to act as a nominee or custodian, as it applies to any other trustee.

Agents, nominees and custodians

10.13 *TA 2000, s 32* deals with the remuneration and expenses of agents, nominees and custodians other than trustees. The trustees are authorised to remunerate the agent, nominee or custodian out of the trust fund for services if he is engaged on terms entitling him to be remunerated for those services, and the amount does not exceed such remuneration as is reasonable in the circumstances for the provision of those services by him to or on behalf of that trust. The trustees may reimburse the agent, nominee or custodian out of the trust funds for any expenses properly incurred by him in exercising functions as an agent, nominee or custodian.

Commencement

10.14 The provisions relating to remuneration and expenses apply to services provided to or on behalf of a trust, or expenses incurred on or after 1 February 2001, regardless of when the trust was created.

Other statutory provisions authorising charging

Judicial trustee

10.15 A judicial trustee appointed by the court may be paid out of the trust property such remuneration, not exceeding the prescribed limits, as the court may assign in each case. Rule 11(1) of the *Judicial Trustee Rules 1983 (SI 1983 No 370)* makes provision for disbursement and remuneration. A person appointed a judicial trustee should be allowed on the examination of his accounts (in addition to such disbursements as have actually and properly been expended in his trusteeship) by way of remuneration, if any, such reasonable remuneration as may be authorised by the court.

The court may direct that such remuneration shall be fixed by reference to such scales or rates of professional charges as it thinks fit provided that such remuneration should not exceed 15% of the capital value of the trust property. Rule 11(2) provides that the capital value should be ascertained from the certificate which the judicial trustee is required by rule 10 to endorse on his annual accounts as to the approximate capital value of the trust property at the commencement of the year of account. It also provides that the court may, if it thinks fit, indicate to a judicial trustee upon his appointment the scale or rate of professional charges that it considers would be appropriate in relation to the appointment.

Public Trustee

10.16 Under the *Public Trustee Act 1906, s 9* the fees chargeable by the Public Trustee are fixed by the Treasury with the sanction of the Lord Chancellor. The Public Trustee may also retain and be paid expenses in the same manner as a private trustee and may determine the incidence as between capital and income of such expenses. The current provisions as to fees are prescribed by the *Public Trustee (Fees) Order 1999 (SI 1999 No 855)*, which deals also with the incidence of the fees as between capital and income. The prescribed fees comprise an executorship fee payable on acceptance by the Public Trustee of any executorship or administration or an acceptance fee upon acceptance of any other trust (other than certain annuity or terminable payments) and on additional property subsequently coming into the trust other than accumulated income; an administration fee payable annually and withdrawal fee upon the Public Trustee ceasing to act or upon the withdrawal of part of the estate or trust property. The executorship or acceptance fee, the administration fee and the withdrawal fee are all calculated as a percentage of the capital of the fund.

There is also provision for fees for special services set out in *Part VI* of the Order, and for a management fee for superannuation schemes and friendly societies (*Part VII*). The Public Trustee has power to postpone payment if it appears just and reasonable and to commute future payments. The Public Trustee also has power to remit fees and settle disputes about his right to a fee or its amount but, save where the fee is remitted in respect of any estate or trust where the whole or any part of the property is in another estate or trust where he is acting, the Public Trustee must have the approval of the Treasury to any compromise or to the remitting of any fee.

Corporation appointed by court to act as trustee

10.17 By the *Trustee Act 1925, s 42* where the court appoints a corporation other than the Public Trustee either solely or jointly with any other person, the court may authorise the corporation to charge such remuneration for its services as trustee as the court may think fit. *Section 42* applies only to the appointment of a corporation, not to the appointment of an individual even if acting in a professional capacity. The section would seem to be largely superseded by the provisions of the *Trustee Act 2000*. The Public Trustee is entitled to charge by virtue of the *Public Trustee Act 1906, s 9*.

Substitute personal representative

10.18 Where the High Court appoints a substitute personal representative to act as a personal representative in place of the existing personal representatives of a deceased person or any of them the court may authorise the person appointed to charge remuneration for his services on such terms as the court may think fit; such terms may include the submission of bills of charges for taxation. [*Administration of Estates Act 1985, s 50(3)*].

Charging by agreement with the beneficiaries

10.19 It is, of course, open to a beneficiary (being of full age and capacity) to authorise a trustee to charge at the expense of the beneficiary's own beneficial interest under the trust providing no other beneficiary's interest is adversely affected. Thus, a life tenant can, without the consent of the remainderman, authorise a trustee to charge against income during the subsistence of the life interest whereas a remainderman cannot (without the concurrence of the life tenant) authorise a trustee to charge against capital during the currency of a life interest, for the diminution of capital would adversely affect the income return. A person with a vested interest in remainder can authorise charges against his expectant share even if he or she was likely to die before it falls into possession (for a person may bind his own estate); a person with a contingent interest in remainder however cannot do so.

The old cases indicate that an agreement by a beneficiary authorising remuneration for a trustee would be looked on jealously and set aside unless shown to be made freely, without pressure and with the benefit of independent advice (see, for example, *Ayliffe v Murray (1740) 2 Atk 58*). In the case of a trust corporation or trustee acting in a professional capacity, the statutory right to charge is likely to obviate any need to make an agreement with the beneficiaries. In the case of a lay trustee or a trust corporation or a professional trustee seeking remuneration of a kind or at a level not authorised by *TA 2000, s 29*, agreements as to remuneration are liable to remain vulnerable to judicial scrutiny if subsequently called into question by the beneficiary since they involve a conflict of interest for the trustee.

Charging authorised by the court

10.20 The court may authorise a trustee to charge by virtue of its inherent jurisdiction and pursuant to certain express statutory provisions. The inherent jurisdiction is likely to become less important in respect of trust corporations and trustees acting in a professional capacity given the statutory power to charge but will remain important for lay trustees.

Inherent jurisdiction

10.21 The basis of the inherent jurisdiction is the good administration of the trust: if, whilst balancing the interests of the beneficiaries against the claims of the trustees, the authorising of remuneration or increased remuneration is beneficial to the trust then the court may authorise the payment of remuneration or increased remuneration to the trustees. The jurisdiction applies both to work already done and to work to be done in the future. Thus in *Re Duke of Norfolk's Settlement Trusts [1982] Ch 61*, where the settlor added blocks of property to the trust fund leading to a substantial redevelopment and the trustees were involved in work unforeseen at the time of the settlement, the charging provision of which had fallen out of date, the trustees sought increased remuneration and it was held that the court had jurisdiction to grant it.

The jurisdiction is not limited to express trustees: in *Re Berkeley Applegate Ltd [1989] Ch 32* a liquidator of a company who was not a trustee but upon whom in practice fell the task of dealing with a pension fund was authorised to charge at the expense of the trusts assets to the extent that the company assets were insufficient to compensate him adequately for his costs, skill and labour. In *Gray v Richards Butler [2001] WTLR 625* a solicitor executor had administered an estate before it transpired that the document which had been admitted to probate as the last will was invalid. He was awarded remuneration under the inherent jurisdiction in respect of work which would, in any event, have fallen to be done under the terms of the penultimate will then admitted to probate. In a similar situation occurring after 1 February 2001 the solicitor would arguably be entitled to remuneration by virtue of *TA 2000, s 29*.

Remuneration may be authorised for part only of the trustee's work. For example, in *Foster v Spencer [1996] 2 All ER 672*, trustees of a disused cricket ground brought about a sale for development and were thereby engaged in work quite out of the ordinary. Remuneration was authorised for that work, however, as the future administration of the funds was not exceptional, and the burden would fall on the trust's solicitors, future remuneration was not authorised.

Constructive trustees

10.22 The jurisdiction to order remuneration is not confined to authorising express trustees to charge, e.g. where a person is held to be a constructive trustee the court may authorise remuneration. So in *Boardman v Phipps [1967] 2 AC 46* a solicitor to the trust and a beneficiary were held liable to account for a personal profit made by them as a consequence of the use of trust assets. They had acted openly, but mistakenly, in a manner which was highly beneficial to the trusts, and were held entitled to 'payment on a liberal scale' (per Lord Cohen at *page 104G*) for their work and skill. However, an order for remuneration, still less one 'on a liberal scale', is by no means inevitable. Where contracts between an entertainer and his manager were set aside on the grounds of restraint of trade and undue influence, the manager was allowed reasonable remuneration albeit less than he might have properly negotiated at the relevant time (*O'Sullivan v Management Agency Ltd [1985] QB 428*). Where a director put himself in a position of conflict of interest with his company, the House of Lords held that there was no prospect of the court (even assuming that the jurisdiction applied) exercising the jurisdiction in his favour (*Guinness plc v Saunders [1990] 2 AC 663 at 702*).

Recouping unauthorised remuneration

10.23 Where a trustee has charged unauthorised remuneration (whether it is said that the remuneration was wholly unauthorised or excessive) a beneficiary is entitled to commence proceedings for an account against the trustee, the effect of which is to put the onus on the trustee to demonstrate that his charges are reasonable and authorised (*Re Wells deceased [1962] 1 WLR 397*). To the extent that they are not reasonable or authorised the trustee is under a duty to reinstate the trust fund together, where appropriate, with interest (whether interest is simple or compound will turn on the facts of the case). The court may send the matter to a costs judge for determination (*Re Park (1889) 41 Ch D 326*).

Chapter 11

Power to Invest

Introduction

11.1 The 19th-century powers of investment were extremely limited. The position was improved by statute and the *Trustee Act 1925, Pt I* set out a list of authorised investments in which a trustee could invest any trust funds in his hands. The *Settled Land Act 1925, Pt III* also set out how capital money could be invested or applied. This effectively incorporated the provisions of the *Trustee Act 1925* in addition to other forms of investment or application which were appropriate to the concept of settled land. A major reform occurred in 1961 with the passing of the *Trustee Investments Act 1961* which introduced the concept of narrower-range investments, wider-range investments, and special-range investments. Narrower-range investments were divided into two – those in which a trustee could invest without advice (e.g. defence bonds, National Savings certificates, etc) and those investments requiring advice (e.g. Government securities, local authority loans, deposits with building societies, mortgages, etc). Wider-range investments included stocks and shares in UK companies, shares in building societies, unit trusts and so forth. A trustee was required to take advice before investing in wider-range investments. Special-range property included investments which the trustee was otherwise authorised to hold. A trustee wishing to invest in wider-range investments (including special-range investments) was required to divide the trust fund equally and maintain at least half the fund in narrower-range investments. The other moiety could be invested in either narrower-range or wider-range investments. In 1996 the proportions were altered to 3:1 wider range: narrower range.

The statutory powers were regarded by most well-advised settlors or testators as being too cumbersome and a wide investment clause became a part of any well-drawn trust deed or will setting up a testamentary trust. Indeed, by October 1982 the Law Reform Committee concluded that the Act had proved 'tiresome, cumbrous and expensive in operation' and recommended revision.

The position has now been substantially simplified by the introduction of a general power of investment by *Part II* of the *Trustee Act 2000* (*TA 2000*). This new statutory power applies to trusts whether created before or after the commencement of that Act (1 February 2001). A provision contained in a trust instrument made before the commencement of the *TA 2000*, which has the effect, under the *Trustee Investments Act 1961, s 3(2)* as a power to invest under that Act, or confers power to invest under that Act, is to be treated as conferring the general power of investment on a trustee (*section 7(3)*).

The general power of investment is in addition to powers conferred on trustees otherwise than by the Act but it may be restricted or excluded by a provision in the trust instrument or by any enactment or any provision of subordinate legislation (*section 6*). However, no provision relating to the powers of a trustee contained in a trust instrument made *before* 3 August 1961 is to be treated as restricting or excluding the general power of investment (*section 7(2)*). The 1961 Act was intended to extend the investment powers of trustees notwithstanding any restrictions in the trust instrument and *TA 2000* preserves that position substituting the general power of investment for the limited power contained in the 1961 Act. However an exclusion or restriction of the statutory power contained in a trust instrument made *after* 3 August 1961 will be effective.

General power of investment

11.2 Subject to the provisions of *TA 2000, Pt II*, a trustee may make any kind of investment that he could make if he were absolutely entitled to the assets of the trust (*section 3*). The general power of investment does not permit a trustee to make investments in land other than a loan secured on land. However, *section 8* of the Act makes specific provision for the acquisition of freehold or leasehold land (see CHAPTER 12: POWERS OF ACQUIRING, SELLING AND LEASING LAND).

Standard investment criteria

11.3 In exercising powers of investment, whether arising under *TA 2000, Pt II* or otherwise, a trustee must have regard to the standard investment criteria. A trustee must from time to time review the investments of the trust and consider whether, having regard to the standard investment criteria, they should be varied. [*TA 2000, s 4*].

The standard investment criteria in relation to a trust are:

(*a*) the suitability to the trust of investments of the same kind as any particular investment proposed to be made or retained, and of that particular investment as an investment of that kind; and

(*b*) the need for diversification of investments of the trust in so far as is appropriate to the circumstances of the trust.

Advice

11.4 Before exercising any power of investment, whether arising under *TA 2000, Pt II* or otherwise, a trustee must obtain and consider proper advice about the way in which, having regard to the standard investment criteria, the power should be exercised. The one exception is that a trustee need not obtain such advice if he reasonably concludes that in all the circumstances it is unnecessary or inappropriate to do so. [*TA 2000, s 5*].

When reviewing the investments of the trust, a trustee must obtain and consider proper advice about whether, having regard to the standard investment criteria, the investment should be varied. Again, the only exception is that a trustee need not obtain such advice if he reasonably concludes that in all the circumstances it is unnecessary or inappropriate to do so.

Proper advice is the advice of a person who is reasonably believed by the trustee to be qualified to give it by his ability in, and practical experience of financial and other matters relating to the proposed investment. [*TA 2000, s 5(4)*]. Again the belief that the adviser is qualified must be reasonable.

The exception

11.5 It should be noted that the exception from the requirement to take advice only applies if the decision not to take advice is reasonable; if it is unreasonable the trustee will be liable for any adverse consequences. The Act is silent as to what does or does not constitute a reasonable decision. Clearly if a fund is very small and the chosen investment a safe one (for example, investing a modest pecuniary legacy until the legatee comes of age), a trustee is hardly likely to be criticised. Except in the plainest cases, a decision not to take advice and the reason for it should be minuted so that there is a contemporary record if the decision is subsequently called into question.

Who may advise

11.6 Beyond stating that proper advice is the advice of a person who is reasonably believed by the trustee to be qualified to give it, the Act does not set out any restrictions on who may or may not give such advice. The Act does not appear to contemplate the trustees taking advice from one of their number or from an employee. However, if a trustee is a qualified person, or employs a qualified person able to give the appropriate advice (e.g. a trust corporation which as part of its ordinary course of business gives investment advice), the matter may fall within the exception, i.e. that in the circumstances it is unnecessary or inappropriate to take further advice. The trustee is, of course, responsible for that decision.

A trustee would be unwise to rely on advice given by a person with a direct financial interest in the implementation of that advice, for in that situation the impartiality and hence reliability of the advice would be open to question.

Form of advice

11.7 The Act does not require the advice to be given in writing. However, given that a trustee may subsequently be called to account and to show that the trustee both took advice and acted upon it, a trustee would be unwise to rely on oral advice.

Following advice

11.8 The Act requires a trustee to 'obtain and consider' proper advice. The Act does not require the advice to be followed in its entirety or at all. A trustee who departs from advice must however be prepared and able to justify so doing. If a major departure from advice is contemplated, the trustee would be well advised to take further advice on the proposed course of action. If the advice given is plainly wrong (e.g. that a fund required to produce income for a life tenant be invested in non-income producing bonds) then the Trustees could hardly plead the advice as a defence to a claim of breach of trust.

The duty of care

11.9 The statutory duty of care (see 3.11 above) applies to a trustee when exercising the general power of investment, or any other power of investment (however conferred). It also applies when carrying out the duty, to which a trustee is subject under *TA 2000, s 4*, to have regard to the standard investment criteria, or the duty under *section 5* to take advice relating to the exercise of a power of investment or to the review of investments. [*TA 2000, Sch 1, para 1*].

Delegation

11.10 The power of investment is a delegable function within the meaning of *TA 2000, s 11*, i.e. it is a power which can be delegated to an agent (see CHAPTER 18: POWER TO DELEGATE). However, investment of assets subject to the trust is an asset management function so that the trustees may not authorise a person to exercise a power of investment as their agent except by an agreement which is in, or evidenced in, writing and unless they have prepared a statement that gives guidance as to how the function should be exercised ('the policy statement'). The trustee must keep that policy statement under review.

Social, ethical or political considerations

11.11 The duty of a trustee is to act in the best interest of his beneficiaries. If the purpose of the trust is the provision of financial benefits, a power of investment has to be exercised so that their funds yield the best return by way of income and capital appreciation, judged in relation to the risks of the investments being considered. That is so whatever a trustee's personal views or moral reservations as to the choice of the most suitable investments, although taking account in exceptional cases of the particular inclinations of the beneficiaries being provided for.

In *Cowan v Scargill [1985] Ch 270* some of the trustees of a large pension fund for coal miners were nominated by the union and the union objected to certain investments including investments in companies involved in competing fuels. The trustees nominated by the union were wrong to hinder the normal operation of the pension scheme by objections or prohibitions which could not be justified on economic grounds or, except remotely, in the interests of the beneficiaries.

It is to be noted that the decision in the *Scargill* case related to trusts the purpose of which was the provision of financial benefits (i.e. pensions to members). The same was the case in *Harries v Church Commissioners for England [1992] 1 WLR 1241*. The Church Commissioners were responsible for managing a fund for the financial assistance of the clergy of the Church of England. It was held that the Commissioners were justified in excluding investments which might be offensive on moral grounds to members of the Church in favour of alternative investments but that they were right to refuse to adopt a more restrictive policy of investment which involved taking into account non-financial considerations to an extent which would give rise to the risk of significant detriment to the proper object of the trust.

Speculative investments

11.12 Although the general power of investment (and many express powers) enables a trustee to make any kind of investment that he could make if he were absolutely entitled to the assets of the trust, the exercise of that power is subject to the duty of care, i.e. a duty to exercise such skill and care as is reasonable in all the circumstances. [*TA 2000, Sch 1, para 1*]. In principle, a trustee should conduct the business of the trust as an ordinary prudent man of business would conduct his own but in *Re Whiteley (1886) 33 Ch D 347*, Lindley LJ observed that the business of the trustee (and of the hypothetical man of business) is that of investing money for persons entitled to it at some future time and not simply the person entitled to income and that the duty is to take such care as would an ordinary prudent man of business who is minded to make an investment for the benefit of other people for whom he felt morally bound to provide.

Accordingly, however wide the scope of the investment clause, the trustee should not be reckless with trust money. Thus, in *Bartlett v Barclays Bank Trust Co [1980] Ch 515* a professional trustee embarked on a speculative development which occasioned loss to the trust fund. The trustee was held liable to make good the loss. The trustee was, however, allowed to offset a profit made on another speculative investment because - and only because - it was made as part of the same policy. The general rule is that a trustee who has committed a breach of trust is liable to account for any profit he has made by virtue of the breach of trust and to make good any loss without the right to offset the profit.

Transactions such as futures, options or the purchase and sales of currency or commodities which depend entirely on predicting future market movements are speculative and thus normally unsuitable as an investment of trust money. Indeed, as the same are incapable of generating income they may well not be investments in the correct sense of that word at all.

Implied or constructive trustees

11.13 Persons who become implied or constructive trustees generally do so unintentionally or against their will. The extent of a trustee's lawful power of investment is, however, relevant to determining whether such persons have occasioned any loss to the beneficiaries and, if so, the extent of that loss.

Bearer securities

11.14 The general power of investment clearly extends to investments in bearer securities, given the provisions of *TA 2000, s 18* which requires a trustee to appoint a person to act as custodian of securities payable to bearer.

Loans secured on land

11.15 A person invests in a loan secured on land if he has rights under any contract under which:

(*a*) one person provides another with credit; and

(*b*) the obligation of the borrower to repay is secured on land.

Credit includes any cash loan, or other financial accommodation, and cash includes money in any form. [*TA 2000, s 3*].

Providing the trustees observe the common duty of care and the standard investment criteria, trustees may invest by lending on mortgage. Trustees should be concerned to see that the property offered as security has a sufficient value to secure the borrower's liability. Particular care must be taken before lending on a second or subsequent charge. The prudent trustee will also have regard to the ability of the borrower to pay the interest under the charge and to repay the capital.

Prior to the changes made by *TA 2000*, a trustee who lent not more than two thirds of the value of real property (valued by a person whom the trustee believed was an able practical surveyor or valuer) was protected by the *Trustee Act 1925, s 8* from being charged with breach of trust only because of the inadequacy of the security. The section also protected a trustee who lent on the security of leasehold property for not investigating the lessor's title and for accepting in the case of any property a shorter title than a person acting with prudence and caution would have accepted. *Section 8* has been repealed by the 2000 Act but the transitional provisions in *Schedule 3* preserve the trustees' protection given by *section 8* in respect of loans or investments made before 1 February 2001. The propriety of loans made after that date falls to be judged by whether the requirements of *TA 2000* have been complied with.

Also preserved (despite its repeal) in respect of investments made before 1 February 2001, is the *Trustee Act 1925, s 9* which limited a trustee's liability to make good an excessive sum lent on an otherwise proper security. The trustee's liability was limited to the amount of the excess.

A trustee should not lend trust money to himself or to a co-trustee and to do so would be a breach of the self-dealing rule even if the loan were fully secured and on commercial terms (see CHAPTER 5: DUTY NOT TO BENEFIT PERSONALLY). A trustee should exercise caution before lending to a beneficiary and, unless the trust instrument provides otherwise, any such loan should be fully secured and on commercial terms. Unless specifically authorised by the trust instrument the trustees should not make unsecured loans.

Rent charges

11.16 Unlike the *Trustee Investments Act 1961* which expressly authorised trustees to invest in perpetual rent charges, perpetual rent charges are excluded from the general power of investment (being an interest in land). They are also excluded from the power to acquire land (see further CHAPTER 12: POWERS OF ACQUIRING, SELLING AND LEASING LAND). However, the transitional provisions in *TA 2000, Sch 3* provide that a trustee shall not be liable for breach of trust merely because he continues to hold a perpetual rent charge.

Chattels

11.17 Historically the court construed a power to invest as a power to purchase property to hold for the income which it produced. On that test, a chattel would not normally qualify as an investment even if it had the potential to yield a profit by capital growth. The Act contains no definition of 'investment' and it therefore remains to be seen whether the court is now prepared to take a broader view of what is capable of constituting an investment. Clearly, a chattel which does not have the potential to yield either income or capital growth cannot constitute an investment. Where a life interest is in being, the trustees' duty to balance the interests of the life tenant in income and remaindermen in capital may of itself make a chattel an unsuitable investment unless proper arrangements can be made for the life tenant to enjoy the chattel in specie.

Application to personal representatives and judicial trustees

11.18 The provisions of *TA 2000* apply in relation to a personal representative administering an estate as they apply to a trustee carrying out a trust for beneficiaries. [*TA 2000, s* 35]. A judicial trustee is a 'trustee' even in respect of the administration of an estate (*Judicial Trustees Act 1986, s 1*) and, therefore, the provisions of *TA 2000* clearly apply to a judicial trustee.

Settled land

11.19 The mode of investment or application of capital monies arising under a strict settlement are dealt with by the *Settled Land Act 1925, s 73*. *Section 73(1)(i)* provides for investment either under the general power of investment under *TA 2000, s 3* or under a power to invest conferred on the trustees of the settlement by the settlement. *Section 73(1)(ii)–(xxi)* then goes on to list other authorised forms of application of capital monies.

The *Settled Land Act, s 75(1)* provides for any capital monies to be paid to the trustees and invested by the trustees (as opposed to the tenant for life). As originally enacted, *section 75(2)* provided for the investment to be according to the direction of the tenant for life or in default according to the discretion of the trustees. *Section 75(2)* has now been replaced (see *TA 2000, Sch 2*).

Section 75(2) now provides that the investment or other application should be according to the discretion of the trustees, but subject to any consent required or direction given by the settlement with respect to investment or other application by the trustees of trust money of the settlement. Furthermore, a duty has been imposed on the trustees (by *subsection (4)*, the existing *subsection (4)* being renumbered *subsection (4A)*) that in exercising their power to invest or apply capital money the trustees should:

(*a*) as far as practicable, consult the tenant for life; and

(*b*) as far as consistent with the general interest of the settlement, give effect to his wishes.

New *subsections 75(4B)* and *(4C)* provide that, on the one hand, the trustees may not delegate their power of investment or application of capital monies on terms that prevent them complying with that duty to the tenant for life but, on the other, that the agent is not subject to the duty. The net effect seems to be that trustees of a strict settlement will not be able to delegate their powers of investment or application of capital money to an agent on terms that the agent consults the tenant for life but can only delegate power to act after consultation with the life tenant and in a manner which gives effect (to the extent required by the Act) to the tenant for life's wishes.

Securing part of the purchase money

11.20 Special provision is made by the *Settled Land Act 1925, s 75A* (introduced by *TA 2000*) where land subject to a strict settlement is sold by the tenant for life or the statutory owner for an estate in fee simple or a term having at least five hundred years to run and the proceeds of sale are liable to be invested. The tenant for life or statutory owner may with the consent of the trustees of the settlement contract that the payment of any part not exceeding two-thirds of the purchase money shall be secured by a charge by way of legal mortgage of the land sold with or without the security of other property.

It should, however, be noted that if any buildings are comprised in the property secured by the charge, the charge *must* contain a covenant by the mortgagor to keep them insured for their full value against loss and damage due in any event.

A person exercising this power or giving consent is not required to take advice under *TA 2000, s 5* and is not liable for any loss incurred merely because the security is insufficient at the date of the charge. The power is subject to the consent of any person whose consent to a change of investment is required by the instrument, if any, creating the trust. Where the sale is made under the order of the court, the power applies only if and as far as the court may by order direct.

Breach of trust

Consequences of making an unauthorised investment

11.21 A trustee who invests outside his power of investment commits a breach of trust. If the consequence of the unlawful investment is to yield a capital and income return as good as, or better than, an authorised investment would have yielded, then damages will be nominal. The trustee must account for all the profit made. A trustee may not set off profits made from one breach of trust against losses resulting from another unless the breaches are connected. In *Bartlett v Barclays Bank Trust Co [1980] Ch 515* where trustees undertook a speculative development and were liable for the loss resulting they were held entitled to set off a gain made on development land because it had been acquired as part of the same policy.

If through making unauthorised investments, the trustee has achieved enhanced income but at the expense of capital growth or vice versa the trustee must account for actual return achieved and make up the shortfall. He may not set off the one against the other unless the beneficial interest is the same (e.g. in a discretionary trust where income is being accumulated).

Consequences of retaining an unauthorised investment

11.22 A trustee who makes an unauthorised investment is under a duty to realise the same even if this crystallises a loss, which he is then liable to make good.

Charities

General

11.23 A trustee of a charitable trust has the same powers and is under the same duties as the trustee of a private trust. However, in the context of a charitable trust, social ethical or political issues may present a more acute and legitimate concern. In the case of charitable trusts, the charitable purpose must inform the exercise of any of the trustees' powers including their power of investment and this may justify trustees excluding from consideration investment in companies whose activities are incompatible with the objects of the charity. It was observed in *Harries v Church Commissioners for England [1992] 1 WLR 1241* the law is not so cynical as to require trustees to behave in a fashion which would bring them or their charity into disrepute, although it was added that their consciences must not be too tender.

Trustees must act prudently and not use property held by them for investment for the purpose of making moral statements at the expense of the charity of which they are trustees. Where moral views differ over whether a particular investment conflicts with the charitable purpose the trustees, when making an investment decision, are not required to decide which view is correct or to prefer one view over another even if in the majority (*Harries*).

Common investment scheme

11.24 The *Charities Act 1993, s 24* provides that on the application of any two or more charities the court or the Charity Commissioners may by order make and bring into effect a common investment scheme. Under a common investment scheme trustees manage a fund to which property is transferred by or on behalf of the charities participating in the scheme and the charities are entitled to the capital and income of the fund in shares determined by the amount or value of the property transferred at the time of transfer. The powers of investment of every charity include a power to invest in a common investment scheme unless that power is specifically excluded in the trusts of the charity.

A common investment scheme will make provision for all matters connected with the establishment, investment, management and winding up of the common investment fund.

TA 2000, Pt II relating to investment (i.e. the general power of investment, the standard investment criteria and the provisions relating to advice) does not (save as mentioned in *TA 2000, s 38(a)*) apply to the trustees managing a fund under a common investment scheme.

Common deposit scheme

11.25 The *Charities Act, s 25* provides for funds to be deposited by participating charities and for them to receive interest thereon. *TA 2000, Pt II* likewise does not apply to the trustees managing a fund under a common deposit scheme.

Pension schemes

11.26 The provisions of the *TA 2000* relating to investment do not apply to pension schemes (*section 36*) the relevant power is be found in the *Pensions Act 1995, s 34* which provides that, subject to any restriction imposed by the scheme, the trustees have the same power to make an investment of any kind as if they were absolutely entitled to the assets of the scheme.

Chapter 12

Powers of Acquiring, Selling and Leasing Land

Introduction

12.1 Historically, trusts of land fell into one of two types – strict settlements and land held on trust for sale. Strict settlements were and are still governed by the *Settled Land Act 1925* (*SLA 1925*). Land that was not settled land was inevitably held on a trust for sale. The strict settlement was used to preserve landed estates and secure their passing in specie from one generation to the next whilst land held on trust for sale was intended to be sold and the proceeds of sale invested in authorised investments. However, the 19th century reforms and the 1925 legislation brought about significant changes.

In the case of a trust for sale the land was vested in the trustees; well-drawn trust powers almost invariably contained a power enabling the trustees to postpone the sale and, in any event, the *Law of Property Act 1925, s 25* implied a power to postpone unless the contrary intention appeared. By contrast, settled land was vested in the tenant for life and the Act gave the tenant for life an unfettered and inalienable right to sell the land if he chose, the trustees' role being to receive and invest the capital money. As a result, in the case of land held on trust for sale, decisions affecting the land rested with the trustees whereas in the case of settled land, decisions rested with the tenant for life. The Gilbertian consequence was that, after 1925, a settlor wishing to see his estate preserved in specie often concluded that the safer course was to settle it on a trust for sale on the basis that the trustees could be relied on to exercise their power to postpone sale indefinitely, rather than to create a strict settlement and expose the land to the self interest of the tenant for life.

Strict settlements came to be seen as archaic and new settlements almost inevitably were drawn on the basis of the trust for sale. Although some strict settlements were no doubt created by choice, others were inadvertently created by defective drafting. The time for reform had come.

The *Trusts of Land and Appointment of Trustees Act 1996* (*TLATA 1996*) provides that no settlement created after the coming into force of the Act (1 January 1997) is a settlement for the purposes of the *SLA 1925* and it introduces the concept of the 'trust of land'. Transitional provisions mean that any existing strict settlement remains such unless and until it ceases to hold any relevant property (i.e. land, and heirlooms to which *SLA 1925, s 67(1)* applies) at which point the settlement permanently ceases to be a settlement for the purpose of the 1925 Act; thereafter any land acquired will be held on a trust of land. [*TLATA 1996, s 2(4), Sch 1*].

An express trust for sale can still be created, but in respect of all new and existing trusts for sale a power to postpone sale is to be implied and the trustees are not liable in any way for postponing sale of the land, in exercise of their discretion, for an indefinite period (see 12.10 below).

A number of statutory provisions imposed a trust for sale of land and by *TLATA 1996, s 5* these are converted into trusts of land. The statutory provisions are listed in *Schedule 2* to the Act. Most commonly encountered are dispositions to tenants in common or joint tenants (*Law of Property Act 1925, ss 34, 36*) and land devolving on intestacy (*Administration of Estates Act 1925, s 33*).

What interest in land can be settled?

12.2 Any property, real or personal, legal or equitable which is capable of being assigned can be made the subject of a trust. Clearly, if the right to assign or part with possession is prohibited or qualified (as for example in a lease) the terms of that prohibition or qualification must be observed.

It does not, however, follow from the fact that there is no restriction on what a settlor may settle that a trustee has the same unlimited power when it comes to investing trust money. A trustee can only invest trust money in the purchase of land if authorised to do so by the trust instrument or statute.

Acquisition of land – express power

12.3 An express power to acquire land will fall to be construed according to its terms. A well-drawn power will make clear whether the trustee is authorised to acquire an equitable interest in land, in particular, an undivided share. Acquisition of an undivided share is not authorised by statute. An express power to invest in an undivided share may, therefore, be of particular use. A common example is the case of the widow or widower entitled to a life interest in the estate of the deceased spouse. The survivor cannot afford to buy a property on his or her own and the trust fund is not large enough to buy a property for him or her to live in, or not large enough to do so without seriously diminishing the income needed for his or her living costs. The obvious solution is for the survivor and the trust to join together to buy a property jointly. However, this can only be done under an express power (or an order of the court (see CHAPTER 21: TAKING ADDITIONAL ADMINISTRATIVE POWERS OR SURRENDERING OR RELEASING POWERS).

Acquisition of land – statutory power

12.4 *TLATA 1996, s 6(3)* (as amended) provides that trustees may acquire land under *TA 2000, s 8*. *Section 8* provides that a trustee may acquire freehold or leasehold land in the United Kingdom:

(*a*) as an investment;

(*b*) for occupation by a beneficiary; or

(*c*) for any other reason.

Section 8 applies whether a trust was created before or after the commencement of the section. It does not, however, apply in relation to a trust of property which consists of or includes land which remains settled land and it does not apply to a trust to which the *Universities and Colleges Estates Act 1925* applies.

Freehold or leasehold land means in England and Wales a legal estate in land, in Scotland its equivalent, and in Northern Ireland a legal estate in land including land held under a fee farm grant (*section 8(2)*). As the power under *section 8* is restricted to the acquisition of a legal estate in the land, it is not possible under the statutory power to buy an equitable interest, e.g. an undivided share in land.

The statutory power to acquire freehold and leasehold land granted by *TA 2000, s 8* is in addition to powers conferred on legal trustees otherwise than by the Act, but subject to any restriction or exclusion imposed by the trust instrument or by any enactment or provision of subordinate legislation. [*TA 2000, s 9*].

Statutory duty of care

12.5 Both *TA 2000* and *TLATA 1996* (as amended) provide that the duty of care applies to trustees when exercising their power to acquire land. The statutory duty of care is set out in *TA 2000, s 1, Sch 1* (see CHAPTER 3: DUTY TO EXERCISE REASONABLE CARE AND SKILL).

Powers of trustees in relation to land

12.6 For the purpose of exercising their functions as trustees, the trustees of land have in relation to the land the subject of the trust all the powers of an absolute owner. In exercising their powers, trustees must have regard to the rights of the beneficiaries. The powers must not be exercised in contravention of, or of any order made in pursuance of, any other enactment or any rule of law or equity. Order includes an order of the court or of the Charity Commissioners. If any other enactment confers authority to act subject to any restriction limitation or condition the power to act remains subject to that restriction limitation or condition. The statutory duty of care applies to a trustee of land when exercising this power. [*TLATA 1996, s 6*].

In respect of land acquired pursuant to the power given by *TA 2000, s 8*, a trustee has all the powers of an absolute owner in relation to the land but subject to any restriction or exclusion imposed by the trust instrument or by any enactment or any provision of subordinate legislation. [*TA 2000, ss 8, 9*].

Delegation of powers relating to land

12.7 The trustees of land may, by power of attorney, delegate to any beneficiary or beneficiaries of full age and beneficially entitled to an interest in possession in land subject to the trust any of their functions as trustees which relate to the land. [*TLATA 1996, s 9*].

Power to sell land

12.8 In the case of every trust of land, the trustees have all the powers of an absolute owner and, accordingly, have power to retain or sell the land as they see fit. If a trust for sale is expressly created by a disposition a power to postpone sale is to be implied, despite any provision to the contrary made by the disposition and the trustees are not liable in any way for postponing the sale of the land, in the exercise of their discretion, for an indefinite period. Statutory provisions which impose a trust for sale are converted to a trust of land without a duty to sell. (See generally *TLATA 1996, ss 4–6* and *Sch 2*).

The *Trustee Act 1925, ss 12, 13* continue to make specific provision with regard to the power of trustees and personal representatives to sell, either by auction or by private treaty, and include the power to sell subject to deprecatory conditions. *Sections 12* and *13*, however, apply only in so far as a contrary intention is not expressed in the trust instrument and has effect subject to the terms thereof. [*Trustee Act 1925, s 69*].

Power to lease land

12.9 As trustees have all the powers of a beneficial owner they have power to grant a lease (or in the case of leasehold land an underlease) of land subject to the trustees' overriding duty to have regard to the rights of the beneficiaries and subject to the trustees' overriding duty of care.

Power to postpone sale

12.10 In the case of every express trust for sale of land there is to be implied, despite any provision to the contrary, a power to postpone sale of the land and the trustees are not to be liable in any way for postponing sale of the land, in exercise of their discretion, for an indefinite period. [*TLATA 1996, s 4*]. This goes beyond the provision in the *Law of Property Act 1925, s 25* under which the statutory power to postpone gave way to any contrary intention. The 1996 Act does not abrogate a liability incurred by a trustee before the commencement of the Act (1 January 1997).

Trustees must obtain the best price

12.11 When selling or leasing land, trustees must obtain the best price. If an offer has been accepted 'subject to contract' and a better offer comes along, the trustees must accept the higher offer, unless they believe that the higher offer is unlikely to result in a sale and that there is a real risk of losing the current offer, i.e. that the adage 'a bird in the hand is worth two in the bush' genuinely applies (*Buttle v Saunders [1950] 2 All ER 193*).

Power to repair and improve property

12.12 By *TLATA 1996, s 6(1)* for the purpose of exercising their functions as trustees, the trustees of land have in relation to land all the powers of an absolute owner. It follows that trustees have power to keep the property in repair and to carry out improvements if the same would be for the benefit of the trust. In principle, the cost of periodic work to a property, such as painting, decorating and minor repairs, should be charged to income whereas major work that will reflect in the value of the property should be charged to capital.

Right of a beneficiary to occupy trust land

12.13 *TLATA 1996, ss 12–14* set out the right of a beneficiary entitled to an interest in possession in land to occupy the land. A right to receive the income from the land would, of course, be an interest in possession. In exercising their powers the trustees are charged to have regard to the intentions of the person or persons (if any) who created the trust, the purposes for which the land is held, and the circumstances and wishes of each of the beneficiaries entitled under the statutory provisions to occupy the land (*section 13(4)*).

A beneficiary is entitled to occupy the land at any time if, at that time, the purposes of the trust include making the land available for his occupation (or for the occupation of beneficiaries of a class of which he is a member or of beneficiaries in general) or the land is held by the trustees so as to be so available (*section 12(1)*). However, a beneficiary does not have a right to occupy land if it is either unavailable or it is unsuitable for occupation by him (*section 12(2)*). If a trust holds a house which is let, it is not available for occupation by him. If a trust holds land used for, say, arable farming it is, presumably, unsuitable for occupation by a beneficiary who has no experience or expertise as a farmer.

The trustees may impose reasonable conditions on a beneficiary in relation to his occupation of the land including a condition to pay any outgoings or expenses in respect of the land, or to assume any other obligation in relation to the land or to any activity that is proposed to be conducted there. [*TLATA 1996, s 13(3), (5)*].

Where two or more beneficiaries would be entitled to occupy land, the trustees may exclude or restrict the entitlement of any one or more (but not all) of them to occupy the land (*section 13(1)*). However, trustees may not unreasonably exclude any beneficiary's entitlement to occupy land, or restrict that right to an unreasonable extent (*section 13(2)*). If the entitlement of a beneficiary is excluded or restricted, then the conditions which may be imposed on a beneficiary who is entitled to occupy the land may include a requirement that he make payments by way of compensation to the beneficiary whose entitlement has been excluded or restricted, or a requirement that he forgo any payment or other benefit to which he would otherwise be entitled under the trust so as to benefit that beneficiary (*section 13(6)*).

Where someone is already in possession of the land, the powers conferred on trustees by *section 13* may not be exercised so as to prevent that person from continuing to occupy the land or in a manner likely to result in any such person ceasing to occupy the land unless he consents or the court has given approval. If asked to approve, the court must have regard to the same matters as those to which the trustees are charged to have regard (*section 13(7), (8)*). This provision is very widely drawn, requiring the trustees to look at the practical consequences of the exercise of their powers, and how they will impact on a person already in possession. The provision is not limited to situations where a person is in possession by virtue of the statutory right to occupy, it applies whenever a person is, for whatever reason, in occupation.

Power to appropriate land and power to partition

12.14 Trustees have powers of appropriation and partition in respect of land and other assets. These powers are dealt with in CHAPTER 17: POWER TO APPROPRIATE AND POWER TO PARTITION.

Settled land

Introduction

12.15 In respect of land which remains settled land the provisions of the *Settled Land Act 1925*, *Pt II* continue to apply. These provisions set out and regulate the powers of a tenant for life. In exercising any power under the *SLA 1925*, a tenant for life (or a statutory owner, i.e. a person having the powers of a tenant for life) shall have regard to the interest of all parties entitled under the settlement and shall, in respect of the exercise of those powers, be deemed to be in the position and to have the duties and liabilities of a trustee for those parties. In a quaint reflection of at least one aspect of the social attitudes underlying the Act, *section 107(2)* expressly provides that the provision by a tenant for life or statutory owner, at his own expense, of dwellings available for the working classes on any settled land shall not be deemed to be an injury to any interest or reversion or remainder in that land, but such provision shall not be made by a tenant for life or statutory owner without the previous approval in writing of the trustees of the settlement. In addition, *Schedule 3* of *Part I* includes the provision of cottages for labourers, farm servants and artisans, whether employed on the settled land or not, as one of the improvements, the cost of which may be funded by capital money.

The powers of the tenant for life are entrenched by *SLA 1925, s 106*. *Subsection (1)* deems to be void any provision in a settlement (or other document) which purports or attempts to forbid a tenant for life or statutory owner from exercising any power under the Act or his right to require the settled land to be vested in him, or attempts to prohibit or prevent him from exercising, or to induce him to abstain from exercising any such power or right. *Subsection (2)* continues an estate or interest that would otherwise cease on the exercise of a power or right as a tenant for life or statutory owner and *subsection (3)* provides that the exercise of a power under the Act shall not occasion a forfeiture.

By *SLA 1925, ss 108, 109* any other powers vested in the tenant for life are preserved and nothing precludes the settlor from conferring on the tenant for life (or, save as provided in the Act, on the trustees of the settlement) any powers additional to or larger than those conferred by the Act. However, the provision contained in *section 106* is overriding.

Where a tenant for life exercises a power which results in capital money arising, then the capital money is paid to the trustees. If reinvested in land which, on acquisition, becomes settled land, then title to the land so acquired is vested in the tenant for life.

Whilst an existing settlement holds relevant property (that is to say, land and personal chattels settled to devolve with settled land [*SLA 1925, s 67*]), then the provisions of the *SLA 1925* will continue to apply to land bought or sold within the settlement. However, once a strict settlement ceases to hold relevant property, then that settlement permanently ceases to be a settlement for the purpose of *SLA 1925*. These transitional provisions mean that the statutory provisions relating to tenants for life will continue to be relevant for a considerable period of time.

Powers of sale and exchange

12.16 A tenant for life may sell the settled land, or any part thereof, or may make an exchange of the settled land or any part thereof for other land and that includes an exchange in consideration of money paid for equality of exchange. The power of sale and exchange extends also to any easement, right or privilege of any kind over or in relation to the land, whether or not newly created. [*SLA 1925, s 38*].

Regulations in respect of sales are set out in *section 39* of the Act. Every sale shall be made for the best consideration in money that can reasonably be obtained. A sale may be made in one lot or several lots and either by auction or by private contract and may be made subject to any stipulation in respect of title or evidence of title or other things. On a sale the tenant for life may fix reserved biddings and the tenant for life may buy in at an auction. For provisions relating to purchase by the tenant for life of settled land, see 12.24 below.

Section 39 also contains provisions relating to sales in consideration of a perpetual or terminable rent and sales to companies incorporated by special Act of Parliament (though not companies incorporated under the *Companies Act 1985*). These situations do not commonly arise and reference should be made to the Act for the detailed provisions.

In the case of an exchange, save as provided in the Act, every exchange shall be made for the best consideration in land, or in land and money, that can reasonably be obtained. *Section 40(3)* imposes an express prohibition on settled land in England and Wales being given in exchange for land out of England and Wales (an exchange for land in Scotland would, therefore, not be permitted). Like a sale, an exchange may be made subject to any stipulations in respect of title, or evidence of title, or other things.

Power to lease

12.17 *SLA 1925* sets out in some detail the power of the tenant for life to lease the settled land or any part thereof, or any easement, right or privilege of any kind over or in relation to the land.

By *section 41* the term of a lease is limited as follows:

(*a*) in the case of a building lease, 999 years;

(*b*) in the case of a mining lease, 100 years;

(*c*) in the case of a forestry lease, 999 years; and

(*d*) in the case of any other lease, 50 years.

In the case of building or mining leases the court may authorise a longer term if either that is the custom in the district or it would otherwise be difficult to make a lease for that purpose. [*SLA 1925, s 46*].

Where a lease is granted at the best rent that can reasonably be obtained without fine (i.e. payment of capital money by way of a premium) and the lessee is not exempted from punishment for waste (e.g. a full repairing lease) then, if the term does not exceed 21 years, the lease may be granted without any notice of an intention to make the lease having been given under the Act by the tenant for life and notwithstanding that there are no trustees of the settlement, and, if the term does not extend beyond three years from the grant, may be given under hand only, rather than by deed. [*SLA 1925, s 42(5)*].

Otherwise, every lease must be by deed and must take effect in possession not later than twelve months after its date or, in reversion, after an existing lease having not more than seven years to run at the date of the new lease. The lease must reserve the best rent that can reasonably be obtained, regard being had to any fine (i.e. capital money in the nature of a premium) taken and to any money laid out or to be laid out for the benefit of the settled land, and generally to the circumstances of the case. The lease must contain a covenant by the lessee for the payment of the rent and a condition of re-entry on the rent not being paid within the time therein specified, not exceeding thirty days. A counterpart of every lease shall be executed by the lessee and delivered to the tenant for life or statutory owner, of which the execution of the lease by the tenant for life or statutory owner shall be sufficient evidence. A statement contained in a lease or in an endorsement thereon signed by the tenant for life or statutory owner, respecting any matter of fact or of calculation under the Act in relation to the lease, shall, in favour of the lessee and of those claiming under him, be sufficient evidence of the matters stated. Any premium paid in respect of a lease shall be deemed to be capital money arising under the *Settled Land Act*. [*SLA 1925, s 42*].

If an existing lease contains an enforceable covenant for renewal, then the leasing power of the tenant for life extends to the grant of a new lease in performance of that covenant. Similarly, if a lease is void or voidable then the tenant for life may grant a new lease confirming that previous lease. [*SLA 1925, s 43*].

Building, mining and forestry leases

12.18 *SLA 1925, ss 44–48* contain detailed provisions relating to building, mining and forestry leases. In view of the specialist nature of these leases the following is simply a summary and reference should be made to the Act for the detailed provisions.

A building lease is a lease for any building purpose or purposes connected therewith. Building purposes include the erection and improving of, and the adding to, and the repairing of, buildings. [*SLA 1925, s 117*]. Every building lease should be made partly in consideration of the lessee (or some other person) having erected or agreeing to erect buildings (new or additional), or having improved or repaired, or agreed to improve or repair buildings, or having executed or agreed to execute on the land leased an improvement authorised by *SLA 1925* for or in connection with building purposes.

The reference to repairing includes something more than just the usual repairing covenant in a lease. A peppercorn rent, or a nominal or other rent less than the rent ultimately payable, may be made payable for the first five years or any lesser part of the term. Where the land is contracted to be leased in lots, the entire amount of the rent to be ultimately payable may be apportioned amongst the lots in any manner provided that the annual rent reserved by any lease shall not be less than 50p and the total amount of the rents reserved on all leases for the time being granted shall not be less than a total amount of the rents which, in order that the leases may be in conformity with *SLA 1925*, ought to be reserved in respect of the whole land for the time being leased, and the rent reserved by any lease shall not exceed one-fifth part of the full annual rent of the land comprised in that lease with the buildings thereon when completed.

In the case of a mining lease, the rent may be made to be ascertainable or vary according to the acreage worked or the quantity of substance mined or by and according to the facilities given. The rent may also be made to vary according to the price of the substance mined. A fixed or minimum rent may be made payable. A lease may also be made partly in consideration of the lessee having executed or agreeing to execute an improvement authorised by the Act or in connection with mining purposes. In the case of a mining lease part of the mining rent falls to be capitalised.

In the case of forestry leases a nominal or reduced rent may be made payable for all or part of the first ten years of the term. The rent can be made to be ascertainable by or vary according to the value of the timber on the land or cut and removed either with or without a minimum rent. Provision can be made for sharing the proceeds or the profits with the Forestry Commissioners.

Leasing miscellaneous powers

12.19 *SLA 1925, s 49* contains miscellaneous powers on the sale or other disposition or dealing with land under the Act. The most important are the right to reserve or grant over or in relation to the settled land or any part thereof, or other land, including the land disposed of, and in the case of exchange the land taken in exchange, any easement, right or privilege of any kind, and a power to impose by covenant, condition or otherwise on the tenant for life or statutory owner and the settled land or any part thereof, or on the other party and any land disposed of to him, a restriction with regard to building or other use of the land or with respect to mines and minerals, and the beneficial working thereof or with respect to any other thing. *Section 50* also permits separate dealing with surface and minerals with or without wayleave.

Power to grant options

12.20 By *SLA 1925, s 51*, a tenant for life may at any time, either with or without consideration, grant by writing an option to purchase or take a lease of the settled land or any part thereof, or any easement, right or privilege over or in relation to the same at a price or rent fixed at the time of the granting of the option. Every such option shall be made exercisable within an agreed number of years, not exceeding ten. This is substantially less than the perpetuity period permitted for the grant of an option, which is 21 years. The consideration for the grant of the option is capital money arising under the Act.

The price or rent prescribed by the option should be the best which, having regard to all the circumstances, can reasonably be obtained and either:

(*a*) may be a specified sum of money or rent, or a specified rate according to the superficial area of land with respect to which the option is exercised, or the frontage thereof or otherwise; or

(*b*) in the case of an option to purchase contained in a lease or agreement for a lease, may be a stated number of years' purchase at the highest rent reserved by the lease or agreement; or

(*c*) if the option is exercisable as regards part of the land comprised in the lease or agreement, may be a proportionate part of such highest rent;

and any aggregate price or rent may be made to be apportionable in any manner, or according to any system, or by reference to arbitration.

An option to take a mining lease may be coupled with the grant of a licence to search for or prove any mines or minerals under the settled land, or any part thereof, pending the exercise of the option.

SLA 1925, ss 52–60 contain a miscellany of powers relating to settled land. *Section 52* contains provisions relating to surrenders and re-grants. *Section 53* permits the acceptance by the tenant for life of a lease of land, mines, minerals or easements, etc, but provides that no fine shall be payable out of capital money in respect of any such lease. *Sections 54–56* empower the tenant for life to make grants to statutory bodies for public and charitable purposes and for dedication of the streets and open spaces, etc. *Section 57* provides for the provision of land for small dwellings, small holdings and dwellings for working classes, and *section 58* gives a power to compromise claims and release restrictions, etc. *Section 59* empowers the tenant for life to vary leases and grants and to give licences and consents and *section 60* empowers the tenant for life to apportion rent.

Section 61 provides that all money other than rent payable by the tenant for life in respect of any transaction to which *SLA 1925, ss 58, 59* or *60* apply (that is to say the power to compromise claims etc, the power to vary leases etc and the power to apportion rents) shall be paid out of capital money and all money not being rent received by the tenant for life on the exercise of any of the powers conferred by those sections shall, unless the court otherwise directs, be capital money. An application for a direction must be made within six months of the receipt of the money unless the court in special circumstances allows further time.

General power of a tenant for life to effect any transaction under an order of the court

12.21 Any transaction affecting or concerning the settled land or any part thereof or any other land (not being a transaction otherwise authorised by the *SLA 1925* or by the settlement) which, in the opinion of the court, would be for the benefit of the settled land, or any part thereof, or the persons interested under the settlement, may, by an order of the court, be effected by the tenant for life if it is one which could have been validly effected by an absolute owner. [*SLA 1925, s 64*].

In *Raikes v Lygon [1988] 1 WLR 281*, the court authorised trustees of settled property to transfer part of the property to a maintenance fund notwithstanding that might have conferred some benefit on persons who were not beneficiaries under the settlement. In *Hambro v Duke of Marlborough [1994] Ch 158*, a transaction was approved, notwithstanding that it varied the interest of an ascertained beneficiary of full age and capacity, notwithstanding the absence of that beneficiary's consent, because the variation was for the benefit of the settled land and all the beneficiaries under the settlement.

Mansion house

12.22 The power to sell or lease settled land conferred by *SLA 1925* on the tenant for life is subject to restriction in respect of any principal mansion house on the settled land. The restrictions also apply to any pleasure grounds and park and any land usually occupied together with a mansion house, or pleasure grounds and park. *Section 65* provides that the power shall not be exercised without the consent of the trustees to the settlement or an order of the court:

(*a*) if the settlement is a settlement made or coming into operation before the commencement of the Act (1 January 1926) and the settlement does not expressly provide to the contrary; or (*b*) if the settlement is a settlement coming into operation after the commencement of the Act and the settlement expressly provides that these powers or any of them shall not be exercised without such consent or order.

Where a house is usually occupied as a farm house, or where the site of any house and the pleasure grounds and park and lands, if any, usually occupied therewith do not exceed 25 acres in extent, the house is not deemed to be a principal mansion house within the meaning of *section 65* and it may accordingly be disposed of in like manner as any other part of the settled land.

Section 66 makes express provision for the cutting and sale of timber and capitalisation of part of the proceeds. Where a tenant for life is impeachable for waste in respect of timber, and there is on the settled land timber ripe and fit for cutting, the tenant for life, on obtaining the consent of the trustees of the settlement or an order of the court, may cut and sell that timber or any part thereof. The proceeds of sale are then divided as to three quarters to capital monies and the remaining quarter as rent and profits. If the tenant for life is not impeachable for waste, then, with the exception of timber planted or left for shelter or ornament, the tenant for life may cut timber for his own use or retain the proceeds of sale.

Heirlooms

12.23 Where personal chattels are settled first to devolve with settled land or as nearly as may be in accordance with the law and practice in force at the date of the settlement, or are settled together with land, or upon trust declared by reference to the trusts affecting land, a tenant for life of the land may sell the chattels or any of them, but only with an order of the court (*section 67*). Any money arising by the sale is capital money arising under the *SLA 1925*. It may be invested in the purchase of other chattels of the same or any other nature which, when purchased, shall be settled and held on the same trusts and devolve in the same manner as the chattels sold.

Dealings between tenant for life and estate

12.24 Generally speaking, a person in a fiduciary position is debarred by the rule against self-dealing from acquiring an interest in any trust property. *SLA 1925*, however, makes specific provision to enable a tenant for life to purchase or otherwise acquire an interest in the settled land. This provision is made by *section 68*. The interests of the other beneficiaries under the settlement are protected by the trustees, who for this purpose are given the powers that would otherwise be vested in the tenant for life.

Section 68 provides that in the manner mentioned, and subject to the provisions contained in that section:

(*a*) the sale, grant, lease, mortgage, charge or other disposition of settled land, or of any easement, right, or privilege, over the same may be made to the tenant for life; or

(*b*) capital money may be advanced or mortgaged to him; or

(*c*) a purchase may be made from him of land to be made subject to the limitations of the settlement; or

(*d*) an exchange may be made with him of settled land for other land; and

(*e*) any such disposition, advance, purchase, or exchange, as aforesaid, may be made to, from, or with any persons of whom the tenant for life is one.

In every such case the trustees of the settlement, in addition to their powers as trustees, have all the powers of a tenant for life in reference to negotiating and completing the transaction and power to enforce any covenants by the tenant for life. Where the tenant for life is himself one of the trustees, then the powers are vested in the other trustee or trustees. The powers of the tenant for life are exercised by the trustees of the settlement in the name and on behalf of the tenant for life.

Section 68 applies notwithstanding that the tenant for life is one of the trustees of the settlement, or an order has been made authorising the trustees to act on his behalf, or that he is suffering from a mental disorder, but does not apply to dealings with any body of persons which includes a trustee of the settlement, not being the tenant for life, unless the transaction is either previously or subsequently approved by the court.

Charity land

Disposition of land

12.25 Prior to the passing of the *Trusts of Land and Appointment of Trustees Act 1996*, the power of charity trustees to deal with land derived from *SLA 1925, s 29*. However, following the passing of that Act, no land held on charitable, ecclesiastical, or public trusts, shall be or be deemed to be settled land even if it was, or was deemed to be, settled land before the commencement of the Act. [*TLATA 1996, s 2(5)*]. It follows that land held by charity trustees is held on a trust of land and the trustees have all the powers of an absolute owner. [*TLATA 1996, s 6(1)*]. However, the powers conferred by *section 6* cannot be exercised in contravention of, or of any order made in pursuance of, any other enactment or rule of law or equity, including an order of any court or of the Charity Commissioners. [*TLATA 1996, s 6(6), (7)*].

The *Charities Act 1993, s 36* imposes restrictions on the disposal of land in England and Wales. The provisions do not apply to the disposition of land held by or in trust for an exempt charity. Nor do they apply to the disposition of land by way of mortgage or other security, or to any disposition of an advowson. There are no restrictions on the disposition of land not situate in England or Wales.

The restrictions fall into two categories. First, of general application is the restriction on the selling, leasing or otherwise disposing of land without an order of the court or of the Charity Commissioners unless certain requirements have been met. The other restrictions relate to land held on trust for a charity, which trust stipulates that it is to be used for the purpose, or any particular purpose, of the charity. These two categories will be dealt with separately below.

General requirements

12.26 Except where the proposed disposition is the granting of a lease for a term not exceeding seven years (as to which see below), the charity trustees must, before entering into an agreement for the sale, or (as the case may be) for a lease or other disposition of the land:

(*a*) obtain and consider a written report on the proposed disposition from a qualified surveyor instructed by the trustees and acting exclusively for the charity;

(*b*) advertise the proposed disposition for such a period and in such manner as the surveyor has advised in his report (unless he has there advised that it would not be in the best interests of the charity to advertise the proposed disposition); and

(*c*) decide that they are satisfied, having considered the surveyor's report, that the terms on which the disposition is proposed to be made are the best that can reasonably be obtained for the charity.

For this purpose a person is a qualified surveyor if he is:

(i) a fellow or professional associate of the Royal Institution of Chartered Surveyors or of the Incorporated Society of Valuers and Auctioneers or satisfies such other requirement or requirements as may be prescribed by regulations made by the Secretary of State; and

(ii) reasonably believed by the charity trustees to have ability in, and experience of, the valuation of land of the particular kind, and in the particular area, in question;

and any report prepared for the purposes of that subsection may contain such information and deal with such matters as may be prescribed by regulations so made.

Where the proposed disposition is the granting of a lease for a term ending not more than seven years after it is granted (other than one granted wholly or partly in consideration of a fine – that is to say, a capital premium), the charity trustees must before entering into an agreement for the lease:

- obtain and consider the advice on the proposed disposition of a person who is reasonably believed by the trustees to have the requisite ability and practical experience to provide them with competent advice on the proposed disposition; and
- decide that they are satisfied, having considered that person's advice, that the terms on which the disposition is proposed to be made are the best that can reasonably be obtained for the charity.

It will be noted that the requirements for advice are less stringent in the case of a proposed grant of a lease for a term of less than seven years (otherwise than for a premium) than for other transactions. The advice need not be given in writing and the adviser is not required to be a qualified surveyor.

Where:

(*a*) any land is held by or in trust for a charity; and

(*b*) the trusts on which it is so held stipulate that it is to be used for the purposes, or any particular purposes of the charity;

then the land shall not be sold, leased or otherwise disposed of unless the charity trustees have previously:

(i) given public notice of the proposed disposition, inviting representations to be made to them within a time specified in the notice, being not less than one month from the date of the notice; and

(ii) taken into consideration any representations made to them within that time about the proposed disposition.

This requirement does not apply to any such disposition of land if:

- the disposition is to be effected with a view to acquiring replacement property; or
- the disposition is the granting of a lease for a term ending not more than two years after it is granted (other than one granted wholly or partly in consideration of a fine).

Further, the Charity Commissioners may direct that the requirements for giving a public notice and consideration of representations shall not apply to dispositions of land held by or in trust for a charity or class of charities (whether generally or only in the case of a specified class of dispositions or land, or otherwise as may be provided in the direction), or that subsection shall not apply to a particular disposition of land held by or in trust for a charity if, on an application made to them in writing by or on behalf of the charity or charities in question, the Commissioners are satisfied that it would be in the interests of the charity or charities for them to give the direction.

The restrictions on dispositions imposed by *section 36* apply notwithstanding anything in the trusts of the charity. However, nothing in *Charities Act 1993, s 36* applies to:

(*a*) any disposition for which general or special authority is expressly given (without the authority being made subject to the sanction of an order of the court) by any statutory provision contained in or having effect under an Act of Parliament or by any scheme legally established; or

(*b*) any disposition of land held by or in trust for a charity which:

  (i) is made to another charity otherwise than for the best price that can reasonably be obtained; and

  (ii) is authorised to be so made by the trusts of the first mentioned charity; or

(*c*) the granting by or on behalf of a charity and in accordance with its trusts of a lease to any beneficiary under those trusts where the lease:

  (i) is granted otherwise than for the best rent that can reasonably be obtained; and

  (ii) is intended to enable the demised premises to be occupied for the purposes, or any particular purposes, of the charity.

Supplementary provisions

12.27 Supplementary provisions relating to dispositions are contained in the *Charities Act 1993, s 37* of which the following is a summary.

Any contract for the sale, or for the lease or other disposition, of land which is held by or in trust for a charity, and any conveyance, transfer, lease or other instrument affecting a disposition of land, shall state the following:

(*a*) that the land is held by or in trust for a charity;

(*b*) whether the charity is an exempt charity and whether the disposition is one falling within paragraphs (*a*), (*b*) or (*c*) of *subsection 36(9)*; and

(*c*) if it is not an exempt charity and the disposition is not one falling within any of those paragraphs, that the land is land to which the restrictions on disposition imposed by that section apply.

The form of the statement is prescribed by *Land Registration Rules 1925, rule 62*.

Where appropriate, the charity trustees shall certify in the instrument by which the disposition is effected that, where a disposition requires an order of the court or of the Commissioners, the disposition has been so sanctioned. Where no such order is required the trustees shall certify in the instrument by which the disposition is effected that they have power under the trusts of the charity to effect the disposition, and that they have complied with the provisions of *section 36* so far as applicable to it.

Where those requirements have been complied with in relation to any disposition of land, then, in favour of a person who (whether under the disposition or afterwards) acquires an interest in the land for money or money's worth, it shall be conclusively presumed that the facts were as stated in the certificate.

There is further protection in favour of a person who (under a disposition or afterwards) *in good faith* acquires an interest in land for money or money's worth, in that, even if the requirements of *section 36* have not been complied with, then, whether or not the disposition has been sanctioned by an order of the court or the Commissioners, or the charity trustees have power under the trusts of the charity to effect the disposition and have complied with the provisions of that section so far as applicable to it, the disposition shall be valid.

Acquisition of land

12.28 Any contract for sale or lease or other disposition of land which will, as a result of the disposition, be held by or in trust for the charity and any conveyance, transfer, lease or other instrument affecting a disposition of such land shall state:

(*a*) that the land will as a result of the disposition be held by or in trust for a charity;

(*b*) whether the charity is an exempt charity; and

(*c*) if it is not an exempt charity, that the restrictions on disposition imposed by *Charities Act 1993, s 36* will apply to the land.

The form of the statement is prescribed by rule the *Land Registration Rules 1925, rule 61*.

In the case of land held by or in trust for a non-exempt charity the Registrar shall enter on to the register a restriction in the form prescribed by *the Land Registration Rules 1925, rule 60*. If the charity becomes an exempt charity, then the charity trustees shall apply to the Registrar for the restriction to be withdrawn. If any registered land is held by or in trust for an exempt charity, and the charity ceases to be an exempt charity, or any registered land becomes, as a result of a declaration of trust by the registered proprietor, land held in trust for a charity (other than an exempt charity), the charity trustees shall apply to the Registrar for a restriction to be entered in the Register in respect of the land. [*Charities Act 1993, s 37(10)*].

Pension fund trustees

12.29 No specific provisions relate to pension fund trustees in respect of land. However, it should be noted that, by the *Pensions Act 1995, s 35(4)*, neither the trust scheme nor any written statement of the principles governing decisions about investments may impose restrictions (however expressed) on any power to make investments by reference to the consent of the employer. Accordingly, the acquisition or sale of land cannot be made subject to the consent of the employer.

Chapter 13

Power to Borrow on the Security of the Trust Property

Express power

13.1 A well-drawn trust deed will usually contain an express power to borrow on the security of the trust property in the widest possible terms. Where an express power is included, the limit, if any, to the trustees' power will turn on the construction of the provision.

Statutory power of trustees to borrow

13.2 The *Trustee Act 1925, s 16* gives trustees express power to mortgage all or any part of the trust property to raise any capital money required for any purpose to be applied in any manner authorised by the trust instrument. The section applies notwithstanding anything to the contrary in the trust instrument but it does not apply to trustees of property held for charitable purposes, or to the trustees of a settlement for the purposes of the *Settled Land Act 1925* (*SLA 1925*), not being also the statutory owners. *Section 16* does not, however, authorise trustees to mortgage the trust property to acquire further property for the trust or to acquire further land with the aid of a mortgage over the land being acquired save possibly to acquire a small piece of land to protect existing land (*Re Suenson-Taylor's Settlement Trusts [1974] 1 WLR 1280*).

However, the general powers of trustees of a trust of land given by the *Trusts of Land and Appointment of Trustees Act 1996, s 6(1)* are not so limited. Trustees of land have in relation to the land subject of the trust, for the purpose of exercising their functions as trustees, all the powers of an absolute owner. The general powers are not unlimited. They do not override any restriction limitation or condition imposed by any other enactment and may be restricted or excluded by the trust instrument or be made subject to the obtaining of consent (*section 8*). In exercising the power given by *section 6(1)*, the trustees must have regard to the rights of the beneficiaries. The power must not be exercised in contravention of, or any order made in pursuance of, any other enactment or any rule of law or equity. However, in principle the provision would appear to be sufficiently broad to enable trustees of land in a proper case to mortgage the land to raise money for the benefit of the trust in circumstances wider than permitted by the *Trustee Act 1925, s 16*.

Similarly, in the case of land acquired pursuant to the power to acquire freehold or leasehold land contained in the *Trustee Act 2000, s 8*, a trustee has all the powers of an absolute owner in relation to that land unless the same have been restricted or excluded by the trust instrument. Again, that appears wide enough to enable the trustee to mortgage any land so acquired to fund further purchases or to acquire further land with the aid of a mortgage, providing, in either case, the land has been or is being acquired for the purposes in *section 8(1)*. The powers given by *section 8* do not apply to land held in the trust otherwise that by acquisition under *section 8(1)* and so, for example, do not apply to any land originally settled as opposed to having been acquired.

Trusts of Land and Appointment of Trustees Act 1996, s 6(1) and *Trustee Act 2000, s 8(1)* apply in relation to trusts whether created before or after the commencement of the respective acts. Neither apply to settled land or to a trust to which the *Universities and Colleges Estates Act 1925* applies. Both are subject to any restriction or exclusion imposed by the trust instrument or by any enactment or any provision of subordinate legislation.

In any case where the trustees do not have power to mortgage either under the terms of the trust instrument or statute, the trustees may seek the authority of the court under the *Trustee Act 1925, s 57* which enables the court to authorise dealings with the trust property. If trustees are required to obtain the consent of a third party before mortgaging property the court has power under the *Trusts of Land and Appointment of Trustees Act 1996, s 14* to relieve them of that obligation.

There is no statutory requirement for trustees (other than charity trustees) to take advice before mortgaging trust land. However, unless excluded or modified by the trust instrument, the trustees, are in the exercise of their powers, subject of the statutory duty of care and, therefore, in a proper case should take advice.

Settled land

13.3 By *SLA 1925, s 71*, the tenant for life of settled land has power to mortgage the settled land or any part thereof for the following specific purposes:

(*a*) discharging an encumbrance on the settled land or part thereof;

(*b*) paying for any improvement authorised by the *SLA 1925* or by the settlement;

(*c*) equality of exchange;

(*d*) redeeming a compensation rent charge in respect of the extinguishment of manorial incidents and affecting the settled land;

(*e*) commuting any additional rent made payable on the conversion of a perpetually renewable leasehold interest into a long term;

(*f*) satisfying any claims for compensation on the conversion of a perpetually renewable leasehold interest into a long term by any officer, solicitor or other agent of the lessor in respect of fees or remuneration that would have been payable by the lessee or under-lessee on any renewal;

(*g*) payment of the costs of any transaction authorised by *SLA 1925, ss 69* or *70* (relating to encumbrances on the settled land) or by *section 71*.

An encumbrance for the purpose of *section 71* does not include any annual sum payable only during a life or lives or during a term of years absolute or determinable. The restrictions imposed by *SLA 1925, Pt II* on the leasing powers of a tenant for life do not apply in relation to a mortgage term created under the Act.

Other statutes confer on the tenant for life the power to raise money by mortgage for certain charges and expenses: for example, expenses of carrying out initial repairs under the *Landlord and Tenant Act 1954, Pt II* and expenses incurred under the *Leasehold Reform Act 1967* and sums recoverable under the *Town and Country Planning Act 1990*.

Where there is an encumbrance affecting any part of the settled land, the tenant for life, with the consent of the encumbrancer, may shift that encumbrance to any other part of the settled land or any part of the capital money or securities representing capital money subject or to become subject to the settlement. [*SLA 1925, s 69*].

Where an encumbrance affects any part of the settled land, the tenant for life may, with the consent of the encumbrancer, vary the provisions of the encumbrance and charge the settled land by way of additional security. [*SLA 1925, s 70*].

Duties and liabilities of tenant for life

13.4 Although the statutory duty of care does not apply to a tenant for life, a tenant for life or statutory owner in exercising any powers under *SLA 1925* is deemed to be in the position of, and to have the duties and liabilities of, a trustee for all parties entitled under the settlement and must have regard to the interests of those parties. [*SLA 1925, s 107*].

Dealings with the tenant for life

13.5 Special provision is made by *SLA 1925, s 68* to enable a mortgage of the settled land to be made to the tenant for life or for capital money to be advanced on mortgage to the tenant for life. In such case the trustees, in addition to their powers as trustees, have all the powers of the tenant for life in reference to negotiating and completing the transaction and power to enforce any covenants by the tenant for life. If the tenant for life is one of the trustees, then the other or others of them have such powers.

Section 68 applies notwithstanding that the tenant for life is one of the trustees or that an order has been made authorising the trustees to act on his behalf (e.g. under *SLA 1925, s 24* – see CHAPTER 21: TAKING ADDITIONAL ADMINISTRATIVE POWERS OR SURRENDERING OR RELEASING POWERS) or that he is suffering from mental disorder. It does not apply to dealings with any body of persons which includes a trustee of the settlement, not being the tenant for life, unless the transaction is either previously or subsequently approved by the court.

Charity trustees

13.6 Charity trustees are in a different position to ordinary trustees in that, with two exceptions, no mortgage or charge of land held by or in trust for a charity may be granted without an order of the court or of the Commissioners (*Charities Act 1993, s 38(1)*) unless specific requirements have been satisfied. 'Land' means land in England or Wales.

The two exceptions are:

(*a*) where the charity is an exempt charity; or

(*b*) if general or special authority is expressly given (without the authority being made subject to the sanction of an order of the court) by any statutory provision contained in or having effect under an Act of Parliament or by any scheme legally established.

The requirements to be observed (set out in *Charities Act 1993, s 38*) are that the charity trustees have, before executing the mortgage, obtained and considered proper advice, given to them in writing, on the following matters:

(i) whether the proposed loan is necessary in order for the charity trustees to be able to pursue the particular course of action in connection with which the loan is sought by them;

(ii) whether the terms of the proposed loan are reasonable having regard to the status of the charity as a prospective borrower; and

(iii) the ability of the charity to repay on those terms the sums proposed to be borrowed.

For this purpose, proper advice is the advice of a person:

- who is reasonably believed by the charity trustees to be qualified by his ability in and practical experience of financial matters; and
- who has no financial interest in the making of the loan in question,

and such advice may constitute proper advice for those purposes notwithstanding that the person giving it does so in the course of his employment as an officer or employee of the charity or of the charity trustees.

Mortgage of land

13.7 Any mortgage of land held by or in trust for a charity must contain the statement prescribed by the *Land Registration Rules 1925, rule 62* (*Charities Act 1993, s 39(1)*) which states:

(*a*) that the land is held by or in trust for the charity and, if it is an exempt charity, that it is an exempt charity;

(*b*) in the case of an non-exempt charity and, where appropriate, that the charge or mortgage is one falling within *section 38(5)* of the Act (i.e. one for which general or special authority has been given as mentioned in *section 36(9)(a)* of the Act); and

(*c*) where the charity is not an exempt charity, and the charge or mortgage is not one falling within *section 38(5)*, that the restrictions of *section 38* of the Act apply.

In the case of a mortgage which requires to be sanctioned by an order of the court or of the Commissioners, the charity trustees must certify in the mortgage that the mortgage has been so sanctioned. Where a mortgage has been taken following advice, the charity trustees must all certify in the mortgage that the charity trustees have power under the trusts of the charity to grant the mortgage and that they have obtained and considered such advice as is mentioned in *section 38(2)* of the Act.

Where the mortgage contains such a certificate, then, in favour of a person who (whether under the mortgage or afterwards) acquires an interest in the land in question for money or money's worth, it is conclusively presumed that the facts were as stated in the certificate.

Where the charity trustees have failed to obtain the sanction of an order of the court or the Commissioners, or to obtain the appropriate advice, then, in favour of a person who (whether under the mortgage or afterwards) in good faith acquires an interest in the land for money or money's worth, the mortgage shall be valid notwithstanding that failure. It is to be noted that this protection is afforded only to a person who acquires an interest *in good faith*. If such a person knew or should have known that the statutory requirements had not been complied with then such a person will not be acting in good faith and will not be protected.

Chapter 14

Power to Insure Trust Property

Power to insure and pay premiums

Trusts other than bare trusts

14.1 A trustee may insure any property, which is subject to the trusts, against risk of loss or damage due to any event, and pay the premiums out of the trust funds (*Trustee Act 1925, s 19* as substituted by *Trustee Act 2000, s 34*). The substituted section applies to trusts created before as well as after the amendment. The 'trust funds' means capital or income.

Unless excluded or modified by the trust instrument, the statutory duty of care imposed by the *Trustee Act 2000* (*TA 2000*) applies to the trustee when exercising any power to insure, whether that power is the power arising under *section 19*, an express power contained in the trust instrument or the general power of an absolute owner conferred on trustees of land by the *Trusts of Land and Appointment of Trustees Act 1996, s 6(1)*.

However the statutory duty of care does not *expressly* impose on trustee *a duty* to insure. It is expressed to apply to a trustee *exercising* the statutory power to insure or any corresponding power (see *TA 2000, Sch 1, para 5*), but it does not in terms apply to the decision whether or not to exercise that power. However, a trustee is under a duty to act in respect of the trust fund as a prudent man of business, and in respect of any trust asset for which insurance is available at reasonable cost, a failure to insure would, prima facie, seem to be a breach of that duty. In the case of a chattel, if insurance is not available at reasonable cost the trustees should take the absence of available insurance into account in making arrangements for its safeguarding.

A power to insure is a delegable function within the meaning of the *TA 2000, s 11* so the trustees may authorise any person to exercise their power to insure as their agent.

Bare trusts

14.2 A bare trust is a trust for a beneficiary who is of full age and capacity and absolutely entitled to the property subject of the trust or for beneficiaries who are of full age and capacity and who (taken together) are absolutely entitled to the property subject to the trust.

In the case of property held on a bare trust, the power to insure is subject to any directions given by the beneficiary or each of the beneficiaries:

(*a*) that any property specified in the direction is not to be insured; or

(*b*) that any property specified in the direction is not to be insured except on such conditions as may be so specified (*TA 1925, s 19(2)*).

If such a direction is given, the power to insure, in so far as it is subject to the direction ceases to be a delegable function for the purpose of *TA 2000, s 11*. [*TA 1925, s 19(4)*].

Settled land

14.3 The *Settled Land Act 1925, s 107(1A)* (substituted by *TA 2000, Sch 2, para 17*) provides that certain provisions apply to the tenant for life as they apply to the trustees of the settlement. The provision includes the power to insure under *section 19*. The effect appears to be that the power to insure is vested in both the trustees and the tenant for life. If responsibility for insurance is undertaken by the tenant for life, the prudent trustee will take steps to ensure that the responsibility has been discharged and that adequate insurance cover has been put in place and is thereafter maintained.

Charities

14.4 Charity trustees should insure trust property against loss and damage. If the charity holds property to which the public has access or engages in public events then public liability insurance should also be held.

In contrast to private trusts, in appropriate cases it may be proper for charity money to be used to fund professional indemnity insurance for trustees in respect of their conduct. The matter is dealt with further in *Tolley's Charities Manual*. In the case of a private trust a trustee may not effect indemnity insurance at the cost of the trust in the absence of an express provision in the trust instrument authorising him to do so or the consent of the beneficiaries at whose expense the premium is paid.

Application of insurance monies

14.5 The application of insurance monies is dealt with by the *Trustee Act 1925, s 20*.

Money received by trustees or any beneficiary under a policy of insurance against loss or damage of any property subject to a trust or to a settlement within the meaning of the *Settled Land Act 1925* shall be capital money for the purpose of the trust or settlement as the case may be. [*Trustee Act 1925, s 20(1)*].

If any such money is receivable by any person other than the trustees of the trust or settlement, that person shall use his best endeavours to recover and receive the money, and shall pay the net residue thereof, after discharging any costs of recovering and receiving it, to the trustees of the trust or settlement, or, if there are no trustees capable of giving a discharge therefore, into court.

An example of trust monies payable to a person other than the trustees would be the case of a tenant for life who is required, under the *Settled Land Act 1925, s 88(1)* to insure against damage by fire buildings or works comprised in improvements paid for out of capital money.

If insurance money is receivable in respect of settled land within the meaning of the *Settled Land Act 1925*, or any building or works thereon, it shall be deemed to be capital money arising under that Act from the settled land, and shall be invested or applied by the trustees, or - if in court - under the direction of the court. A similar provision applies in respect of personal chattels settled as heirlooms within the meaning of the *Settled Land Act*.

If insurance money is receivable in respect of land subject to a trust of land or personal property held on trust for sale, it should be held on the trusts and subject to the powers and provisions applicable to money arising by a sale under such trust. [*TA 1925, s 20(3)(c)*].

In any other case, insurance money shall be held on trusts corresponding as nearly may be with the trusts affecting the property in respect of which it was payable. [*TA 1925, s 20(3)(d)*].

Insurance money or any part thereof may be applied by the trustees or - if in court - under the direction of the court, in rebuilding, reinstating, replacing or repairing the property lost or damaged. Any such application by the trustees shall be subject to the consent of any person whose consent is required by the instrument, if any, creating the trust to the investment of capital money subject to the trust. In the case of money which is deemed to be capital money arising under the *Settled Land Act 1925*, it will be subject to the provisions of that Act with respect to the application of capital money by the trustees of the settlement.

Third parties

14.6 Nothing in the *Trustee Act 1925, s 20* prejudices or affects the right of any person to require any insurance monies or any part thereof to be applied in rebuilding, reinstating or repairing the property lost or damaged, or the rights of any mortgagee, lessor or lessee, whether under any statute or otherwise. Accordingly, if the trust property includes property let under a landlord's covenant to insure, and the landlord is required to lay out the insurance monies in the reinstatement of the property, the right of the lessee to require the insurance monies to be so laid out overrides any provision in *TA 1925* relating to the application of those monies.

It should also be noted that any person having an interest in any house or other building burned down, demolished or damaged by fire, may require the *insurer* to cause the insurance money to be laid out on rebuilding or repairing the house, unless the persons claiming the money give a sufficient security to the insurers that the money will be so laid out, or unless the insurance money is disposed of to or amongst all the contending parties to the satisfaction of the insurers. (*Fires Prevention (Metropolis) Act 1774, s 83,* which applies throughout England and Wales. See also *Sinnott v Bowden [1912] 2 Ch 414.*)

Where property is in the course of being sold or exchanged, then, subject to any provision to the contrary in the contract or to any requisite consents of the insurers, insurance money becoming payable after the date of the contract is held or receivable by the vendor on behalf of the purchaser and to be paid over on the date of completion or so soon thereafter as the same is received by the vendor. The purchaser must pay the proportionate part of the premium from the date of the contract. [*Law of Property Act 1925, s 47*].

Chapter 15

Power to Carry on a Business

Introduction

15.1 Trust property may include a business or an interest in a business in one of two forms. If the business has been incorporated, the trust property will be the shares in the company and the trustees will be in the position of shareholders. Shareholders are not normally concerned with the day-to-day conduct of the business and their liability is limited to the amount unpaid on the share capital. However, if a trust's holding of shares is such that the trustees have power to control or influence the conduct of the company, then their duties as trustees may require them to take an active, as opposed to a passive, interest in the running of the company.

Alternatively, a business may be unincorporated. In that event, liability will be unlimited and if the business is continued by the trustees, the trustees will, as regards creditors of the business, incur a personal liability. It is very unusual for an unincorporated business to form part of a trust fund in relation to a trust created during the lifetime of a settlor. However, it is not unusual for personal representatives to have to deal with a business that had been run by the deceased, and to continue the business whilst the decision is made whether it should be wound up or disposed of as a going concern.

The issues that arise in respect of an unincorporated and an incorporated business are very different and it is proposed to deal with them separately.

Unincorporated business

Trustees should not generally commence to trade

15.2 As a general principle, trustees have no power to commence an unincorporated business and to trade at the risk of the trust. Trustees should not do so unless there is a clear power in the trust instrument both enabling them to do so and to indemnify themselves out of the trust assets. Trustees should always remember that as regards creditors of the business they are personally liable, regardless of the ability of the trust to indemnify them against liability.

Continuing an existing business

15.3 If trustees are put in possession of an existing business then they have power to continue the same for such reasonable time as is necessary to enable them to sell it as a going concern. Trustees should not continue a business, other than for the purpose of a sale, unless there is a clear authority entitling them to do so and to indemnify themselves against liability. In all other cases, the trustees should take steps to wind up the business as quickly as possible.

It should be noted that, whilst an authority in the trust instrument to carry on a business may justify the trustees in doing so as against the beneficiaries, if the assets of the trust are required for paying other creditors, the trustees may not be entitled to be reimbursed in priority unless those creditors have consented to the continuation of the business (*Dowse v Gorton [1891] AC 190*). If the creditors have given consent, then the trustees are entitled to assert their right of indemnity against the trust assets in priority to those creditors. The mere fact that creditors stand by knowing that a business is being continued by the trustee does not necessarily constitute consent (*Dowse v Gorton*). In respect of trade creditors incurred during the course of trade, trustees will normally have a contractual liability regardless of whether the trust assets are sufficient to cover the liability.

A trustee who has properly carried on a business is entitled to a lien on the trust assets to reimburse himself against liabilities properly incurred. If the trustee goes bankrupt, the right vests in the trustee in bankruptcy, although creditors owed money in respect of liabilities incurred on behalf of the trust (though not the trustee's other creditors) may be subrogated to the rights of the trustee (*Re Richardson [1911] 2 KB 705*). If a trustee has conducted a business without proper authority then no right of indemnity arises (*Re Oxley [1914] 1 Ch 604*).

The special position of the Public Trustee as regards the management or carrying of a business is considered at 15.6 below.

Incorporated business

15.4 It is, of course, commonplace for a trust fund to include a holding of shares in a private company.

If the holding is a comparatively small proportion of the total issued share capital, then it is unlikely that trustees will have the ability to influence the day-to-day running of the company. If, however, the trust holding is substantial, then the trustees may be under a duty to consider whether their voting power is such that they can, and should, influence the running of the company.

If the trustees' holding is a controlling interest, then the trustees, being under a duty to act as prudent men of business, should act so as to safeguard the trust's investment. If, therefore, it comes to the trustees' knowledge that the company's affairs are not being conducted as they should be, or the trustees are put on inquiry, the trustees should take appropriate action.

Appropriate action may consist in the first instance of inquiry and consultation with the directors but, in the last resort, may require the convening of a general meeting to replace one or more of the directors. The trustees should not content themselves with the receipt of such information on the affairs of the company that a shareholder ordinarily receives at annual general meetings. As the trustees have the power to do so, they should go further and see that they have sufficient information to enable them to make a responsible decision from time to time, either to let matters proceed as they are, or to intervene if the trustees are dissatisfied. The foregoing is a précis of the statement of principles set out by Brightman J in *Bartlett v Barclays Bank Trust Co [1980] Ch 515 at 532*. In that case, professional trustees were held liable for breach of trust in respect of a loss making development pursued by a company virtually all the shares of which were held by the trust.

The other principal authority in this area is *Re Lucking's Will Trust [1968] 1 WLR 866 at 874* where Cross J made clear that trustees holding a controlling interest ought to ensure so far as they can that they have such information as to the progress of the company's affairs as directors would have. He went on to add that if trustees sit back and allow the company to be run by the minority shareholder and receive no more information than shareholders are entitled to, they do so at their peril.

The trustee's duty to intervene in the running of a private company can be excluded or modified by an appropriately drafted exemption clause. Examples of this are to be found in *Bogg v Raper (1998/9) 1 ITELR 267* and *Walker v Stones [2000] WTLR 975*.

Information relating to a company

15.5 If the trust assets include all, or substantially all, the shares in a private company, then a beneficiary may be entitled, in a proper case, to see company documents in the hands of the trustee as director, not merely documents in the hands of the trustee as trustee or shareholder (see further CHAPTER 8: PROVISION OF INFORMATION AND DISCLOSURE OF TRUST DOCUMENTS).

A trustee who is a director of a company is, of course, subject to precisely the same duties and responsibilities as any other company director. Such duties and responsibilities may also fall on a shadow director being 'any person in accordance with whose directions or instructions the directors of the company are accustomed to act'. [*Companies Act 1985, s 741(2)*]. Therefore, if a trustee exercises his duty as trustee to intervene in the running of a company for the benefit of the trust without becoming a director he may be regarded as a shadow director and, in either case, must pay full regard to the duties and responsibilities imposed by company law.

Company law matters are outside the ambit of this book (reference may be made to *Tolley's Company Law*). It may, however, be appropriate to note that if a company of which a trustee has been acting as director or shadow director becomes insolvent (whether while he was a director or subsequently) and the trustee's conduct as a director (or shadow director) makes him unfit to be concerned in the management of the company, the court may make a disqualification order against him under the *Company Directors Disqualification Act 1986*.

The Public Trustee

15.6 The Public Trustee shall not accept any trust that involves the management or carrying on of any business except in cases where he may be authorised to do so by the Public Trustee Rules. [*Public Trustee Act 1906, s 2(4)*]. Rule 7 of the Public Trustee Rules authorises the Public Trustee to act in two situations. The first is to act as a custodian trustee for the trust that involves the management or carrying on of any business. The important words to note are 'custodian trustee' and the rules state specifically that if the Public Trustee thinks fit to act it must be on the condition that:

(*a*) he shall not act in the management or carrying on of such business; and

(*b*) he shall not hold any property of such a nature as will expose the holder thereof to any liability except under exceptional circumstances and when the Public Trustee is satisfied that he is fully indemnified or secured against loss.

The other circumstance is that the Public Trustee may accept as ordinary trustee, under exceptional circumstances, a trust which involves the management or carrying on of any business, but upon conditions that, except with the consent of the Treasury, he shall only carry on the same:

(i) for a short time not exceeding 18 months; and

(ii) with a view to a sale, disposition or winding up; and

(iii) if he is satisfied that the same can be carried on without risk of loss.

The rules are silent as to whether the Public Trustee may accept a trust which holds a controlling interest in a trading company, and where the trust does not contain any provision relieving the trustee from the responsibility for overseeing and directing the management of the business.

Chapter 16

Power to Compromise and Power to Litigate

Compromise

16.1 The *Trustee Act 1925, s 15* gives power to personal representatives and trustees to compromise claims and compound liabilities. The section specifically authorises them to do any of the following:

(*a*) accept any property, real or personal, before the time at which it is made transferable or payable;

(*b*) sever and apportion any blended trust funds or property;

(*c*) pay or allow any debt or claim on any evidence that he or they think sufficient;

(*d*) accept any composition or any security, real or personal, for any debt or for any property, real or personal, claimed;

(*e*) allow any time of payment of any debt; or

(*f*) compromise, compound, abandon, submit to arbitration, or otherwise settle any debt, account, claim, or thing whatever relating to the testator's or intestate's estate or to the trust.

Section 15 continues that for any of these purposes a trustee may enter into, give, execute, or do any such agreements, instruments of composition or arrangement, releases and any other things as to him or them seem expedient, without being responsible for any loss occasioned by any act or thing so done by him or them if he or they have discharged the duty of care set out in the *Trustee Act 2000, s 1(1)*.

The jurisdiction under *section 15* is no different to any other power of the trustees and, in the case of a private (as opposed to a charitable) trust, all the trustees must act together as a majority cannot bind a minority. A sole trustee, who under the trust instrument or statute is authorised to execute the trusts and powers, can act alone providing he is not required to give a receipt for capital monies. In contrast to a trustee, a sole executor may act alone. Therefore, one executor has power to compromise a claim by his co-executor against the estate (*Re Houghton [1904] 1 Ch 622*) although the position of such an executor was described in that case as 'a delicate one', and an executor in a similar situation would be well advised to seek the directions of the court if the beneficiaries are not in agreement.

Duty of care

16.2 It is to be noted that, in exercising the power given by *Trustee Act 1925, s 15*, a trustee must discharge the common duty of care. This requirement was introduced by the *Trustee Act 2000* in place of the requirement in the section as originally enacted that the power be exercised 'in good faith'. The statutory duty of care, of course, embraces an obligation to act in good faith, but goes further and requires a trustee to exercise such skill and care as is reasonable in the circumstances. The duty of care also applies to a trustee when exercising any corresponding power, however conferred, and so, for example, would apply in the case of an express power to compromise set out in the trust instrument.

Desirable and fair to all beneficiaries

16.3 The section has been given the widest construction. It will apply even if the terms of compromise involve a surrender of a beneficial interest by a party to the compromise, although it gives the trustees no power to vary beneficial interests against the wishes of the beneficiaries (*Re Earl of Strafford deceased [1980] Ch 28*). However, *Trustee Act 1925, s 15* does not apply to a dispute between beneficiaries or to vary the trusts of the settlement.

In order to justify the exercise of the power under *section 15* it is not necessary to show that the claim, if it had not been compromised, would have succeeded (*Re Ridsdel [1947] Ch 597*). However, there must be a real dispute or the power of compromise does not arise (*Sneath v Valley Gold Ltd [1893] 1 Ch 477*).

The interests of all the beneficiaries must be considered before exercising the power of compromise and the compromise must be desirable and fair to all the beneficiaries, but it is not necessary for the beneficiaries to consent before the power under *section 15* can be exercised (*Earl of Strafford*).

Surrendering trustees' discretion to the court

16.4 The trustees may surrender their power under *Trustee Act 1925, s 15* to the court. If they do so, then, although the court would pay due attention to the wishes of the beneficiaries, it will not necessarily follow those wishes but will make up its own mind whether to sanction a compromise (*Re Ezekiel's Settlement Trusts [1942] Ch 230*). Although *section 15* gives a wide measure of protection to trustees, in a difficult or marginal case, or in a matter involving a substantial sum of money, the trustees might be well advised to seek the directions of the court, whether or not the trustees are minded to surrender their discretion to the court.

Litigation

16.5 Trustees, of course, have the title and authority to bring or defend legal proceedings on behalf of the trust. Legal proceedings may be divided broadly into two categories. The first category (which can be termed 'hostile litigation') comprises actions which are necessary to get in trust assets or to assert rights on behalf of the trust against third parties or to defend the trust or the trust assets from adverse claims. The second category (which may broadly be called 'administration actions') comprise applications to the court in respect of the administration of the trust or the construction of the trust instrument.

Beddoe applications

16.6 In the case of hostile litigation, save in the clearest cases, trustees should not litigate either as claimants or defendants without the specific authority of the beneficiaries or the authority of the court sought on an application for directions (such an application is called a 'Beddoe application' after the decision in *Re Beddoe [1893] 1 Ch 547*).

A trustee who litigates under the authority of a Beddoe order will be entitled to an indemnity out of the trust fund in respect of any costs properly incurred by him in respect of the litigation whether or not the litigation is successful. However, a trustee who engages in hostile litigation without the authority of the beneficiaries or the protection of a Beddoe order, may be deprived of his right to an indemnity as to the costs if it is subsequently determined that the action should not have been brought or defended – see for example *Singh v Bhasin [2000] WTLR 275*. It should be noted that there is not an absolute bar on a trustee litigating without authority, but the trustee does so at risk of a finding that the proceedings should not have been brought or defended. A Beddoe order will not protect a trustee beneficiary in his capacity as beneficiary or in respect of his beneficial interest. A Beddoe order does not impact on the right of the trustee to seek an order for costs against another party or on the right of another party to seek an order for costs against the trustee; nor does a Beddoe order limit the trustees' exposure to an adverse costs order to the amount of the trust fund.

A Beddoe application is made in a separate action to the litigation which it concerns (*Alsop Wilkinson v Neary [1996] 1 WLR 1220*). The Beddoe application is an application between the trustees and the beneficiaries of the trust, it is not a matter that concerns the other party or parties to the litigation in question. If that other party is also a beneficiary then, although he should be made a party to the Beddoe application, any material which, as against him, in the litigation would be privileged should not be put in evidence as exhibits to the trustee's witness statement unless the trustee considers that no harm would be done by its disclosure and the party may be excluded from part of the hearing including that which is devoted to the evidence withheld (see the Practice Direction to RSC Order 85, to be replaced from 2 December 2002 by CPR Pt 64 and a new Practice Direction).

Evidence

16.7 A Beddoe application should be supported by an advice of an appropriately qualified lawyer as to the prospects for success, which advice should either set out the basis on which it is given or the instructions should also be put in evidence. There should also be put in evidence:

(*a*) any other matters relevant to the taking of proceedings including a costs estimate, any known facts concerning the means of the opposing party and a draft of the proposed statement of case;

(*b*) the value of the trust assets and the significance of the proposed litigation or other course of action for the trust and why the court's directions are necessary;

(*c*) in the case of a pension fund, the latest actuarial valuation, and should describe the membership profile and, if a deficit on winding up is likely, the priority provisions and their likely effect;

(*d*) whether:

 (i) any pre-action protocol has been followed; and

 (ii) whether the trustees have proposed or undertaken, or intend to propose, mediation by ADR and (in each case) if not why not.

The evidence must explain what, if any, consultation there has been with beneficiaries, and with what result. The Practice Direction sets out further guidance (paragraph 7.7).

Consultation

16.8 In summary, in the case of a private trust, the trustees will be expected to have canvassed the proposed or possible courses of action with the beneficiaries who are adult, identified, and traceable, even if those adult beneficiaries do not represent the whole of the beneficial interest. In the case of a charitable trust, the trustees must have consulted the Attorney-General, through the Treasury Solicitor, as well as the Charity Commissioners. The consent of the Commissioners will have been needed under the *Charities Act 1993, s 33*. In relation to a pension trust, unless the members are very few in number, no particular steps by way of consultation with the beneficiaries (including where relevant employers) or their representatives are required in preparation for the application, however, the trustees' evidence should describe any consultation that has, in fact, taken place. If no consultation has taken place, the court may direct that meetings of one or more classes of beneficiaries be held to consider the subject matter of the application, particularly as a preliminary to deciding whether a member of a particular class ought to be joined as a defendant; although in that event, steps may need to be considered to protect privileged material from too wide disclosure.

Directions for review

16.9 In all but the simplest cases, leave to bring or defend proceedings, if given, will be given up to a certain stage in the litigation when the prospects for success may be revisited. The court may direct that the directions be reviewed at a particular stage without hearing if the beneficiaries obtain and lodge the written advice of an appropriately qualified lawyer stating that he or they support the continuation of the directions. If the court gives directions for review after disclosure of documents and it is necessary to show the court in the Beddoe proceedings documents obtained by disclosure in the main litigation, it may be necessary to obtain permission to do this from the court in which the primary litigation is proceeding. However, the implied undertaking limiting the use of documents disclosed by another party to the litigation does not preclude their use on an application by trustee parties for directions since that is used for the purpose of the litigation (*White v Biddulph* (Hart J, 22 May 1998, unreported)).

In a case of urgency, for example where a limitation period or period for service of proceedings is about to expire, the court may be able to give directions on a summary consideration of the evidence to cover the steps which need to be taken urgently, but limiting those directions so that the application is reviewed on fuller consideration at an early stage.

Child beneficiary

16.10 The Practice Direction makes clear that if in any application for directions a child is a defendant, the court will expect to have put before it the instructions to and advice of an appropriately qualified lawyer as to the benefits and disadvantages that were proposed and any other relevant courses of action from the point of view of the child beneficiary.

Assets

16.11 It appears that a trustee will be protected by a Beddoe order in respect of costs properly incurred and will retain his indemnity on the assets comprising the trust fund even if the consequence of the litigation is to establish that those assets are not subject of the trust at all (*Re*

Dallaway [1982] 1 WLR 756). However, if the beneficiaries are all adult and of full capacity the more appropriate way to proceed may be for the beneficiaries to be joined as parties to defend the claim or not, as they think fit, at their own risk as to costs (*Evans v Evans [1986] 1 WLR 101* – where the trustees also had beneficial interests).

A trustee will not be compelled to continue litigation where the trust fund may be exhausted leaving the trustee exposed to personal risk without sufficient assets against which to seek an indemnity (*Bradstock Trustee Services Ltd v Nabarro Nathanson [1995] 1 WLR 1405*).

Administration actions

16.12 A Beddoe application is generally not appropriate in respect of an administration action. If a doubt or dispute arises over the correct construction of the trust instrument or the administration of the trust, the trustees' duty is to seek the determination or guidance of the court. In such proceedings the relevant beneficiaries will be joined as parties and the trustees role will usually be one of neutrality. A trustee may, however, be asked to assist the court both in making a clear presentation of the facts and circumstances giving rise to the dispute or drawing the court's attention to relevant principles of law. A trustee may also have a duty to represent absent or unborn interests. A trustee properly discharging those duties will not be deprived of his costs. However, a trustee who otherwise abandons a neutral stand and enters the arena on one side or the other does so at risk as to costs.

In respect of claims against an estate under the *Inheritance (Provision for Family and Dependants) Act 1975* the usual course is to join the beneficiaries who might be adversely affected and for the personal representative to assume a role of neutrality. An executor who is also a beneficiary may, of course, defend his beneficial interest but does so at risk as to costs.

A Beddoe application is also not appropriate in the case of a claim by a beneficiary against a trustee for breach of trust. In such a case the trustee defends to protect himself against a claimant pursuing a personal claim.

Measure of costs

16.13 Where a person is or has been a party to any proceedings in the capacity of trustee or personal representative, the general rule is that where he is entitled to be paid his costs of the proceedings out of any fund held by him as trustee or personal representative, those costs shall be assessed on the indemnity basis. However, the court retains its discretion in respect of costs and, in particular, may order otherwise if the trustee or personal representative has acted for a benefit other than that of the trust fund (CPR r 48.4).

Trustees should normally be represented as a body rather than separately and will normally be allowed only one set of costs. Different considerations apply where one or more trustees have a separate interest, for example, as a beneficiary or where one only of several trustees is charged with wrongdoing. In such a case, it may be necessary and appropriate for that individual trustee to be separately represented.

Appeals

16.14 A trustee who has sought the directions of the court in respect of any matter affecting the trust and who then appeals the order made normally does so at his personal risk as to costs and, unless there are special circumstances, will be ordered to pay the costs of an unsuccessful appeal. The reason is that the trustee is protected by the order at first instance and, therefore, has no need to appeal (*Re Londonderry's Settlement [1965] Ch 918* – although the court was divided about the propriety of the appeal in that case).

Pre-emptive costs orders

16.15 The court has an exceptional jurisdiction to make an order at an early stage in the proceedings regarding the ultimate incidence as to costs. The jurisdiction may be exercised, for example, where a representative beneficiary is joined to advance the arguments of a particular class of persons even though the benefit to the individual might be so small that he or she would not personally contemplate the risk in costs. The four relevant considerations are:

(*a*) the strength of the party's case;

(*b*) the likely order as to costs at the trial;

(*c*) the justice of the application;

(*d*) any special circumstances.

As to the second consideration, save in respect of derivative actions and actions relating to pension funds, it must appear that the judge at trial could properly exercise his discretion only by ordering that the applicant's costs be paid out of the trust estate (see *Alsop Wilkinson v Neary [1996] 1 WLR 1220 at 1226*).

In the case of trustees, it will usually be appropriate to seek a Beddoe order rather than a pre-emptive costs order. If, however, the nature of the litigation is such as may result in a third party establishing title as against the trust to all the assets (as in *Re Dallaway [1982] 1 WLR 756*) it may be convenient to include an alternative claim to a pre-emptive costs order in the Beddoe application.

Settled land

16.16 The foregoing considerations apply as much to *Settled Land Act* trustees and the tenant for life as to other trustees.

The *Settled Land Act 1925, s 92* gives the court express power to approve of proceedings taken or to be taken for the recovery of land being, or alleged to be, subject to a settlement and to direct that the costs be paid out of the property subject of the settlement. An order can be made retrospectively. In the case of *Re Wilkie's Settlement [1914] 1 Ch 77*, the court made an order to recoup to the tenant for life the costs of proceedings funded out of income, even though by the time of the application, the proceedings had been abandoned.

Section 93 of the Act gives express power to the tenant for life, statutory owner or trustees of the settlement or any other person interested in the settlement to refer questions to the court for its decision or directions. It applies if any question arises or doubt is entertained:

(*a*) respecting the exercise or intended exercise of any of the powers conferred by the Act or settlement or any matter relating thereto;

(*b*) as to the person in whose favour a vesting deed or assent ought to be executed, or as to the contents thereof; or

(*c*) otherwise in relation to the property subject to a settlement.

Charities

16.17 In the case of a charitable trust it is important to consider at the outset whether proceedings or proposed proceedings are charity proceedings within the meaning of the *Charities Act 1993, s 33(8)*. The importance is twofold. First, the persons who may commence charity proceedings is delimited. Second, with certain exceptions, unless the proceedings have the consent of the Charity Commissioners or, following a refusal of consent, the permission of the court, the proceedings may not be entertained or proceeded with.

Charity proceedings defined

16.18 'Charity proceedings' are proceedings in any court in England or Wales brought under the court's jurisdiction with respect to charities, or brought under the court's jurisdiction with respect to trusts in relation to the administration of a trust for charitable purposes. [*Charities Act 1993, s 33(8)*].

The following are not charity proceedings:

- Proceedings concerning charities established outside England and Wales in accordance with the law of a foreign state (*Gaudiya Mission v Brahmachary [1998] Ch 341*).
- An action to enforce common law rights or to enforce individual equitable rights not relating to the administration of a charitable trust (*Rendall v Blair (1890) 45 Ch D 139*). However, an application for judicial review of a decision of a charitable public body exercising its discretionary powers in the management of trust property does fall within the definition of charity proceedings (*Ex p Scott [1998] 1 WLR 226*).
- Proceedings to determine whether or not a trust is charitable or whether, in the case of a testamentary document, a provision is effective to create a charitable trust (*Re St Giles' and St George's, Bloomsbury, Volunteer Corps (1858) 25 Beav 313; Re Belling [1967] Ch 425*).

Who may take charity proceedings?

16.19 Charity proceedings may be taken with reference to a charity either by the charity or by any of the charity trustees, or by a person interested in the charity, or by any two or more inhabitants of the area of the charity if it is a local charity, but not by any other person. [*Charities Act 1993, s 33(1)*]. A local authority may be 'a person interested' within the meaning of *section 33(1)* if, but only if, it has a sufficient interest in the proper administration of the particular charity (*Re Hampton Charity [1989] Ch 484*, where there was a close nexus between the functions of the Council and the functions of the charity in respect of assistance to needy residents particularly the elderly).

Authorisation necessary

16.20 Save with certain exceptions, no charity proceedings relating to a charity shall be entertained or proceeded with in any court unless the taking of the proceedings is authorised by order of the Commissioners. [*Charities Act 1993, s 33(2)*]. The exceptions are:

(*a*) proceedings relating to an exempt charity (exempt charities are listed in *Schedule 2* to the Act);

(*b*) the taking of proceedings in a pending cause or matter or for the bringing of an appeal;

(*c*) the taking of proceedings by the Attorney-General with or without a relator;

(*d*) the taking of proceedings by the Commissioners under *section 32* of the Act.

Unless the matter falls within one or other of the exemptions the authority of the Commissioners must be obtained and proceedings commenced without that authority will be struck out or stayed until consent is obtained.

The Commissioners are expressly charged by *section 33(3)* not, without special reason, to authorise the taking of charity proceedings where, in their opinion, the case can be dealt with by them under the powers of the *Charities Act 1993*.

If authority has been applied for and refused, then the proceedings may be entertained or proceeded with if, after authority was refused, leave to take the proceedings is obtained from one of the judges of the High Court attached to the Chancery Division. [*Charities Act 1993, s 33(8)*]. The application must be made within 21 days after the refusal by the Commissioners of an order authorising proceedings. (RSC Order 108(2)).

The Commissioners may refer a matter to the Attorney General with a view to the Attorney taking proceedings with reference to the charity (other than an exempt charity) or its property or affairs. [*Charities Act 1993, s 33(7)*].

If charity trustees consider that it would be appropriate to bring or defend proceedings in respect of the charity or its assets and wish to have the protection of a Beddoe order, the application for a Beddoe order is itself a charity proceeding for which the authority of the Commissioners is required, even if the contemplated litigation is not.

Jurisdiction

16.21 Under the *Charities Act 1993, s 16*, the Commissioners have concurrent jurisdiction with the High Court for the following purposes:

(*a*) establishing a scheme for the administration of the charity;

(*b*) appointing discharging or removing a charity trustee or trustee for a charity or removing an officer or employee;

(*c*) vesting or transferring property, or requiring or entitling any person to call for or make any transfer of property or any payment.

An appeal against any order of the Commissioners under *section 16* may be brought in the High Court by the Attorney-General. The right of the Attorney-General to appeal is not limited.

Such an appeal may also be brought by the charity or any of the charity trustees, or by any person removed from any office or employment by the order (unless he is removed with the concurrence of the charity trustees or with the approval of the special visitor, if any, of the charity). In the case of a scheme, a person interested in the charity shall have the like right of appeal as a charity trustee, and in the case of a local charity, so shall any two or more inhabitants in the area and the parish council or (in Wales) any community comprising the area or any part of it.

However, in contrast to the unfettered right of the Attorney-General to appeal, such an appeal must be brought within three months beginning with the day following that on which the order is published and it shall only be brought with a certificate of the Commissioners that it is a proper case for an appeal or with the leave of one of the judges of the High Court attached to the Chancery Division. [*Charities Act 1993, s 16(12), (13)*]. An application may not be made for permission to appeal against an order of the Commissioners unless the applicant has requested the Commissioners to grant a certificate and they have refused to do so. (RSC Order 108(3)).

Pension funds

16.22 The same considerations apply to the powers and duties of trustees of pension funds as apply to the trustees of a private trust. Trustees should seek the protection of a Beddoe order (or the consent of the beneficiaries) if they are not to litigate at their own risk as to costs. If the resolution of the point at issue requires a class of beneficiaries to be represented, a representative party may be entitled to a pre-emptive costs order in order that he is not exposed to a personal risk as to costs properly incurred (see 16.15 above).

Trustees of an occupational pension scheme must secure that such arrangements as are required by or under the *Pensions Act 1995, s 50* for the resolution of disagreements between prescribed persons about matters in relation to the scheme are made and implemented. Failure to do so may attract a fine (up to £1,000 in the case of an individual or £10,000 in any other case) under *section 10* of the Act. Applications for decisions under such arrangements and the procedure for reaching and giving such decisions are prescribed by regulations, currently the *Occupational Pension Schemes (Internal Dispute Resolution Procedures) Regulations 1996 (SI 1996 No 1270)*.

The prescribed persons as defined by the regulations are:

(*a*) the active, deferred and pensioner members of the scheme;

(*b*) the widow, widower or surviving dependant of a deceased member of the scheme;

(*c*) prospective members of the scheme;

(*d*) persons who ceased to be within any of the categories of person referred to in subparagraphs (*a*) to (*c*) above within six months immediately preceding the date of an application for a decision;

(*e*) a person claiming to be within (*a*) to (*d*) above where there is a disagreement which relates to whether or not he is within those paragraphs.

The regulations set out the particulars to be included in an application and what is to be included in a notice of decision.

The requirements of *section 50* of the Act do not apply to schemes in which all members are trustees or schemes with no more than one member. Nor do the requirements of *section 50* apply to a disagreement if in respect of that disagreement proceedings have been begun in any court or tribunal or the Pensions Ombudsman has commenced an investigation into a complaint made or a dispute referred to him.

Chapter 17

Power to Appropriate and Power to Partition

Introduction

17.1 This chapter deals with the power of trustees to appropriate assets in specie to beneficiaries and the questions whether and to what extent the beneficiaries have a right to call for their share in trust property to be satisfied by the appropriation of assets in specie as opposed to the sale of the assets and a distribution of the proceeds of sale. It also deals with the power of a trustee to partition land in order that it can be distributed in specie.

Powers

Implied power

17.2 A trustee has an implied power to appropriate assets in satisfaction of a beneficiary's share (*Re Ruddock (1910) 102 LT 89*).

Express power

17.3 If a trust instrument contains an express power it is normally in clear terms to that effect. However, an express power to appropriate may be found in lcss dircct words. For cxamplc, in *Rc Nicholson's Will Trusts [1936] 3 All ER 832*, a direction that in the event of the remarriage of the testator's widow his trustees should set apart from the trust fund a sum sufficient to secure to the wife an annual income of £300 was held to authorise the trustees to appropriate for that purpose such of the investments authorised by the will as they should think fit.

Appropriation under AEA 1925, s 41

Personal representatives

17.4 *Section 41* of the *Administration of Estates Act 1925* (*AEA 1925*) expressly authorises a personal representative to appropriate any part of the real or personal estate of the deceased in or towards satisfaction of any legacy bequeathed by the deceased or of any other interest or share in his property, whether settled or not, as to the personal representative may seem just and reasonable according to the respective rights of the persons interested in the property of the deceased. There is no restriction on the type of assets which may be appropriated. However, an appropriation shall not be made so as to affect prejudicially any specific demise or bequest.

Section 41 applies whether a deceased died intestate or not and extends to property over which the testator exercised a general power of appointment, including the statutory power to dispose of an entailed interest (*Law of Property Act 1925, s 176*) and authorises the setting apart of a fund to answer an annuity by means of the income of such fund or otherwise.

The power to appropriate under *section 41* is not confined to appropriations to an individual absolutely entitled but extends to property held on a settled share. Any property duly appropriated to a trust under the powers conferred by *section 41* shall thereafter be treated as an authorised investment and may be retained and dealt with accordingly (*section 41(2)*). Property appropriated to a settled legacy share or interest remains subject to all trusts and powers of leasing, disposition and management or varying investments which would have been applicable thereto (or to such legacy, share or interest in respect of which the appropriation is made) if no such appropriation had been made (*section 41(6)*).

Consents required

17.5 An appropriation under *AEA 1925, s 41* must be by consent. When made for the benefit of a person absolutely and beneficially entitled in possession, the consent must be of that person. When made in respect of any settled legacy, share or interest, the consent must be either of the trustee thereof, if any (not being also the personal representative) or the person who may for the time being be entitled to the income.

If the person whose consent is required is an infant, the consent may be given on his behalf by his parents or parent or testamentary or other guardian. If there is no such parent or guardian consent may be given by the court on the application of his litigation friend. No consent (save of a trustee) shall be required on behalf of a person who may come into existence after the time of appropriation or who cannot be found or ascertained at that time. So, for example, if property is left for the benefit of a person or persons as yet unborn, the only consent required is that of the trustee of the fund.

If the person whose consent is so required is incapable by reason of mental disorder within the meaning of the *Mental Health Act 1983* of managing and administering his property and affairs then consent may be given by his receiver. If no receiver is acting, then, if the appropriation is of an investment authorised by law or by the will of the deceased for the investment of money subject to the trust, no consent is required. In the case of an appropriation of an unauthorised asset, where there is no receiver, the consent of a nominated judge (or other authorised person) under the *Mental Health Act 1983, Pt VII* is required.

In the case of a settled legacy, share or interest, if, independently of the personal representative, there is no trustee, and no person of full age and capacity is entitled to the income thereof, no consent shall be required to an appropriation in respect of such legacy, share or interest, providing that the appropriation is of an investment authorised by law or by the will of the deceased for the investment of money subject to the trust.

County court – jurisdiction

17.6 Where the consent of the court is required, then the county court has jurisdiction where the estate in respect of which the application is made does not exceed the amount or value of the county court limit (presently £30,000).

Protection of purchasers

17.7 If land is appropriated in exercise of the powers, and the person to whom it was conveyed disposes of it, or any interest therein, then, in favour of a purchaser, the appropriation shall be deemed to have been made in accordance with the requirements of *AEA 1925, s 41* and after all requisite consents, if any, have been made. 'Purchaser' means a purchaser for money or money's worth (*section 41(8)* – contrast the general definition of 'purchaser' in *section 55*).

Trustee must determine value before appropriation

17.8 If a trustee appropriates property without ascertaining its value he may commit a breach of trust. In *Re Brookes [1914] 1 Ch 558* an estate was divisible between two families. The trustee appropriated a mortgage in satisfaction of the share of one family and the other assets in satisfaction of the share of the other family. The trustee had not inspected the premises upon which the mortgage was secured and they were found to be derelict, unoccupied and in a dilapidated condition and practically worthless as security. The trustee was held liable to the family to which it had been appropriated.

Date of valuation

17.9 The value is determined at the date of appropriation not the date of death (see *Re Collins [1975] 1 WLR 309*).

For the purpose of an appropriation under *AEA 1925, s 41*, the personal representative may ascertain and fix the value of the respective parts of the real and personal estate and the liabilities of the deceased as he may think fit and shall for that purpose employ a duly qualified valuer in any case where such employment may be necessary, and may make any conveyance (including an assent which may be requisite for giving effect to the appropriation). [*AEA 1925, s 41(3)*]. *Subsections (4)* and *(5)* of *section 41* expressly provide that an appropriation made pursuant to the section shall bind all persons interested in the property of the deceased whose consent is not thereby made requisite. The personal representatives, however, must, in making the appropriation, have regard to the rights of any person who may come into existence, or who cannot be found or ascertained at the time of the appropriation, and of any other person whose consent is not required by the section.

Right of trustee to compel a beneficiary to take land by appropriation

17.10 The *Trusts of Land and Appointment of Trustees Act 1996, s 6(2)* provides that where each of the beneficiaries interested in the land is of full age and capacity and absolutely entitled to the land, the general powers of trustees include the power to convey the land to the beneficiaries even though they have not required the trustees to do so; the beneficiaries must do whatever is necessary to secure that the land vests in them and if they fail to do so the court may make an order requiring them to do so.

Right of a beneficiary to compel a trustee to appropriate an asset

17.11 Where persons who, between them, hold the entirety of the beneficial interest in a particular trust fund are all of age and mentally competent, they are entitled to act together and direct the trustees to hand over the trust assets in specie, subject, of course, to the right of the trustee to be fully protected against any actual or contingent liabilities to which he is exposed and in respect of which he is entitled to an indemnity out of the trust assets. Furthermore, where one of several beneficiaries has an absolute interest, that beneficiary is entitled to an aliquot share of each and every asset of the trust fund, providing the assets present no difficulty so far as division is concerned (e.g. cash, money at the bank or unsecured loan stock, quoted securities and the like).

However, in respect of land, shares in a private company, and other assets where division may be complicated, the beneficiary is not entitled to call on the trustees, as of right, to appropriate a share of the asset (*Stephenson v Barclays Bank Trust Co Ltd [1975] 1 WLR 882 at 889–890*). (See also *Crowe v Appleby [1975] 1 WLR 1539*.)

Where a will specifically directed that private company shares were to be retained in specie and not sold, beneficiaries entitled absolutely to one-half of the estate were entitled to have one half of the shareholding transferred to them, notwithstanding that the will authorised the trustees 'to retain [the shares] so long as they [the trustees] in their absolute and uncontrolled discretion shall think fit' (*Re Sandeman's Will Trusts [1937] 1 All ER 368*). The trustees had argued that it was for the benefit of all the beneficiaries that they retained control of the shares and that it was the intention of the testator that the trustees should retain the whole of the shares until they all fell into possession. The court, whilst accepting that in special circumstances the trustees might be justified in refusing to transfer shares, pointed out that the right of the trustees to maintain control of the company was a right exercisable for the benefit of the beneficiaries and, vis-à-vis the beneficiaries (they being absolutely entitled to one half of the shares), the trustees had no right to refuse to transfer them. That case was followed in *Re Weiner's Will Trusts [1956] 1 WLR 579*, where a beneficiary had become absolutely entitled to 45% of the income and capital of the residuary personal estate and successfully sought an order directing the trustees to pay and transfer to him a 45% share of the trust's holding of shares in a private company.

However, it is not in every case that a beneficiary is entitled to call for an appropriation of assets. In *Lloyds Bank plc v Duker [1987] 1 WLR 1324*, the defendant, who was managing director of a private company which owned a luxury hotel, was entitled to 46/80ths of the testator's estate. He called upon the executors to transfer to him 574 shares in the company, which was the nearest whole number to a similar proportion of the estate's holding of shares. The court held that the general principle requiring trustees to treat all beneficiaries equally was not necessarily displaced by the general rule entitling a beneficiary to call for the transfer to him of his share in divisible personalty. Such a distribution broke up the controlling interest, thus reducing the value of the whole. On the evidence, the block of 574 shares was worth more per share than any minority holding and it followed that the transfer to the defendant would give him markedly more than 46/80ths of the total value of all the shareholdings. Accordingly, to ensure equality among the beneficiaries, the defendant was under a duty to sell all 999 shares on the open market so that the first defendant took 46/80ths of the residuary estate by value. The report discloses that the judge, however, directed that the defendant should be left free to bid for the shares on their sale.

Similar considerations may apply in respect of land where, to divide up an estate would diminish the value of the whole (*Re Marshall [1914] 1 Ch 192 at 199*).

Self-dealing

17.12 Where the same person is both trustee or personal representative, and beneficiary, then the rule against self-dealing applies and, with the exception of cash or assets equivalent to cash, such as quoted securities, the trustees or personal representative is not entitled to appropriate assets in specie towards his share without the consent of the other beneficiaries affected or an order of the court. If an appropriation is made in breach of the self-dealing rule, then a beneficiary is entitled to have the appropriation set aside as of right.

Thus, in *Kane v Radley-Kane [1999] Ch 274*, a widow took a grant of letters of administration to the estate of her late husband. The estate included a number of shares in a private company. The shares were valued for the purpose of the grant at £50,000 so that the estate was within the statutory widow's legacy and the widow treated herself as being absolutely entitled to all the assets of the estate, including the shares, and took them in specie. Within two years of the death, the widow had sold the shares for a sum in excess of £1.1m. One of the sons of the deceased by a previous marriage successfully applied to have the appropriation set aside, the court holding that the proceeds of sale of the shares formed part of the estate, for which the widow was accountable.

Intestacy and the matrimonial home

17.13 The surviving husband or wife of a person dying intestate may require the personal representative (in exercise of the statutory power of appropriation under *AEA 1925, s 41*) to appropriate the estate's interest in the dwelling house in which the surviving husband or wife was resident at the time of the intestate's death in or towards satisfaction of any absolute interest of the surviving husband or wife in the real or personal estate of the intestate. [*Intestates' Estates Act 1952, s 5, Sch 2*]. The absolute interest of the surviving husband or wife includes the statutory legacy, or the reference to or the capital value of the life interest which the surviving husband or wife has, under *AEA 1925, s 47A*, elected to have redeemed. Where part of a building was at the date of death of the intestate occupied as a separate dwelling, that dwelling shall for this purpose be treated as a dwelling house.

Unless the context otherwise requires, references to a dwelling house include references to any garden or portion of ground attached to and usually occupied with the dwelling house or otherwise required for the amenity or convenience of the dwelling house (*Intestates' Estates Act 1952, Sch 2, para 7*).

The right does not apply to an interest in a tenancy which, at the date of the death of the intestate, has less than two years to run or which the landlord could bring to an end within a period of two years by notice.

In certain cases (set out in *paragraph 2* of the *Schedule*), the right of the surviving husband or wife shall not be exercisable unless the court so orders. The court must be satisfied that the exercise of the right is not likely to diminish the value of assets in the residuary estate (other than the said interest in the dwelling house) or make them more difficult to dispose of. The cases are where:

(*a*) the dwelling house forms part of a building and an interest in the whole of the building is comprised in the residuary estate; or

(*b*) the dwelling house is held with agricultural land and an interest in the agricultural land is comprised in the residuary estate; or

(*c*) the whole or part of the dwelling house was at the time of the intestate's death used as a hotel or lodging house; or

(*d*) a part of the dwelling house was at the time of the intestate's death used for purposes other than domestic purposes.

The right to have the matrimonial home appropriated is not exercisable after the death of the surviving husband or wife. It is also not exercisable after the expiry of twelve months from the first taking out of representation with respect to the intestate's estate, although this period can be extended in the following circumstances, if the husband or wife satisfies the court that the period of twelve months would operate unfairly. The circumstances are:

(i) the representation first taken out was probate of a will subsequently revoked on the ground that the will was invalid;

(ii) in consequence of a question whether a person had an interest in the estate not having been determined at the time when representation was first taken out; or

(iii) in consequence of some other circumstances affecting the administration or distribution of the estate.

[*Administration of Estates Act 1925, s 47A(5)* applied by *Intestates' Estates Act 1952, Sch 2, para 3*].

The right must be exercised, except where the husband or wife is the sole personal representative, by notifying the personal representative (or, where there are two or more personal representatives of whom one is the surviving husband or wife, all except the surviving husband or wife) in writing. Once notification in writing has been given, it is not revocable except with the consent of the personal representative. The surviving husband or wife may require the personal representative to have the said interest in the dwelling house valued in accordance with *AEA 1925, s 41* and to inform him or her of the result of that valuation before he or she decides whether to exercise the right.

During the period of twelve months the personal representative shall not without the written consent of the surviving husband or wife sell or otherwise dispose of the interest in the dwelling house except in the course of administration owing to want of other assets.

In the case where an application to the court is required under *paragraph 2* of *Schedule 2* (see above) the application may be made by a personal representative as well as by the surviving husband or wife and the court may authorise the personal representative to dispose of the interest in the dwelling house within the said period of twelve months. The court, if extending the period of twelve months, may direct that the paragraph shall apply during that extended period.

The *Intestates' Estates Act 1952, Sch 2, para 5* provides an express exemption from the self-dealing rule (see CHAPTER 5: DUTY NOT TO BENEFIT PERSONALLY). It provides that, where the surviving husband or wife is one of two or more personal representatives, the rule that a trustee may not be a purchaser of trust property shall not prevent the surviving husband or wife from purchasing out of the estate of the intestate an interest in a dwelling house in which the surviving husband or wife was resident at the time of the intestate's death. If the surviving husband or wife is the sole personal representative then he or she should seek the written approval of the beneficiaries or an order of the court.

Paragraph 5 also provides in *subparagraph (2)* that the power of appropriation under *AEA 1925, s 41* shall include power to appropriate an interest in the dwelling house in which the surviving husband or wife was resident at the time of the intestate's death partly in satisfaction of an interest of the surviving husband or wife in the real and personal estate of the intestate and partly in return for a payment of money by the surviving husband or wife of the personal representative. Accordingly, if the value of the dwelling house exceeds the value of the spouse's interest in the estate, the difference can be paid to the estate by way of a money payment (*Re Phelps [1980] Ch 275*).

Where the surviving husband or wife is a person suffering from mental disorder, a requirement or consent under *Schedule 2* may be made or given by his or her receiver or by the court. A requirement or consent made or given under the *Schedule* by a surviving husband or wife who is an infant shall be as valid and binding as it would be if he or she were of age, and the provisions of *AEA 1925, s 41* as to obtaining the consent of the infant's parent or guardian, or of the court on behalf of the infant, shall not apply. [*Intestates' Estates Act 1952, Sch 2, para 6*].

Power to partition

17.14 The *Trusts of Land and Appointment of Trustees Act 1996, s 7* provides a statutory power of partition in respect of land. The trustees of land may, where beneficiaries of full age are absolutely entitled in undivided shares to land subject to the trust, partition the land, or any part of it, and provide (by way of mortgage or otherwise) for payment of any equality money.

Before exercising their power to convey partitioned land the trustees must obtain the consent of each of the beneficiaries (*section 7(3)*). However, the provisions of the *Trusts of Land and Appointment of Trustees Act 1996, s 14* enable the court to make an order relieving the trustee of the obligation to obtain consent. That power is unrestricted and so is exercisable either in a situation in which consent cannot be obtained because for example the beneficiary is missing, or in a situation where a beneficiary unreasonably withholds consent.

If a beneficiary does not have the mental capacity to consent, then a nominated judge of the Court of Protection can exercise the power to consent. [*Mental Health Act 1983, s 96*].

Although the section requires the beneficiaries to be of full age it goes on to provide that if a share in the land is absolutely vested in a minor, the statutory provisions for partition apply as if he were of full age except that the trustees may act on his behalf and retain land or other property representing his share in trust for him.

The trustees give effect to such partition by conveying the partitioned land in severalty, i.e. as opposed to jointly. If a legal mortgage has been created for raising equality money it may be conveyed subject to that mortgage. The conveyance should be either absolutely or in trust in accordance with the rights of those beneficiaries. Where a share in the land is affected by an encumbrance, the trustees may either give effect to it or provide for its discharge from the property allotted to that share as they think fit.

Chapter 18

Power to Delegate

Introduction

18.1 In considering the power of a trustee to delegate there are two quite distinct matters to consider. The first is whether and to what extent an individual trustee may delegate his powers to a third party to exercise on his behalf. The second is whether the trustees as a body may delegate to one or some only of their number or to a third party the exercise of their powers and the discharge of their duties as trustees.

Equity drew a distinction between the primary duties of a trustee which were regarded as incapable of delegation and the engagement of others to assist in the management of a trust fund which was permitted (see the classic statement of Lord Fitzgerald in *Speight v Gaunt (1883) 9 App Cas 1 at 29*). However, trustees who employed an agent to conduct trust business were expected to exercise the same care that an ordinary prudent man of business would exercise in respect of his own affairs in the selection and supervision of the agent, and a failure to do so could lead to personal liability for loss to the trust fund resulting (*Re Lucking's Will Trusts [1968] 1 WLR 866*).

Wider and more defined powers of delegation could be granted by the trust instrument or by statute. In the case of delegation by trustees as a body a statutory power to employ agents was created by the *Trustee Act 1925, s 23, Pt IV* which has now been superseded by the more comprehensive provisions in the *Trustee Act 2000* (*TA 2000*).

In the case of delegation by an individual trustee, the *Trustee Act 1925, s 25* gave a limited power to delegate trustee functions by power of attorney during his absence abroad. *Section 25* was recast by the *Powers of Attorney Act 1971* which removed the limit of its application to delegation whilst abroad. When enduring powers of attorney were introduced by the *Enduring Powers of Attorney Act 1985, s 2(8)* it was expressly provided that a power of attorney granted under *section 25* could not be an enduring power of attorney. However, *section 3(3)* of the 1985 Act provided that, subject to any condition or restriction in the instrument, an attorney under an enduring power, whether general or limited, might execute or exercise all or any of the trust powers or discretions vested in the donor as trustee and might give a valid receipt for capital or other money paid.

There was, therefore, an illogical inconsistency between the limited power in the Trustee Act 1925 and the broad power in the *Enduring Powers of Attorney Act 1985*. Matters have now been rationalised by the *Trustee Delegation Act 1999* which came into force on 1 March 2000.

In the case of trusts of land, liberal powers of delegation by power of attorney are available. First, a trustee who has a beneficial interest may delegate any of his trustee functions to a third party. Second, the trustees may delegate to any beneficiary or beneficiaries of full age and beneficially entitled to an interest in possession in land any of their functions which relate to the land.

Delegation by an individual trustee

Delegation of trustee functions under the Trustee Act 1925, s 25

18.2 An enduring power of attorney which is not made under the *Trustee Act 1925, s 25* created after 1 March 2000 does not entitle the donee to exercise the donor's functions as trustee or to give a receipt for capital monies. [*Trustee Delegation Act 1999, s 4(1)*]. In the case of powers granted before 1 March 2000, the power to exercise donee functions will continue in respect of *registered* powers but in the case of powers where application to register had been made before that date or within one year thereafter, will cease to apply when the registration of the instrument is cancelled under the *Enduring Powers of Attorney Act 1985, s 8(4)* or is finally refused. [*Trustee Delegation Act 1999, s 4(3)* – see also *subsections (4)–(6)*].

A power of attorney created under the *Trustee Act 1925, s 25* after 1 March 2000 can be an enduring power of attorney. [*Trustee Delegation Act 1999, s 6*].

The *Trustee Act 1925, s 25* (as substituted by the *Trustee Delegation Act 1999, s 5(1), (2)* in relation to powers of attorney granted after 1 March 2000) provides that, notwithstanding any rule of law or equity to the contrary, a trustee may, by power of attorney, delegate the execution or exercise of all or any of the trusts, powers and discretions vested in him as trustee either alone or jointly with any other person or persons. The provisions of *section 25* apply also to a personal representative and, in respect of settled land, a tenant for life or a statutory owner.

Duration of period of delegation

18.3 A delegation under *section 25* is limited to a maximum period of 12 months. It commences as provided in the instrument creating the power or, if the instrument makes no provision as to the commencement of the delegation, with the date of the execution of the instrument by the donor, and continues for a period of 12 months or any shorter period provided by the instrument creating the power. [*Trustee Act 1925, s 25(2)*].

Who may be a donee?

18.4 *Section 25* does not impose any restriction on the persons who may be appointed a donee; it expressly provides that a trustee may delegate by power of attorney trustee functions to a trust corporation. [*Trustee Act 1925, s 25(3)*].

Requirements for notice

18.5 Before or within seven days after giving a power of attorney under *section 25*, the donor shall give written notice of it (specifying the date on which the power comes into operation and its duration) to the donee of the power, the reasons why the power is given and, where some only are delegated, the trusts, powers and discretions delegated to:

(*a*) each person (other than himself), if any, who under any instrument creating the trust has power (whether alone or jointly) to appoint a new trustee; and

(*b*) each of the other trustees, if any.

[*Trustee Act 1925, s 25(4)*].

In the case of a personal representative, notice should be given to each of the other personal representatives except an executor who has renounced. In the case of a tenant for life, notice should be given to the trustees of the settlement and the person, if any, who, together with the person giving notice, constitutes the tenant for life. In the case of a statutory owner, notice should be given to the person, if any, who together with the person giving the notice constitutes the statutory owner and in the case of a statutory owner by virtue of the *Settled Land Act 1925, s 23(1)(a)* (person of full age on whom powers of a tenant for life are by the settlement expressed to be conferred) the trustees of the settlement. [*Trustee Act 1925, s 25(10)*].

Failure to give notice does not, in favour of a person dealing with the donee of the power, invalidate any act done, or instrument executed, by the donee.

Form of power

18.6 A power of attorney given under *section 25* must be in the form set out in *subsection (6)*, or in a form to the like effect, but expressed to be made under *section 25(5)*. [*Trustee Act 1925, s 25(5)*].

Donee's power to delegate

18.7 *Section 25(8)* permits an attorney to exercise any of the powers conferred on the donor by statute or by the instrument creating the trust including the power to delegate the transfer of any inscribed stock; however, the *donee* is not empowered to exercise the power of delegation imposed by *section 25*.

Power of attorney not to be notice of a trust

18.8 The fact that it is apparent, in dealing with any shares and stock, that the donee is acting in execution of a trust shall not be deemed to affect a person in whose books the shares are, or stock is, registered or inscribed (*Trustee Act 1925, s 25(9)*; by *section 68(1)*, 'stock' includes fully paid up shares).

Acts in relation to land – delegation by power of attorney

Trustee Delegation Act 1999, s 1

18.9 In the case of a trust of land, capital monies arising from a dealing with land or income from land, delegation by ordinary power of attorney unlimited in time is permitted by the *Trustee Delegation Act 1999, s 1* if the donor also has a beneficial interest. *Section 1* appears to have been intended to relax the limitations of the *Trustee Act 1925, s 25* for co-owners of land (who of course occupy the dual positions of trustee and beneficiary) but it is not confined to co-owners.

The section provides that the donee of a power of attorney (created after 1 March 2000) is not prevented from doing an act in relation to land, capital proceeds of a conveyance of land, or income from land by reason only that the act involves the exercise of a trustee function of the donor if, at the time when the act is done, the donor has a beneficial interest in the land, proceeds, or income. 'Conveyance' has the same meaning as in the *Law of Property Act 1925, s 205* and so includes any assurance of property or an interest therein, other than by will.

If a donee of a power of attorney is acting under power of attorney given under a statutory provision or under a provision of the trust instrument by which the donor of the power is expressly authorised to delegate the exercise of all or any of his trustee functions by power of attorney, then the donee of the power is not to be regarded as exercising a trustee function by virtue of the *Trustee Delegation Act, s 1*.

Save in the case of enduring powers of attorney registered before 1 March 2000 or within one year thereafter, the section applies only to powers of attorney created after 1 March 2000.

18.9 *Power to Delegate*

A general power of attorney in the form set out in the *Powers of Attorney Act 1971, Sch 1* or a similar form will now confer on the donee of the power an authority to exercise a trustee function to the extent permitted by the *Trustee Delegation Act 1999, s 1*. This is expressly provided by *section 3* and reverses *Walia v Michael Naughton Ltd [1985] 1 WLR 1115*.

Doctrine of conversion

18.10 The statutory power to delegate is extended to persons who have a beneficial interest in the proceeds of sale of land where (by way of exception to the *Trusts of Land and Appointment of Trustees Act 1996, s 3(1)*) the doctrine of conversion continues to operate. [*Trustee Delegation Act, s 1(7)*].

Contrary intention

18.11 The section applies only if and so far as the contrary intention is not expressed in the instrument creating the power of attorney and subject to the terms of that instrument (*Trustee Delegation Act 1999, s 1(3)*) and only if and so far as a contrary intention is not expressed in the instrument (if any) creating the trust and subject to the terms of such instrument. [*Trustee Delegation Act, s 1(5)*]. Co-ownership may, of course, arise without a trust instrument, e.g. by joint payment of the purchase price.

Donor remains responsible

18.12 The donor of the power of attorney is liable for the acts or defaults of the donee in exercising any function by virtue of *subsection (1)* in the same manner as if they were acts or defaults of the donor, but is not liable by reason only that a function is exercised by the donee by virtue of that subsection. [*Trustee Delegation Act 1999, s 1(4)*].

Protection of purchaser

18.13 Where the interest of a purchaser depends on the donee of a power of attorney having power to do an act in relation to any property by virtue of the *Trustee Delegation Act 1999, s 1(1)* an appropriate statement is, in favour of the purchaser, conclusive evidence of the donor of the power having a beneficial interest in the property at the time of the doing of the act (*section 2(1)*). 'Purchaser' has the same meaning as in the *Law of Property Act 1925, Pt I*. 'An appropriate statement' means a signed statement made by the donee when doing the act in question, or at any other time within the period of three months beginning with the day on which the act is done, that the donor has a beneficial interest in the property at the time of the donee doing the act (*section 2(3)*). If the appropriate statement is false, the donee is liable in the same way as he would be if the statement were contained in a statutory declaration (*section 2(4)*).

Land includes an undivided share in land

18.14 By the *Trustee Delegation Act 1999, s 10*, where a donee of a power of attorney is authorised by the power to do an act of any description in relation to any land, his authority to do an act of that description includes authority to do it for any interest in the land which is held at that time by the donor (whether alone or jointly with any other person or persons). In other words, a power to deal with land includes a power to deal with an undivided share of land in conjunction with a co-owner. *Section 10*, however, applies only if and in so far as the contrary intention is not expressed in the instrument creating the power of attorney and has effect subject to the terms of that instrument. It applies only to powers of attorney created after 1 March 2000.

Receipts for capital monies

18.15 The requirement for two persons or a trust corporation to give a valid receipt for capital monies is preserved by the *Trustee Delegation Act, s 7*. Where an attorney is acting either as both trustee and attorney for one or more other trustees, or as attorney for two or more trustees, and is not acting together with any other person or persons, that attorney cannot give a valid receipt for capital money and, in order for an interest or power to be overreached, execute a conveyance or deed, unless that attorney is a trust corporation within the meaning of the *Trustee Act 1925*. This provision applies whether a relevant attorney is acting under a power created before or after 1 March 2000, subject, in the case of an attorney acting under an enduring power created before that date, to the continuing application of the *Enduring Powers of Attorney Act 1985, s 3(3)* (which enabled an attorney acting under an enduring power without the concurrence of any other person to give a valid receipt for capital monies).

Delegation by the trustees as a body

18.16 *TA 2000, Pt IV* permits trustees as a body to authorise any person to exercise as their agent what are called in the Act 'delegable functions'. The definition of this term differs as between a private trust and a charitable trust; otherwise the provisions are common to both.

Sole trustees

18.17 *TA 2000, s 25* provides that the provisions of *Part IV* of the Act apply to a trust having a sole trustee.

Express provisions in the trust document

18.18 The powers conferred by *TA 2000* are in addition to powers conferred on trustees other than by the Act but subject to any restriction or exclusion imposed by the trust instrument or by any enactment or any provision of subordinate legislation. [*TA 2000, s 26*]. Trustee functions of the donor are functions which the donor has as trustee, either alone or jointly with any other person or persons. *Subsection (1)* applies only if and so far as a contrary intention is not expressed in the instrument creating the power of attorney, and has effect subject to the terms of that instrument. [*TA 2000, s 1(3)*].

Delegable functions

Non-charitable trust

18.19 In the case of a private trust, delegable functions consist of any function other than:

(*a*) any functions relating to whether, or in what way, any assets of the trust should be distributed;

(*b*) any power to decide whether any fees or other payment due to be made out of the trust funds should be made out of income or capital;

(*c*) any power to appoint a person to be a trustee of the trust; or

(*d*) any power conferred by any enactment, or the trust instrument, which permits the trustees to delegate any of their functions or to appoint a person to act as a nominee or custodian.

[*TA 2000, s 11(2)*].

In the case of a private trust, therefore, the statutory approach is that any function is capable of delegation other than those specifically excluded. The exclusions in paragraphs (*a*) and (*b*) above relate to matters which bear directly on the interests of the beneficiaries of the trusts. The exclusion in paragraph (*c*) bears directly on the selection of new trustees who will bear future responsibility for the conduct of the trust including, of course, any decision whether any function should remain delegated, or be delegated to a particular person or company. The exclusion in paragraph (*d*) prohibits delegation of the power to delegate. Consistent with this is the restriction on delegating on terms which permit the appointment of a substitute (see 18.28 below).

In the case of settled land, the power to employ agents (but not nominees or custodians) applies to the tenant for life as it applies to trustees. [*TA 2000, Sch 2, para 17*].

Charitable trust

18.20 In the case of a charitable trust, the trustees' delegable functions are:

(*a*) any function consisting of carrying out a decision that the trustees have taken;

(*b*) any function relating to the investment of assets subject to the trust (including, in the case of land held as an investment, managing the land and creating or disposing of an interest in the land);

(*c*) any function relating to the raising of funds for the trust otherwise than by means of profits of a trade which is an integral part of carrying out the trust's charitable purpose;

(*d*) any other function prescribed by order made by the Secretary of State.

[*TA 2000, s 11(3)*].

The approach in the case of a charitable trust is therefore the opposite of that for a private trust in that no function is delegable unless it is designated by the statute (or by statutory instrument) to be a delegable function.

Paragraph (*a*) above draws a distinction between making a decision, which is not delegable, and carrying out a decision, which is.

Paragraph (*b*) permits delegation of any function relating to investments including land; the power to create or dispose of an interest in land would appear to permit the delegation of matters such as creating and disposing of leases of land.

Paragraph (*c*) permits the delegation of fund raising but does not permit the delegation of the running of a business which is an integral part of the trust's charitable purpose. For the purpose of this section a trade is an integral part of carrying out a trust's charitable purpose if, whether carried on in the United Kingdom or elsewhere, the profits are applied solely to the purpose of the trust and either:

(i) the trade is exercised in the course of the carrying out of a primary purpose of the trust, or

(ii) the work in connection with the trade is mainly carried out by the beneficiaries of the trust.

[*TA 2000, s 11(3)*].

As to paragraph (*d*) above no statutory instrument has been made.

Duties or restrictions attached to the delegated function

18.21 A person who is authorised to exercise a delegable function is (whatever the terms of the agency) subject to any specific statutory duty or restriction attached to the function. The Act gives the example of a person who is authorised under *TA 2000, s 11* to exercise the general power of investment; that person is subject to the duties under *section 4* of the Act in relation to that power, i.e. a duty to have regard to the standard investment criteria and from time to time to review the investments of the trust and consider whether, having regard to the standard investment criteria, they should be varied.

If a delegable power is subject to a requirement to obtain advice, then the person to whom that function is delegated is subject to that requirement unless he is the kind of person from whom it would have been proper for the trustees, in compliance with the requirement, to obtain advice. Thus if a general power of investment is delegated to an investment adviser, the investment adviser is not under a duty to take advice from another investment adviser; however, if the same power is delegated to a person with no professional expertise in investment, the agent must take advice from an appropriate adviser before exercising the delegated powers.

Duty to consult beneficiaries

18.22 Where there is a duty to consult beneficiaries and give effect to their wishes pursuant to the *Trusts of Land and Appointment of Trustees Act 1996, s 11(1)* the trustees may not authorise an agent to exercise any of their functions on terms that prevent them (i.e. the trustees) from complying with *section 11(1)* of the Act. [*TA 2000, s 12(2)*]. It should be noted that a duty to consult is imposed not on the agent, but remains with the trustees; the onus is on the trustees when appointing an agent to preserve their (the trustees') duty to consult.

Who may act as agents?

18.23 Subject to the provisions of the Act, any person may act as an agent. [*TA 2000, s 11(1)*]. This includes any one or more of the trustees. [*TA 2000, s 12(1)*]. To give an example, if trustees comprise professional and non-professional persons, the trustees can delegate any delegable function to the professional trustee. It also includes a person who is appointed to act as the nominee or custodian for the trustee whether under the provisions of the 2000 Act or any other provision (the relevant provisions in *TA 2000* are *sections 16, 17* and *18*). Trustees may not authorise two or more persons to exercise the same function unless they are to exercise the function jointly. [*TA 2000,* s *12(2)*]. Trustees may not authorise a beneficiary to exercise any function as their agent even if the beneficiary is also a trustee. [*TA 2000, s 12(3)*].

Terms of agency

18.24 The terms of the agency are, subject to specific provisions of the Act, a matter for the trustees to determine. [*TA 2000, s 14*]. However, the trustees may not authorise a person to exercise functions as their agent on any of the following terms unless it is reasonably necessary for them to do so:

(*a*) a term permitting the agent to appoint a substitute;

(*b*) a term restricting the liability of the agent or his substitute to the trustees or any beneficiary;

(*c*) a term permitting the agent to act in circumstances capable of giving rise to a conflict of interest.

[*TA 2000, s 14(2), (3)*].

Asset management functions

18.25 *Section 15(5)* of *TA 2000* provides that the asset management functions of trustees are their functions relating to:

(*a*) the investment of assets subject to the trust;

(*b*) the acquisition of property which is to be subject to the trust; and

(*c*) managing property which is subject to the trust and disposing of, or creating or disposing of an interest in, such property.

Need for writing

18.26 The agreement authorising a person to exercise any of the trustees' asset management functions as their agent must be in, or evidenced in, writing. [*TA 2000, s 15(1)*].

Policy statement

18.27 Trustees may not authorise a person to exercise any of their asset management functions as their agent unless:

(a) they have prepared a statement that gives guidance as to how the functions should be exercised (a policy statement); and

(b) the agreement under which the agent is to act includes a term to the effect that he will secure compliance with:

  (i) the policy statement; or

  (ii) if the policy statement is revised or replaced under *section 22*, the revised or replacement policy statement.

The trustees must formulate any guidance given in the policy statement with a view to ensuring that the functions will be exercised in the best interests of the trust. [*TA 2000, s 15(3)*].

The trustees duty to keep under review the arrangements under which an agent acts includes, in particular, duties to consider whether there is a need to revise or replace the policy statement (and, if there is, to do so) and whether the policy statement is being complied with (see 18.34 below).

Nominees and custodians

Nominees

18.28 *Section 16* of the Act enables the trustees to appoint a person to act as their nominee in relation to such of the assets of the trust as they determine (other than settled land) and to vest those assets in the person so appointed. [*TA 2000, s 16(1)*]. An appointment must be in, or evidenced in, writing. [*TA 2000, s 16(2)*]. The power, however, does not apply to any trust having a custodian trustee, or in relation to any assets vested in the Official Custodian for Charities. [*TA 2000, s 16(3)*]. In the case of settled land, it applies neither to the tenant for life (in whom, under the provisions of the *Settled Land Act 1925*, the settled land falls to be vested) nor to the trustees. (See the exception from *TA 2000, s 16(1).* Note also *section 16* is omitted from the list of sections applying to the tenant for life by *TA 2000, Sch 2, para 17.*)

Custodians

18.29 *Section 17* provides that trustees may appoint a person to act as their custodian in relation to such of the assets of the trust as they may determine. A custodian is defined as a person who undertakes the safe custody of the assets, or of any documents or records concerning the assets. [*TA 2000, s 17(1), (2)*]. An appointment must be in or evidenced in writing (*section 17(3)*). The power does not apply to any trust having a custodian trustee or in relation to any assets vested in the Official Custodian for Charities (*section 17(4)*). Seemingly, *section 17* is not extended to a tenant for life of settled land (although it does apply to the trustees), albeit that provisions of the *Settled Land Act 1925* envisage that the tenant for life will have custody of the title deeds (see the *Settled Land Act 1925, ss 24, 98* and *111*) and the title deeds to settled land are clearly within the ambit of the section, being 'documents or records concerning the assets'.

Bearer securities

18.30 If trustees, except for a sole trustee which is a trust corporation (*section 25(2)*), retain or invest in securities payable to bearer they must appoint a person to act as a custodian of the securities unless the trust instrument or any statutory provision otherwise permits. An appointment must be in, or evidenced in, writing (*section 18(3)*). The provision does not apply to any trust having a custodian trustee, or in relation to any assets vested in the Official Custodian for Charities. [*TA 2000, s 18(4)*].

Who may be appointed nominees or custodians?

18.31 A person may not be appointed a nominee or custodian unless:

(*a*) the person carries on a business which consists of or includes acting as a nominee or custodian;

(*b*) the person is a body corporate which is controlled by the trustees;

(*c*) the person is a body corporate recognised under the *Administration of Justice Act 1985, s 9* (incorporated solicitors practice).

The question of control of a body corporate is determined in accordance with the *Income and Corporation Taxes Act 1988, s 840* (see *TA 2000, s 19(3)*).

In the case of a charitable trust which is not an exempt charity (institutions which are exempt charities are listed in the *Charities Act 1993, Sch 2*), it must act in accordance with any guidance given by the Charity Commissioners concerning the selection of a person for nomination for appointment as a nominee or custodian. [*TA 2000, s 19(4)*].

Trustees as nominees or custodians

18.32 Persons whom trustees may appoint as a nominee or custodian include any one of their number, if that one is a trust corporation, or two or more of their number if they are to act as joint nominees or joint custodians (*section 19(5)*). The trustees may appoint the same person to act as a nominee and custodian and appoint a person to act as nominee or custodian who is also authorised to exercise functions as their agent. [*TA 2000, s 19(6), (7)*].

Terms of appointment

18.33 Trustees may not appoint a person to act as a nominee or custodian (including a custodian of bearer securities) on terms which include the following unless it is reasonably necessary for them to do so. The terms are:

(*a*) a term permitting the nominee or custodian to appoint a substitute;

(*b*) a term restricting the liability of the nominee or custodian, or his substitute, to the trustees or to any beneficiary;

(*c*) a term permitting the nominee or custodian to act in circumstances capable of giving rise to a conflict of interest.

[*TA 2000, s 20*].

Subject to that, and to the provisions relating to remuneration (*sections 29–32*), the trustees may appoint a person to act as a nominee or custodian on such terms as to remuneration and other matters as they may determine. [*TA 2000, s 20(1)*].

Review of agents, nominees and custodians

18.34 Subject to any other provision in the trust instrument, or any other statutory provision, while the agent, nominee or custodian continues to act for the trust, the trustees must:

(*a*) keep under review the arrangements under which the agent, nominee or custodian acts and how those arrangements have been put into effect;

(*b*) if circumstances make it appropriate to do so, consider whether there is a need to exercise any power of intervention that they have; and

(*c*) if they consider that there is a need to exercise such power, do so.

[*TA 2000, s 22*].

If the agent has been authorised to exercise asset management functions, duties thereunder include in particular:

(i) a duty to consider whether there is any need to revise or replace the policy statement made for the purposes of *section 15*;

(ii) if they consider that there is a need to revise or replace the policy statement, a duty to do so; and

(iii) a duty to assess whether the policy statement (as it has effect for the time being) is being complied with.

[*TA 2000, s 22(2)*].

A power of intervention includes a power to:

- give directions to the agent, nominee or custodian;
- revoke the authorisation or appointment.

[*TA 2000, s 22(4)*].

Liability for agents, nominees and custodians etc

18.35 A trustee is not liable for any act or default of the agent, nominee or custodian unless he has failed to comply with the duty of care applicable to him under *TA 2000, Sch 1, para 3* when:

(*a*) entering into the arrangement under which the person acts as agent, nominee or custodian; or

(*b*) carrying out his duties under *section 22* (i.e. the duties (i) to keep the arrangements – and how they are being put into effect – under review and, in particular, to assess whether the policy statement is being complied with and to consider whether there is any need to revise or replace it (and to revise or replace it if he thinks it necessary), (ii) to consider whether there is a need to exercise any power of intervention, and (iii) if necessary, to intervene).

If a trustee has agreed a term under which the agent, nominee or custodian is permitted to appoint a substitute, the trustee is not liable for any act or default of the substitute, unless he has failed to comply with the duty of care applicable to him under *TA 2000, Sch 1, para 3* when:

(i) agreeing that term; or

(ii) carrying out his duties under *section 22* so far as they relate to the use of the substitute.

The duty of care is the statutory duty of care set out in the *Trustee Act 2000, s 1*, i.e. a duty to exercise such skill and care as is reasonable in the circumstances, having regard in particular:

- to any special knowledge or experience that the trustee has, or holds himself out as having; and
- if he acts as a trustee in the course of a business or profession, to any special knowledge or experience that it is reasonable to expect of a person acting in the course of that kind of business or profession.

When entering into arrangements under which a person is authorised to exercise functions as an agent, the duty of care applies in particular to:

- selecting the person who is to act;
- determining any terms on which he is to act; and
- if the person is being authorised to exercise asset management functions, the preparation of a policy statement under *section 15*.

If a trustee has agreed a term under which the agent, nominee or custodian is permitted to appoint a substitute, the trustee is not liable for any act or default of the substitute unless he has failed to comply with the duty of care applicable to him when agreeing that term, or when carrying out his duties of review in so far as they relate to the use of the substitute. [*TA 2000, s 23(2)*].

The absolving of a trustee from liability in respect of the acts or defaults of an agent, nominee or custodian, or a substitute, does not of course relieve the trustee of the duty to bring proper proceedings against the agent, nominee, custodian or substitute, as the case may be, to recover any loss occasioned to the trust fund.

Trustees exceeding their powers

18.36 A failure by the trustees to act within the limits of the powers conferred by *TA 2000, Pt IV* in authorising a person to exercise a function of theirs as an agent, or in appointing a person to act as a nominee or custodian, does not invalidate the authorisation or appointment. [*TA 2000, s 24*]. It would, however, expose the trustee to liability for breach of trust and the exoneration from liability given by *section 23* would not apply.

Delegation by power of attorney to the beneficiaries of a trust of land

18.37 Trustees of land may, by power of attorney, delegate to any beneficiary or beneficiaries (of full age and beneficially entitled to an interest in possession in land subject to the trust) any of their functions as trustees which relate to the land. This includes a person who has a beneficial interest in the proceeds of sale of land where (by way of exception to the *Trusts of Land and Appointment of Trustees Act 1996, s 31(1)*) the doctrine of conversion continues to operate. [*Trusts of Land and Appointment of Trustees Act 1996, s 9(1)*].

A third party dealing with a person to whom trustees have purported to delegate functions by power of attorney under the *Trusts of Land and Appointment of Trustees Act 1996, s 9(1)* are protected under *subsection (2)* in that the person to whom the functions have been delegated shall be presumed in favour of that other person to have been a person to whom the functions could be delegated, unless that other person has knowledge at the time of the transaction that he was not such a person. It is also provided that it shall be conclusively presumed in favour of any purchaser whose interest depends on the validity of that transaction that the other person dealt in good faith and did not have such knowledge if that other person makes a statutory declaration to that effect before or within three months after the completion of the purchase.

A power of attorney under *section 9(1)* shall be given by all the trustees jointly and (unless expressed to be irrevocable and to be given by way of security) may be revoked by any one or more of them; and such power is revoked by the appointment as a trustee of a person other than those by whom it is given (though not by any of those persons dying or otherwise ceasing to be a trustee) (*section 9(3)*).

Where a beneficiary to whom functions are delegated by a power of attorney under *section 9(1)* ceases to be a person beneficially entitled to an interest in possession in land subject to the trust if the functions are delegated:

(*a*) to him alone, the power is revoked;

(*b*) to him and to other beneficiaries to be exercised by them jointly (but not separately), the power is revoked if each of the other beneficiaries ceases to be so entitled (but otherwise functions exercisable in accordance with the power are so exercisable by the remaining beneficiary or beneficiaries); and

(*c*) to him and to other beneficiaries to be exercised by them separately (or either separately or jointly), the power is revoked in so far as it relates to him.

[*Trusts of Land and Appointment of Trustees Act 1996, s 9(4)*].

A delegation under *section 9(1)* may be for any period, or indefinite (*section 9(5)*).

A power of attorney under *section 9(1)* cannot be an enduring power within the meaning of the *Enduring Powers of Attorney Act 1985* (*section 9(6)*).

Beneficiaries to whom functions have been delegated under *section 9(1)* are, in relation to the exercise of the functions, in the same position as trustees (with the same duties and liabilities); but such beneficiaries shall not be regarded as trustees for any other purposes (including, in particular, for the purposes of any enactment permitting the delegation of functions by trustees or imposing requirements relating to the payment of capital money). [*Trusts of Land and Appointment of Trustees Act 1996, s 9(7)*].

The duty of care imposed by the *TA 2000, s 1* applies to trustees of land in deciding whether to delegate any of their functions under *section 9* (*section 9A* inserted by *TA 2000, Sch 2*).

If the trustees of land delegate any of their functions under *section 9*, and the delegation is not irrevocable, then, while the delegation continues, the trustees:

(i) must keep the delegation under review;

(ii) if circumstances make it appropriate to do so, must consider whether there is a need to exercise any power of intervention that they have; and

(iii) if they consider there is a need to exercise such a power, must do so.

[*Trusts of Land and Appointment of Trustees Act 1996, s 9A(2), (3)*].

A power of intervention includes a power to give directions to the beneficiary, and a power to revoke the delegation (*section 9A(4)*). The duty of care under *TA 2000, s 1* applies to trustees in carrying out any duty to keep the delegation under review, to consider whether there is a need to exercise any power of intervention, and, if there is such a need, to exercise that power of intervention (*section 9A(5)*). A trustee of land is not liable for any act or default of the beneficiary, or beneficiaries, unless the trustee fails to comply with the duty of care in deciding to delegate any of the trustee's functions under *section 9* or in carrying out any duty *under subsection (3)*. [*Trusts of Land and Appointment of Trustees Act 1996, s 9A(6)*].

Chapter 19

Power to Accumulate Income

Introduction

19.1 A trustee may accumulate income if authorised to do so by the trust instrument or by statute. At common law there was no limit on the period during which income might be accumulated, other than the general perpetuity period which limited the life of the trust itself. Thus in *Thellusson v Woodford (1805) 11 Ves 112*, the testator directed that income be accumulated during the lifetimes of his sons grandsons and great grandchildren living at his death, a direction which was held valid confined, as it was, to the common law perpetuity period. The *Accumulations Act 1800* was the first Act to place a greater restriction on the permitted period of accumulation and is commonly called the 'Thellusson Act'. The present restriction is to be found in the *Law of Property Act 1925, ss 164–166* (as amended). However, it should be noted that the restrictions in *section 164* do not apply to accumulations directed in trusts created by a company as opposed to an individual.

Statutory power to accumulate

19.2 The *Trustee Act 1925, s 31(2)* applies during the infancy of any person for whom property is held in trust for any interest whatsoever, whether vested or contingent. Subject to any prior interests or charges, trustees are directed to accumulate any income not applied for that person's maintenance education or benefit. The accumulation is to be effected by investing the income (and any income therefrom) in authorised investments.

When income has been accumulated and the time for distribution arrives the question arises who is entitled to the accumulations. This is also dealt with by *section 31(2)*.

If the person during whose infancy the income has been accumulated attains the age of 18 or marries under that age, he is entitled to the accumulated income if:

- his interest in income during infancy is a vested interest; or

- on attaining the age of 18 years or marrying under that age he becomes entitled to the property from which such income arose, if it is land in fee simple (absolute or determinable) if not land absolutely, or (in either case) for an entailed interest.

After marriage an infant can give a good receipt for that income although still an infant. Although in the case of land entitlement to a determinable fee is sufficient to entitle the person to the accumulated income, in the case of a trust fund other than land a vested interest capable of being defeated by the exercise of a power or condition subsequent does not satisfy the requirement that the person becomes entitled to the property 'absolutely' and the person during whose infancy the income has been accumulated is not entitled to the accumulated income (*Re Sharpe's Settlement [1973] Ch 331*). In that situation the accumulated income is added to the corpus of the fund; the different treatment of accumulated income in respect of a trust of land and a trust of personalty appears to be anomalous (*Re Sharpe's Settlement*).

In any other case the accumulations are held as an accretion to the capital of the property from which the income arose and in the case of settled land the accumulations are held as if they were capital money arising therefrom. If, therefore, an infant dies unmarried and under the age of 18 his estate is not entitled to the accumulations of income even though under the terms of the trust his interest in that income was vested. However, *section 31* is subject to any contrary provision in the trust instrument or appointment made thereunder and, therefore, gives way to an inconsistent provision (see *Re Delamere's Settlement [1984] 1 WLR 813*).

In the case of a trust for a class, although an addition to the class has no claim on income arising in the fund before his birth for the purpose of its application for his education, maintenance or benefit, he is entitled to share in any such income which has been accumulated and added to the capital of the fund (*Re Joel's Will Trusts [1967] Ch 14*).

Section 31 applies in the case of a contingent interest only if the limitation or trust carries the intermediate income of the property, which it will generally do unless the contrary intention appears (see *Law of Property Act 1925, s 175* extending the position at common law). However, where a gift is expressly deferred, the intermediate income will not be carried in the absence of words indicating the contrary (*Re Geering [1964] Ch 136* – where, in the event, the income fell to be accumulated under an express provision). In the case of a future or contingent legacy by a parent of, or person standing *in loco parentis* to, the legatee, such legacy carries interest from the date of death and *section 31* applies to such interest. (See generally *section 31(3)*.)

Section 31 applies to a vested annuity in the same manner as if the annuity were income arising from the property. Accumulations made during the infancy of the annuitant are held in trust for the annuitant or the personal representatives of the annuitant absolutely (*section 31(4)*).

Law of Property Act 1925, s 164

19.3 By *section 164* of *Law of Property Act 1925* (*LPA 1925*) the accumulation of income is restricted to one of the following four periods:

(*a*) the life of the grantor or settlor; or

(*b*) the term of 21 years from the death of the grantor, settlor or testator; or

(*c*) the duration of the minority or respective minorities of any person or persons living or *en ventre sa mère* (conceived but unborn) at the death of the grantor, settlor or testator; or

(*d*) the duration of the minority or respective minorities only of any person or persons who under the limitations of the instrument directing the accumulations would, for the time being, if of full age, be entitled to the income directed to be accumulated.

Two further periods were added by the *Perpetuities and Accumulations Act 1964*:

- the term of 21 years from the making of the disposition; and
- the minority or respective minorities of any person in being at that date.

In every case where any accumulation is directed which would fall outside that period, then the direction, in so far as it exceeds one or other of the permitted periods, shall be void and the income of the property directed to be accumulated shall go to, and be received by, the person or persons who would have been entitled thereto if such accumulation had not been directed. If on a construction of the trust deed there is no beneficial interest capable of taking, then the income will be held on resulting trust.

Unborn children

19.4 *LPA 1925, s 164* permits accumulation during successive minorities and the minority or minorities of persons as yet unborn (*Re Cattell [1914] 1 Ch 177*). Thus, a settlement on grandchildren providing for the accumulation of income during the minority of any grandchildren is valid both in respect of grandchildren alive at the date of the settlement and also in respect of future born – see *Re Maber [1928] Ch 88* (in which Counsel in the course of argument demonstrated how an accumulation might continue for 63 years).

The statutory exceptions to *section 164* are as follows:

(*a*) the payment of debts of any grantor, settlor, testator or other person;

(*b*) raising portions for:

(i) any child, children or remoter issue of any grantor, settlor or testator; or

(ii) any child, children or remoter issue of any person taking any interest under any settlement or other disposition directing the accumulations or to whom any interest is thereby limited;

(*c*) respecting the accumulation of the produce of timber or wood.

In the case of the exceptions above the common law provision still applies, which is merely that the accumulation must be limited to the perpetuity period. A trust for accumulation (except to pay debts) which offends the rule against perpetuities is wholly void – *Southampton v Marquis of Hertford (1813) 2 Ves & B 54* and the 'wait and see' provisions of the *Perpetuities and Accumulations Act 1964, s 3*, under which it is possible to wait and see if a disposition is void for remoteness, would not appear to apply to a provision for accumulation. Accordingly a direction for accumulation which might offend the common law perpetuity period is wholly void, even if events have or might occur to prevent it doing so, whereas a provision for accumulation confined to the perpetuity period but for a period longer than that permitted by *section 164*, is void as to the excessive period only – *Leake v Robinson (1817) 2 Mer 363* (the rationale being that the Thellusson Act imposed a restriction on an antecedent liberty and thus it was only as to the excess that the statute was transgressed (see *page 389*)). In the case of a direction to accumulate for an excessive period, the most appropriate period is treated as applicable (*Re Ransome [1957] Ch 348 at 361*). Strictly speaking the test is which period the testator 'seemingly selected, determining that question according to the language employed and the facts of the case' (*Re Watt's Will Trusts [1936] 2 All ER 1555 at 1562* – but that test was described in *Ransome* as 'artificial and difficult').

An accumulation for the payment of debts is not commonly encountered; an old example is a direction to accumulate income for the payment of mortgage debts (*Bateman v Hotchkin (1847) 10 Beav 426*). The exception applies only to debts in existence as a legal liability (albeit contingent) when the instrument providing for accumulation took effect; it does not extend to liabilities which might arise in the future (*Re Rochford's Settlement [1965] Ch 111* – where a direction in effect to accumulate income to pay future liabilities to estate duty was held not within the exception). However, it seems that a trust to accumulate income to meet a claim for dilapidations at the end of a lease is within the exception (*Re Hurblatt [1910] 2 Ch 553*).

Other provisions not falling under section 164

19.5 Other provisions which might at first sight appear to be directions to accumulate but which have been held not to fall within *LPA 1925, s 164* are as follows:

- The payment of premiums in respect of a policy of insurance on a life out of the income of the residuary estate (*Bassil v Lister (1851) 9 Hare 177*).
- Unit trusts conducted under a trust deed which provide that the surplus income in any accounting period, over and above that available for distribution to unit holders, should be added to the capital and should thereupon cease to be available for distribution (*Re AEG Unit Trust (Managers) Ltd [1957] Ch 415*).
- The application of income for the upkeep of a house or other property; also outside the scope of the Act is a provision for the replacement of leaseholds as they expire. Similarly, it does not apply to a fund for the accumulation of income for the improvement of land or by the construction of buildings on it (*Vine v Raleigh [1891] 2 Ch 13*; *Re Gardiner [1901] 1 Ch 697*).
- The retention of income of a will trust to satisfy future payments of an annuity bequeathed by the will (*Re Berkeley [1968] Ch 744*).

By *section 165*, where accumulations of surplus income are made during a minority under any statutory power or under the general law, then the period for which such accumulations are made is not to be taken into account in determining the periods for which accumulations are permitted to be made under *section 164*. The *Trustee Act 1925, s 31* provides that income not applied for the maintenance, education or benefit of an infant beneficiary shall be accumulated and that period is ignored when determining whether an express direction for accumulation of income is or is not valid within the provisions of *section 164*.

Accumulation for the purchase of land

19.6 *LPA 1925, s 166* sets out a specific restriction on accumulation for the purchase of land. No person may settle, or dispose of, any property in such manner that the income thereof shall be wholly or partly accumulated for the purchase of land only, for any longer period than the duration of the minority or respective minorities of any person or persons who, under the limitations of the instrument directing the accumulation, would for the time being, if of full age, be entitled to the income so directed to be accumulated. This restriction is limited to a direction to accumulate income for the purchase of land only and not where the direction is to apply accumulated income to other modes of application (*Re Knapp [1929] 1 Ch 341*).

Section 166 does not apply to accumulations to be held as capital money for the purposes of the *Settled Land Act 1925* whether or not the accumulations are primarily laid out in the purchase of land. [*LPA 1925, s 166(2)*].

Company settlors

19.7 Where the settlor is a company then the provisions of *LPA 1925, s 164* do not apply. In *Re Dodwell & Co's Trust [1979] Ch 301*, a company gave certain monies to trustees to apply in the purchase of shares in the capital of the company and to pay the dividends on such trust shares to certain of the company's employees at the discretion of the Board. By clause 3, the trustees were empowered to accumulate dividends and apply them in the purchase of further shares which should then form part of the trust holding. The duration of the trust was limited within the perpetuity period. It was held that the company (which was, of course, the settlor) was not a 'person' within the meaning of *section 164(1)*, that section referring only to individuals and not to bodies corporate. Therefore, the shares purchased with the accumulated dividends formed part of the capital of the trust and not income to be distributed among the beneficiaries.

Right of beneficiaries to stop accumulations

19.8 Persons who are between them absolutely entitled to the trust fund may stop accumulation under the principle in *Saunders v Vautier (1841) Cr & Ph 240*. The possibility, however remote, of an addition to the class by the birth of further children may stop *Saunders v Vautier* applying. The *Perpetuities and Accumulations Act 1964, s 14* ameliorates this unsatisfactory position by applying the provisions of *section 2* of that Act which sets out presumptions and provides for evidence in respect of the ability of a person to have a child which applies in respect of a question relating to perpetuities.

By *section 2*, in the case of a living person, evidence may be given to show that he or she will not be able to have a child at the time in question. Subject to that it shall be presumed that a male can have a child at the age of 14 years and over, but not under that age and that a female can have a child at the age of 12 years or over, but not under that age or over the age of 55 years. References to having a child include the possibility of having a child by adoption, legitimation or (as the statute has it) 'other means'. Once the question is decided, it applies in relation to the same disposition in any subsequent proceedings. If a person is held unable to have a child at a particular time and the person does have a child, then by *section 2(2)* the High Court may make such order as it thinks fit for placing the persons interested in the property comprised in the disposition, so far as may be just, in the position they would have held had the question not been so decided.

The *Human Fertilisation and Embryology Act 1990, ss 27–30* makes comprehensive provision for the determination of who is to be treated as the mother and father respectively of a child conceived by artificial insemination (see CHAPTER 23: CONSTRUCTION OF DISPOSITIVE POWERS).

Charities

19.9 The rule against accumulation applies as much to a charitable trust as to a private trust. However, if the trusts of a charitable fund provided for excessive accumulation, then, in principle, a scheme could be settled by the court or the Charity Commissioners for the application of the surplus income (see, for example, *Re Bradwell [1952] Ch 575*).

Pension funds

19.10 Unit trusts are not subject to the restrictions on accumulation imposed by *LPA 1925, s 164* (*Re AEG Unit Trust (Managers) Ltd [1957] Ch 415*). The opening words of *section 164,* 'No person may by instrument or otherwise settle or dispose of any property in such manner that …' govern the ambit of its application. An investor purchasing units in a unit trust does not 'settle or dispose of property' within the ambit of those words. Nor is a unit trust within the mischief sought to be addressed by the section.

Chapter 20

Powers of Appointment and Retirement

Number of trustees

Maximum number

20.1 In the case of a trust of land or the proceeds of the sale of land or a settlement which remains a strict settlement subject to the *Settled Land Act 1925*, the maximum number of trustees is four. [*Trustee Act 1925, s 34(1)*]. There is no maximum number in the case of a trust of pure personalty.

The limit on the number of trustees does not apply in the case of land or the proceeds of the sale of land held for charitable, ecclesiastical or public purposes. The section also exempts from the maximum limit trusts of a term of years absolute limited by a settlement on trusts for raising money or of a like term created under the statutory remedies relating to annual sums charged on land set out in the *Law of Property Act 1925, s 121*.

Providing the maximum permitted number of trustees is not exceeded, a power of appointment express or statutory may be used to increase the number of trustees. [*Trustee Act 1925, s 37(1)*]. No power to appoint new trustees authorises an appointment in excess of the maximum number.

Unless the trust instrument states otherwise, there is no obligation to fill a vacancy providing there remain the minimum number of trustees.

Minimum number

20.2 Notwithstanding anything to the contrary in the trust instrument, a single trustee other than a trust corporation cannot give a good receipt for proceeds of sale or other capital monies arising from a trust of land or capital money arising under the *Settled Land Act 1925*. [*Law of Property Act 1925, s 27(2)*; *Settled Land Act 1925, ss 18(1), 94*; *Trustee Act 1925, ss 14, 37*].

In practical terms, therefore, save in the case of a trust of pure personalty, the minimum number of trustees is two unless the sole trustee is a trust corporation. This contrasts with the position of a single personal representative who during the administration of the estate can give a good receipt.

A trust corporation is defined in *section 68(18)* of the *Trustee Act 1925* (*TA 1925*) as:

> 'the Public Trustee or a corporation either appointed by the court in any particular case to be a trustee, or entitled by rules made under subsection (*3*) of section 4 of the Public Trustee Act 1906 to act as custodian trustee'.

Similar definitions appear in the *Law of Property Act 1925, s 205*; the *Settled Land Act 1925, s 117(1)(xxx)*; the *Administration of Estates Act 1925, s 55(1)* and the *Supreme Court Act 1981, s 128(1)*.

It is not obligatory to appoint more that one new trustee when only one trustee was originally appointed or to fill up the original number where more than two were originally appointed. However, a trustee will not be discharged from his trust unless there will be either a trust corporation or at least two persons to act as trustees to perform the trust (*TA 1925, s 1(c)* as amended by the *Trusts of Land and Appointment of Trustees Act 1996*) except in the case where only one trustee was originally appointed and a sole trustee when appointed will be able to give a valid receipt for all capital money (e.g. a trust of pure personalty). The 1996 Act substituted the word 'persons' for 'individuals'; a person includes a company, so a company (not a trust corporation) may act as a trustee together with at least one other company or individual.

Separate trustees

20.3 A separate set of trustees not exceeding four may be appointed for any part of the trust property held on trusts distinct from those relating to any other part or parts of the trust property notwithstanding that no other new trustee or trustees is or are to be appointed for other parts of the trust property. [*TA 1925, s 37(1)(b)*].

Retirement without replacement

20.4 A trustee may retire without being replaced providing that his co-trustees consent and after his retirement there will be at least two persons to act as trustees or a trust corporation. [*TA 1925, s 39*]. The retirement is effected by a deed. The retiring trustee and the continuing trustees must take all necessary steps to vest the property in the names of the continuing trustees. A deed of retirement may contain a vesting declaration in respect of such property for which a vesting declaration is appropriate (see 20.27 below).

Appointment of additional or replacement trustees

Appointment out of court

20.5 *Section 36* of the *Trustee Act 1925* provides:

> 'Where a trustee, either original or substituted, and whether appointed by the court or otherwise, is dead, or remains out of the United Kingdom for more than twelve months, or desires to be discharged from all or any of the trusts or powers reposed in or conferred on him, or refuses or is unfit to act therein, or is incapable of acting therein, or is an infant, then, subject to the restrictions imposed by this Act on the number of trustees,—
>
> (*a*) the person or persons nominated for the purpose of appointing new trustees by the instrument, if any, creating the trust; or
>
> (*b*) if there is no such person, or no such person able and willing to act, then the surviving or continuing trustees or trustee for the time being, or the personal representatives of the last surviving or continuing trustee;
>
> may, by writing, appoint one or more other persons (whether or not being the persons exercising the power) to be a trustee or trustees in the place of the trustee so deceased, remaining out of the United Kingdom, desiring to be discharged, refusing, or being unfit or incapable, or being an infant, as aforesaid'.

Dead trustee

20.6 An appointment out of court can be made not only where a trustee has died during the life of a trust but, in the case of a will trust, where a person nominated in the will to act as a trustee has predeceased the testator.

Trustee remaining outside the UK

20.7 Such a trustee may be removed against his will (*Re Stoneham Settlement Trusts, Popkiss v Stoneham [1953] Ch 59*). However, the power to remove a trustee who remains outside the UK does not imply any legal bar to such a person remaining a trustee or being appointed a trustee in a proper case (*Re Whitehead's Will Trusts [1971] 1 WLR 833*). Observations were made in that case (at *page 837*) that an appointment of a foreign resident would not be proper save in exceptional circumstances but such observations may well now be out of date and it is unlikely that a court would interfere with such an appointment unless so inappropriate that no reasonable trustee could entertain it.

Unfit to act

20.8 A trustee who is adjudicated bankrupt will generally be regarded as unfit to act (*Re Barker's Trusts (1875) 1 Ch D 43*). Conviction of a criminal offence involving dishonesty or which is otherwise serious would be regarded as rendering a trustee unfit. A trustee guilty of defalcations is unfit to act (*Re Sichel's Settlements [1916] 1 Ch 358*). However, if such a trustee is unwilling to retire voluntarily the better course may well be to seek his removal or replacement by the court under *TA 1925, s 41* rather than out of court under *section 36*.

Incapable of acting – mental disorder

20.9 Where a trustee is incapable, by reason of mental disorder within the meaning of the *Mental Health Act 1983, s 1* and does not have a beneficial interest under the trust, that trustee can be replaced under *TA 1925, s 36*. However, if such trustee is also entitled in possession to a beneficial interest in the trust property, no appointment of a trustee in his place shall be made by the surviving or continuing trustees or the personal representative of the last surviving trustee unless leave to make the appointment has been given by the Court of Protection. [*TA 1925, s 36(9)*]. It should be noted, however, that this restriction does not apply to appointments made by a person nominated by the trust instrument for the purpose of appointing new trustees.

An attorney acting under an enduring power of attorney granted by a trustee or trustees, which has been registered under the *Enduring Powers of Attorney Act 1985, s 6*, who intends to exercise any function of the trustee or trustees by virtue of the *Trustee Delegation Act 1999, s 1(1)*, or intends to exercise any function of the trustee or trustees in relation to any land, capital proceeds of a conveyance of land or income from land by virtue of the delegation to him under *TA 1925, s 25* (as substituted by the *Trustee Delegation Act 1999*) or the instrument (if any) creating the trust, may make an appointment of an additional trustee or trustees on behalf of the trustee or trustees provided certain conditions are satisfied. Those conditions are:

- a contrary intention is not expressed either in the power of attorney or the trust instrument; and
- that he is either:
  - (*a*) both a trustee and attorney for the other trustee or both the other trustees (if two others) under a registered power; or
  - (*b*) attorney under a registered power for the trustee (if one) or for both or each of the trustees (if two or three).

The power does, therefore, not apply if there is another trustee in addition to the grantor or grantee of the power. In that event there is no necessity to appoint an additional trustee in order that the delegated functions can be exercised (see generally *TA 1925, s 36(6A)–(6D)*).

Other instances of incapability

20.10 A trustee unable to attend to business as a consequence of severe illness or disability may be incapable of acting (*Re Barber (1888) 39 Ch D 187*). An enemy alien, being unable to sue, is incapable of acting as a trustee (*Re Sichel's Settlements [1916] 1 Ch 358*).

A corporation which is being, or has been, dissolved is deemed incapable of acting as trustee. [*TA 1925, s 36(3)*].

Appointment by the person nominated by trust instrument

20.11 It is clear from the wording of *TA 1925, s 36* that the person or persons exercising a power of appointment may appoint themselves to be a replacement trustee (unless the trust instrument states otherwise). However, such person cannot appoint himself to be an additional trustee (*Re Power's Settlement Trusts [1951] Ch 1074*). A person nominated to appoint new trustees cannot be compelled to exercise the power. A power given to two or more persons must, unless the trust deed states otherwise, be exercised jointly by all the persons nominated or, if any have died, by the survivor or survivors. If the power to appoint is a power to appoint on a particular event then the nominee is not empowered to appoint on any other event and the appointment should be by the continuing trustees (*Re Wheeler and De Rochow [1896] 1 Ch 315*).

It seems that an infant can validly exercise a power of appointment but the appointment is liable to be set aside if it is imprudent or prejudicial to his interests (*Re Parsons [1940] Ch 973*).

Person nominated suffering from mental disorder

20.12 The Court of Protection has power to exercise the functions of the patient in the administration of a trust including the power to appoint a new trustee. [*Mental Health Act 1983, s 96(1)(k)*]. If the patient does not have a beneficial interest in the trust then, if the trust instrument so permits, the remaining trustees may make the appointment or an application may be made to the Chancery Division.

Appointment by the continuing or surviving trustees or the personal representative of the last survivor

20.13 A refusing or retiring trustee, if willing to do so, should join in the appointment of a new trustee (*TA 1925, s 38(8)*) but it is not essential for him to do so (*Re Norris, Allen v Norris (1884) 27 Ch D 333*). A sole or last surviving executor intending to renounce or all the executors if they intend to renounce, at any time before renouncing, may (but are not obliged to) exercise their power to appoint a new trustee or trustees without thereby accepting the office of executor (*section 36(5)*). However, where a grant of probate or letters of administration has been granted, the power of appointment is exercisable by the proving executor or administrator to the exclusion of an executor who has renounced or does not prove (*section 6(4)*). Personal representative includes an executor by representation (*section 68*). A surviving or continuing trustee cannot appoint his successor by will – the appointment must be made during his life (*Re Parker's Trusts [1894] 1 Ch 707*).

Increasing the number of trustees

20.14 *TA 1925, s 36* confers a power to appoint (up to the maximum number) an additional trustee or trustees. A person nominated by the trust instrument to appoint a new trustee cannot (unless the trust instrument provides) appoint himself to be an additional (as opposed to a replacement) trustee (*Re Power's Settlement Trusts [1951] Ch 1074*). *Section 36* does not permit the replacement of two trustees by one; if a reduction in the number of trustees is to be made, those who are not replaced must retire under *section 39*, the requirements of which must be satisfied (*Adam & Co International Trustees Ltd v Theodore Goddard (a firm) [2000] WTLR 349*).

Power to act

20.15 The authority of a trustee appointed under *TA 1925, s 36* speaks from the moment of his appointment and he has the same powers, authorities and discretions as any other trustee whether or not the trust property has yet been vested in him. [*TA 1925, s 36(7)*].

Delegation of the power to appoint a trustee

20.16 The appointment of a new trustee is not a delegable function, so the trustees as a body may not delegate the power to any other person to exercise on their behalf. [*Trustee Act 2000, s 11*]. However, a person appointed to act on behalf of a trustee by a power of appointment under *TA 1925, s 25* can join in the exercise of an appointment of a new trustee, just as he can exercise any other power or discretion vested in the grantor as trustee. Similarly, a donee of a power of attorney granted by a person with a beneficial interest in land or the capital proceeds of land or income from land can exercise any of the donor's powers in relation thereto, which would appear to include the appointment of a new trustee. [*Trustee Delegation Act 1999, s 1*].

Appointment by the court

Inherent power

20.17 The court has an inherent power to appoint a trustee but *TA 1925, s 41* is so widely drawn as in practical terms to render unnecessary any recourse to the inherent power.

Statutory power

20.18 By *TA 1925, s 41*, the court has a statutory power to appoint a new trustee or trustees whenever it is expedient to do so and it is inexpedient, difficult or impracticable to do so without the assistance of the court. *Section 41* does not give power to appoint an executor or administrator (but see below).

The jurisdiction under *section 41* is very wide. Just two examples of its use where there are administrative difficulties in the way of an appointment out of court are where:

- no original trustees were appointed (or those appointed disclaimed or were otherwise incapable of acting) and there was no effective power of appointment (*see Dodkin v Brunt (1868) LR 6 Eq 580* where the order was in fact made under the inherent jurisdiction and *Re Moore (1882) 21 Ch D 778*); and
- joint donees of a power of appointment were unable to agree (*Re Sheppard's Settlement Trusts [1888] WN 234*).

Section 41 is not confined to circumstances of administrative difficulty but empowers the court to remove a trustee against his will and appoint a new trustee in substitution for him (*Re Henderson [1940] Ch 764*). Where a trustee had committed a breach of trust at the instigation of a beneficiary and therefore had a right to impound the beneficial interest under *TA 1925, s 62*, the right to impound was not limited to the case where the trustee was an existing trustee and this was, therefore, not a ground for resisting replacement under *section 41* (*Re Pauling's Settlement Trusts (No 2), Younghusband v Coutts & Co [1963] Ch 576*).

Section 41 expressly empowers the court to make an order appointing a new trustee in substitution for a trustee who is incapable by reason of mental disorder within the meaning of the *Mental Health Act 1983* of exercising his functions as trustee or is bankrupt or is a corporation which is in liquidation or has been dissolved.

The county court has jurisdiction under *section 41* where the amount of value of the trust, estate or fund to be dealt with does not exceed the county court limit (currently £30,000, see *County Courts Act 1984, s 23*) – subject thereto, the court means the High Court (*TA 1925, s 63A*). In the case of trusts of a deed of arrangement within the meaning of the *Deed of Arrangements Act 1914* the power may be exercised either by the High Court or by the court having jurisdiction in bankruptcy in the district in which the debtor resided or carried on business at the date of execution of the deed. [*TA 1925, s 41(2)*].

An order under *section 41* does not operate as a discharge to any former or continuing trustee further or otherwise than an appointment under an express power would have operated; every trustee appointed by the court has the same powers, authorities and discretions and may in all respects act as if he had been originally appointed a trustee by the instrument, if any, creating the trust. [*TA 1925, s 41(3)*].

TA 1925, s 42 empowers the court, when it appoints a corporation other than the Public Trustee to be a trustee either solely or jointly with any other person, to authorise the corporation to charge such remuneration for its services as trustee as the court may think fit. However, unless the trust instrument otherwise provides, the more general provisions of *Part V* of the *Trustee Act 2000*, entitling a trust corporation or a trustee who is acting in a professional capacity to receive remuneration, will enable such a trustee appointed by the court to charge without the express authority of the court.

Appointment at the direction of the beneficiaries

No inherent power

20.19 Prior to the passing of the *Trusts of Land and Appointment of Trustees Act 1996*, the beneficiaries, even if between them they were entitled to bring the trust to an end under the principle of *Saunders v Vautier (1841) 4 Beav 115*, had no power to appoint new trustees or to compel the retirement of any or all of the trustees; their only remedy was to apply to the court for an order under the court's inherent or statutory power (*Re Brockbank [1948] Ch 206*).

Statutory power

20.20 By the *Trusts of Land and Appointment of Trustees Act 1996, s 19*, the beneficiaries may give a direction or directions of either or both of the following descriptions:

(*a*) a written direction to a trustee or trustees to retire from the trust; and

(*b*) a written direction to the trustees or a trustee for the time being (or if there are none to the personal representative of the last person who was a trustee) to appoint by writing to be a trustee or trustees the person or persons specified in the direction.

The statutory power does not create a new power of appointment, rather it enables the beneficiaries to direct the person who otherwise holds the power of appointment to exercise that power as directed by the beneficiaries. It follows that if the person holding the power of appointment cannot be found or refuses to act pursuant to the direction an application to the court must still be made. Similarly if the beneficiaries are not *ad idem* as to the identity of the person to be appointed no direction can be given under *section 19*.

The *Trusts of Land and Appointment of Trustees Act, s 19* only applies where:

(*a*) there is no person nominated for the purpose of appointing new trustees by the instrument (if any) creating the trust; and

(*b*) the beneficiaries under the trust are of full age and capacity and (taken together) are absolutely entitled to the property subject to the trust.

Therefore, if there are persons who take or might take (e.g. under a default provision) who are not of full age and capacity, *section 19* will not apply.

Excluding the statutory power

20.21 The provisions of the *Trusts of Land and Appointment of Trustees Act, s 19* may be excluded by express provision. In the case of a deed created after the commencement of the Act, the exclusion must be contained in the deed. In the case of a trust created before the commencement of the Act, it may be excluded by deed executed (where the trust was created by one person) by that person if he is of full capacity or (where a trust was created by more than one person) by such of the persons who created the trust as are alive and of full capacity. A deed executed for this purpose is irrevocable. A deed excluding the provisions of *section 19* does not affect anything done to comply with a direction under *section 19* before the deed was executed; however, a direction which has been given but not complied with before the deed was executed shall cease to have effect (see generally *Trusts of Land and Appointment of Trustees Act, s 21*).

Direction to retire

20.22 Where a trustee has been given a direction to retire from the trust then, if three conditions are satisfied, it is mandatory that he make a deed declaring his retirement and shall be deemed to have retired and be discharged from the trust. [*Trusts of Land and Appointment of Trustees Act, s 19(3)*]. If the conditions are not satisfied then the obligation to make a deed declaring his retirement does not arise. The three conditions are:

(*a*) that reasonable arrangements have been made for the protection of any rights of his in connection with the trust;

(*b*) that after he has retired there will be either a trust corporation or at least two persons to act as trustees to perform the trust; and

(*c*) either another person is to be appointed to be a new trustee on his retirement (whether in compliance with a direction under *section 2(b)* of the Act or otherwise) or the continuing trustees by deed consent to his retirement.

Where a trustee retires under *section 19(3)* he and the continuing trustees (together with any new trustee) shall (subject to arrangements for the protection of his rights) do anything necessary to vest the trust property in the continuing trustees or the continuing and new trustees.

Mental disorder

20.23 The *Trusts of Land and Appointment of Trustees Act 1996, s 20* also gives to the beneficiaries power to direct the appointment of a trustee or trustees in place of a trustee who is incapable by reason of mental disorder of exercising his functions as a trustee. As with *section 19*, the beneficiaries under the trust must be of full age and capacity and (taken together) be absolutely entitled to the property subject of the trust. It follows that *section 20* has no application if the mentally disordered trustee has a beneficial interest in the trust property. Such a trustee may be replaced under *TA 1925, s 25* or by the court under *TA 1925, s 41*.

The direction must be in writing and given to:

(*a*) a receiver of the trustee; or

(*b*) an attorney acting for him under the authority of a power of attorney created by an instrument which is registered under the *Enduring Powers of Attorney Act 1985, s 6*; or

(*c*) a person authorised for the purpose by the Court of Protection.

The provisions of *section 20* may be excluded by express provision in the trust instrument or in the case of a trust created before 1 January 1997 by separate deed executed by the creator (or, in the case of a trust created by more than one person, the creators or surviving creator) of the trust. [*Trusts of Land and Appointment of Trustees Act 1996, s 21(5)–(8)*].

Form of direction

20.24 A direction given under *section 19* or *section 20* may be given jointly by all the beneficiaries or, providing each specifies the appointment of the same person or persons, by each of them (solely or jointly with one or more) and may be withdrawn before it has been complied with. A direction must not contravene *TA 1925, s 35* or the *Law of Property Act*

1925, s 24(1) which requires that the same persons shall become trustees of a conveyance on trust for sale as become trustees of the settlement of the proceeds of sale. [*Trusts of Land and Appointment of Trustees Act 1996, s 21*].

The authority of a trustee appointed pursuant to a direction under *section 19* or *section 20* speaks from the moment of his appointment and he has the same powers authorities and discretions and may in all respects act as if he had been originally appointed a trustee by the instrument if any creating the trust. [*Trusts of Land and Appointment of Trustees Act 1996, s 21(3)* applying *TA 1925, s 36*]. This applies before as well as after all the trust property becomes vested in him.

Formalities

Retirement with no replacement

20.25 A retirement of a trustee without the appointment of a replacement must be by deed. [*TA 1925, s 39(1)*].

Additional trustee

20.26 An appointment of new trustees in addition to or in place of an existing trustee must be made in writing. It need not be made by deed. However, an appointment made by deed has the advantage that, subject to an express provision to the contrary, it will operate as if it contained a vesting declaration extending to all the estates, interests or rights with respect to which the declaration could have been made. [*TA 1925, s 40(1)*].

Vesting declaration

20.27 A vesting declaration operates without conveyance or assignment to vest in the continuing or new trustees the estate, interest or right to which the declaration relates. However, the following property cannot be transferred by a vesting declaration:

- mortgages (except land conveyed on trust to secure debentures or debenture stock);
- leases (including underlease or an agreement for a lease or underlease) containing a covenant condition or agreement against assignment or disposing of the land without licence or consent;
- stocks and shares.

These assets must be specifically transferred. In the case of a lease any necessary consent must be obtained first.

Appointment of trustees of land and trustees of proceeds of sale

20.28 Appointments of new trustees of land on the one hand and of the settlement of the proceeds of sale on the other hand, shall, subject to any order of the court, be effected by separate instrument. The reason is to keep the beneficial interests off the legal title. However, the appointment should be in such manner as to secure that the same persons shall become the trustees of land as become the trustees of the settlement of the proceeds of sale. [*TA 1925, s 35(1)* as amended].

Memorandum of current trustees

20.29 A memorandum of the persons who are, for the time being, the trustees of land, must be endorsed on or annexed to the conveyance. [*TA 1925, s 35(3)* as amended]. In the case of settlements which remain subject to the provisions of the *Settled Land Act 1925*, the memorandum should be endorsed on or annexed to the last or only principal vesting instrument.

Mental health

20.30 Where a trustee is incapable by reason of mental disorder within the meaning of the *Mental Health Act 1983, s 1* of exercising his functions as a trustee and is also entitled in possession to some beneficial interest in the trust property, no appointment of a new trustee in his place shall be made pursuant to the *TA 1925, s 36(1)(b)* (i.e. an appointment out of court), unless leave to make the appointment has been given by an authority having jurisdiction under *Part VII* of the *Mental Health Act 1983*. [*TA 1925, s 36(9)*]. An application should be made to the Court of Protection by the person or persons who propose to make the appointment (*Court of Protection Rules 2001, r 16*). The patient must be served with notice of the application unless the court otherwise directs and, if the receiver is not the applicant, he should be given notice.

A fair copy of the proposed draft deed of appointment should be filed for the court to approve. Leave is given by way of certificate.

Providing the trust is not subject to an order for administration made by the High Court, the Court of Protection has concurrent jurisdiction with the High Court to appoint a new trustee in relation to:

(*a*) mortgaged property of which the patient has become trustee merely by reason of the mortgage having been paid off;

(*b*) any provision made by the Court of Protection for the exercise of a power of appointing trustees or retiring from a trust;

(*c*) any provision made by the Court of Protection for the carrying out of any contract entered into by the patient;

(*d*) any property or interest in property to which the patient is beneficially entitled but which is held by the patient under an express, implied or constructive trust.

Of these four situations, the most common is (*d*) above, i.e. where the patient has a beneficial interest in the property. The Court of Protection may exercise its concurrent jurisdiction even though there are other persons beneficially interested who are not patients. However, if there is a substantial part of the trust property in which the patient has no interest, application should be made to the Chancery Division (*Re Jackson (1928)* unreported).

Vesting orders

20.31 *TA 1925, ss 44–56* set out the power of the court to make vesting orders in a variety of circumstances where the court's assistance is necessary to procure the vesting of land or other assets into the names of the person entitled thereto. The power of the court extends to all property in any part of Her Majesty's dominions except Scotland. [*TA 1925, s 56*].

In respect of land the power is exercisable:

- on the appointment of a new trustee either by the court or out of court under a statutory or express power;
- where a trustee is:
  - (*a*) under a disability; or
  - (*b*) out of the jurisdiction of the High Court; or
  - (*c*) cannot be found or being a trust corporation has been dissolved;
- when it is uncertain who was the survivor of two or more trustees jointly entitled to possession of any interest in land;
- where it is uncertain whether the last survivor of two or more trustees is living or dead;
- where there is no personal representative of a deceased trustee or where it is uncertain who is the personal representative of a deceased trustee;
- when a trustee, for a period of 28 days after being required to do so by a person entitled to require a conveyance of land or interest in land or a release of a contingent right therein, wilfully neglects or refuses to convey the land or interest or to release the right;
- where it appears to the court to be expedient.

A vesting order has the same effect as a proper conveyance of the land for such estate and interest as the court directs. [*TA 1925, s 49*].

In respect of stock and things in action the court has power to make an order vesting the right to transfer or call for a transfer of stock (including shares in ships registered under the Acts relating to merchant shipping) or to receive the dividends or income thereof, or to sue for or recover the thing in action in any of the following situations:

- on the appointment of a new trustee either by the court or out of court under a statutory or express power;
- where a trustee is
  - (*a*) under a disability; or
  - (*b*) out of the jurisdiction of the High Court; or
  - (*c*) cannot be found or being a trust corporation has been dissolved; or
  - (*d*) neglects or refuses to transfer stock or receive dividends or income thereof or to sue for or recover a thing in action according to the directions of the person absolutely entitled thereto for 28 days next after a request in writing has been made to him by the person so entitled; or
  - (*e*) neglects or refuses to transfer stock or receive dividends or income thereof or to sue for or recover a thing in action according to the directions of the person absolutely entitled thereto for 28 days next after an order of the court for that purpose has been served on him;
- when it is uncertain whether a trustee entitled alone or jointly with another person to stock or a thing in action is alive or dead;
- where stock is standing in the name of a deceased person whose personal representative is under a disability;
- where it appears to the court to be expedient.

[*TA 1925, s 51*].

Appointing a person to convey

20.32 As an alternative to a vesting order, the court may:

- in the case of land, an interest in land or release or disposal of a contingent right, appoint a person to convey the land or interest or release the contingent right [*TA 1925, s 50*]; or
- in the case of a transfer of stock or thing in action, make or join in the making of the transfer. The proper person to make or join in making a transfer of stock shall be some proper officer of the bank or the company or society whose stock is to be transferred. The order binds the Bank of England or relevant company and after notice in writing of an order it shall not be lawful for the Bank of England or company to transfer any stock or pay any dividends except in accordance with the order [*TA 1925, s 51*].

Property of an infant

20.33 Where an infant is beneficially entitled to any property the court may, with a view to the application of the capital or income thereof for the maintenance, education or benefit of the infant, make an order:

(*a*) appointing a person to convey such property; or

(*b*) in the case of stock, or thing in action, vesting in any person the right to transfer or call for the transfer of such stock, or to receive the dividends or income thereof, or to sue for and recover such thing in action, upon such terms as the court may think fit [*TA 1925, s 53*].

Conclusive evidence

20.34 A statement in an instrument appointing a new trustee to the effect:

- that a trustee has remained out of the United Kingdom for more than 12 months or refuses or is unfit to act, or is incapable of acting, or
- that he is not entitled to a beneficial interest in the trust property in possession,

shall, in favour of a purchaser of a legal estate, be conclusive evidence of the matter stated. Any appointment of a new trustee depending on that statement, and any vesting declaration express or implied, consequent on that appointment, shall be valid in favour of such a purchaser. [*TA 1925, s 38*].

Similarly where a vesting order is made as to any land founded on an allegation of any of the following matters, namely:

- the personal incapacity of a trustee or mortgagee,
- that a trustee or mortgagee or the personal representative of or other person deriving title under a trustee or mortgagee is out of the jurisdiction of the High Court or cannot be found, or being a corporation has been dissolved,
- that it is uncertain which of two or more trustees, or which of two or more persons interested in a mortgage, was the survivor,
- that it is uncertain whether the last trustee or the personal representative of or other person deriving title under a trustee or mortgagee, or the last surviving person interested in a mortgage is living or dead, or
- that any trustee or mortgagee has died intestate without leaving a person beneficially interested under the intestacy has died and it is

not known who is his personal representative or the person interested,

the fact that the order has been made shall be conclusive evidence of the matter so alleged in any court upon any question as to the validity of the order. [*TA 1925, s 55*]. The court may, however, direct a reconveyance or surrender or the payment of costs occasioned by any such order if improperly obtained.

Trust corporation

Meaning

20.35 A trust corporation means the Public Trustee or a corporation either appointed by the court in any particular case to be a trustee or entitled to act as a custodian trustee by the rules made under the *Public Trustee Act 1906, s 4(3)*. [*TA 1925, s 68(18)*; see also *Law of Property Act 1925, s 205(1)(xxviii)*; *Settled Land Act 1925, s 117(1)(xxx)* and *Administration of Estates Act 1925, s 55(1)(xxvi)*; *Supreme Court Act 1981, s 128(1)*].

Public Trustee

20.36 The Public Trustee is a corporation sole established by the *Public Trustee Act 1906* empowered to act in the administration of estates of small value, to act as custodial trustee or to act as an ordinary trustee or to be appointed a judicial trustee. It can act alone or jointly with another person or body of persons. Its fees are fixed pursuant to provisions in the statute. The Public Trustee is regulated by the *Public Trustee Rules 1912*.

The Public Trustee shall not accept any of the following:

- a trust which involves the management of or carrying on of any business (save as authorised by the rules);
- any trust under a deed of arrangement for the benefit of creditors nor the administration of an estate believed by the Public Trustee to be insolvent; or
- any trust for religious or charitable purposes.

[*Public Trustee Act 1906, s 2(4), (5)*].

Where the Public Trustee is appointed sole trustee it may act as such notwithstanding any requirement in the trust instrument as to the minimum number of trustees (*Re Duxbury's Settlement Trusts [1995] 1 WLR 425*).

Charities

20.37 An application for the appointment, replacement or removal of a trustee of a charitable trust constitutes 'charity proceedings' within the meaning of the *Charities Act 1993, s 33(8)* and cannot be entertained, or proceeded with, unless the taking of proceedings has been authorised by the Charity Commissioners. If authority has been applied for and refused, an application for permission may be made to the High Court (*section 33(5)*). However, no order is required for the taking of proceedings in a pending cause or matter. [*Charities Act 1993, s 33(4)*].

By *section 16* of the Act, the Commissioners have concurrent jurisdiction with the High Court for purposes including appointing, discharging or removing a charity trustee or trustees; the Charity Commission can also remove an officer or employee. The Commissioners also have concurrent jurisdiction and power for the purpose of vesting or transferring property or requiring or entitling any person to call for or make any transfer of property or any payment. *Sections 16(11)–(13)* make specific provisions with regard to appeals to the High Court from the exercise of the Commissioners of their jurisdiction under this section.

As the Commissioners are charged not, without special reason, to authorise the taking of charity proceedings, where in their opinion the case can be dealt with under the powers of the *Charities Act 1993*, the appointment, replacement or removal of a trustee in a plain case will normally be dealt with by the Commissioners. Conversely, it is expressly provided that the Commissioners should not exercise their jurisdiction in any case (not referred to them by order of the court) which the Commissioners may consider more fit to be adjudicated by the court; this may be by reason of its contentious character or because it involves a special question of law or fact or for other reason. [*Charities Act 1993, s 16(10)*]. The Commissioners do not have jurisdiction under *section 16* to try or determine the title at law or in equity to any property as between a charity or trustee for a charity and a person holding or claiming the property or an interest in it adversely to the charity, or to try or determine any question as to the existence or extent of any charge or trust. [*Charities Act 1993, s 16(3)*].

Save in the case of small charities (see 20.38 below) the Commissioners may only exercise their jurisdiction:

- on the application of the charity;
- on an order of the court under the *Charities Act 1993, s 33(2)* (i.e. directing a scheme);
- in the case of a charity other than an exempt charity, on the application of the Attorney-General (exempt charities are listed in the *Charities Act 1993, Sch 2*).

[*Charities Act 1993, s 16(4)*].

Because charity trustees may act by majority, the Commissioners' jurisdiction can be invoked by the charity acting on the vote of the majority of the trustees.

The Commissioners may, on the application of any charity trustee or trustee for a charity, exercise their jurisdiction under *section 16* for the purpose of discharging him from his trusteeship. [*Charities Act 1993, s 16(8)*].

Small charities

20.38 In the case of a charity which is not an exempt charity whose income from all sources does not exceed £500 a year, the Commissioners may exercise their jurisdiction on the application of:

- any one or more of the charity trustees;
- any person interested in the charity;
- any two or more inhabitants of the area of the charity if it is a local charity (local charities are dealt with in the *Charities Act 1993, ss 76–79*).

[*Charities Act 1993, s 16(5)*; exempt charities are listed in *Schedule 2* to the Act].

The Official Custodian for Charities is an officer of the Charity Commissioners and a corporation sole whose function is to act as a holding trustee. He performs his duties in accordance with the general or special directions given to him by the Commissioners (see generally *Charities Act 1993, s 2*).

Personal representatives

20.39 The power to appoint a new trustee does not permit the appointment of a new personal representative, i.e. an executor or administrator. If a sole surviving executor dies during the course of an administration the devolution of the power and responsibility for completing the administration depends upon whether the chain of representation is complete. The chain of representation is only complete if the deceased executor had by his will appointed an executor who takes probate; the chain will continue through any number of executors who die testate naming an executor who proves.

However, the chain is broken if the deceased executor dies intestate or without naming an executor or if the named executor does not prove the will; in that event then an application for a grant *de bonis non* must be made by the person or persons intending to complete the administration. There is also power to apply for the appointment of a judicial trustee or for the substitution or removal of a personal representative under the *Administration of Justice Act 1985, s 50*; however, these are matters beyond the scope of this book.

Where, under a will, property is left in trust and the original executors are named also as trustees, it is important to determine whether the administration has been concluded and they are holding the trust property in their capacity as trustees (in which case the powers and provisions relevant to trustees apply) or whether they are still holding as executors. In the case of land this change of capacity is marked by the executors assenting to the vesting of the land in themselves as trustees (*Re King's Will Trusts [1964] Ch 542*; *cf Re Edwards' Will Trusts [1982] Ch 30*).

Chapter 21

Taking Additional Administrative Powers or Surrendering or Releasing Powers

Taking additional administrative powers

Introduction

21.1 The trustees' powers are prescribed by the terms of the trust deed or by statute or the general law. If a trustee acts outside those powers then the trustee commits a breach of trust which, if it causes loss, can give rise to personal liability on the part of the trustee. The question whether a particular course of action is or is not authorised is, therefore, a matter of fundamental importance. The common law and previous statutory powers were subject to a number of restrictions not compatible with the efficient running of a modern trust, and so a well-drawn trust instrument usually conferred much wider administrative powers. Some trusts have gone further and incorporate a provision purporting to authorise the trustees by resolution to take powers in addition to those in the trust instrument, although quite how a court would regard a provision for self empowerment has yet to be seen. Less radical are provisions which enable a third party (e.g. the settlor, a beneficiary or, in the case of overseas trusts, the protector) to confer on trustees, or to consent to the trustees adopting, additional or wider powers.

The reforms brought about by the *Trusts of Land and Appointment of Trustees Act 1996*, the *Trustee Delegation Act 1999* and the *Trustee Act 2000* (*TA 2000*) have removed a number of restrictions on trustees' powers and so a trustee is now less likely to find that the available powers are inadequate for the proper running of the trust.

Consent of the beneficiaries

21.2 If there is an administrative step not authorised by the trust instrument or by statute, then, if all the beneficiaries who would be affected are of full age and capacity and agree, they may authorise the trustee to act. The beneficiaries, even if between them absolutely entitled to the trust funds, cannot compel a trustee against his wish to exercise an administrative power or discretion; in that situation their choice is:

- to accept the trustee's decision; or
- to put an end to the trust (*Stephenson v Barclays Bank Trust Company [1975] 1 WLR 882 at 889D*); or
- if the *Trusts of Land and Appointment of Trustees Act 1996, s 19* applies, to require the trustees to retire in favour of new trustees.

Right to confer administrative powers inherent in a power of appointment

21.3 If a trust deed confers a power of appointment over all or part of a trust fund, the power of appointment may authorise the donee of the power when exercising the power to confer on the trustees in respect of that part of the trust fund being appointed different or additional management powers from those contained in the trust deed (*Re Rank's Settlement [1979] 1 WLR 1242*). Whether or not a power of appointment does so authorise is a matter of construction.

Applications to the court

Power of the court

21.4 The court has an inherent jurisdiction to authorise acts of management or administration of the trust property if the same are not otherwise authorised and if the consent of the beneficiaries cannot be obtained. Recourse to the inherent jurisdiction is now rare, given the wide jurisdiction conferred by statute.

Court's jurisdiction under Trustee Act 1925, s 57

21.5 Where in the management or administration of any property vested in trustees, any sale, lease, mortgage, surrender, release or other disposition, or any purchase, investment, acquisition, expenditure or other transaction, is in the opinion of the court expedient, but the same cannot be effected by reason of the absence of any power for that purpose vested in the trustees by the trust instrument, if any, or by law, the court may by order confer upon the trustees, either generally or in any particular instance, the necessary power for the purpose, on such terms, and subject to such provisions and conditions, if any, as the court may think fit and may direct in what manner any money authorised to be expended, and the costs of any transaction, are to be paid or borne as between capital and income.

The enlargement of administrative powers by statute has diminished the importance of *section 57*. If it is doubtful whether a transaction is authorised, then a trustee can seek the directions of the court as to whether he has power, and, in the alternative, for the exercise of the court's jurisdiction under *section 57*.

Settled land

21.6 The jurisdiction equivalent to *TA 2000, s 57* is conferred in respect of settled land by the *Settled Land Act 1925, s 64*. The court must be satisfied that the transaction will be for the benefit of the settled land or any part thereof, or the persons interested under the settlement.

Section 64 has been construed as authorising transactions which involve a variation of the beneficial trusts. For example, in *Hambro v Duke of Marlborough [1994] Ch 158*, the court authorised the transfer of settled land into another settlement under which the life tenant's elder son would take a protected life interest under a trust for sale. The consent of the ascertained adult beneficiaries was not regarded as a pre-requisite (as would have been the case if an application had been made under the *Variation of Trusts Act 1958*).

The *Settled Land Act, s 93* also provides for the reference of questions to the court. *Section 93* applies if a question or doubt is entertained:

- respecting the exercise or intended exercise of any of the powers conferred by the *Settled Land Act*, or the settlement or any matter relating thereto; or
- as to the person in whose favour a vesting deed or assent ought to be executed, or as to the contents thereof; or
- otherwise in relation to property subject to the settlement.

The application can be made by the tenant for life, the statutory owner or the trustees of the settlement, or any person interested under the settlement. The application may be to the court for its decision or directions or the sanction of any conditional contract. The court may make such order or give such directions respecting the matter as the court thinks fit. However, *section 93* does not empower the court to compel one of two life tenants of settled land to concur in a sale of the land at least in the absence of bad faith (*Re 90 Thornhill Road [1970] Ch 261*).

Paper applications to the court

21.7 The *Administration of Justice Act 1985, s 48* provides that where any question of construction arises out of the terms of a will or trust and an opinion in writing has been obtained from a person who has a ten-year High Court qualification on that question by the personal representatives or trustees under the will or trust, the High Court may, on the application of the personal representatives or trustees and without hearing argument, make an order authorising those persons to take such steps in reliance on the said opinion as are specified in the order. The application proceeds as a purely paper application. The reference to a person who has a ten-year High Court qualification means a person who has a right of audience in relation to all proceedings in the High Court and has had that right for at least ten years (not necessarily continuous). [*Courts and Legal Services Act 1990, s 71*].

The section provides that the court shall not make an order it if appears that a dispute exists which would make it inappropriate for the court to make an order without hearing argument.

Procedure

21.8 The procedure for paper applications is set out in the Chancery Guide paragraphs 26.36 to 41 and is as follows.

1. The application should be made by Part 8 Claim Form without naming a defendant, under rule 8.2A. No separate application for permission under rule 8.2A need be made. The claim should be supported by a witness statement or affidavit to which are exhibited:

   (*a*) copies of all relevant documents;

   (*b*) instructions to a person with a ten-year High Court qualification within the meaning of the *Courts and Legal Services Act 1990* ('the qualified person');

   (*c*) the qualified person's opinion; and

   (*d*) draft terms of the desired order.

2. The witness statement or affidavit (or exhibits thereto) should state:

   (*a*) the names of all persons who are, or may be, affected by the order sought;

   (*b*) all surrounding circumstances admissible and relevant in construing the document;

   (*c*) the date of qualification of the qualified person and his or her experience in the construction of trust documents;

   (*d*) the approximate value of the fund or property in question;

   (*e*) whether it is known to the applicant that a dispute exists, and, if so, details of such dispute.

3. When the file is placed before the Master, he considers whether the evidence is complete and, if it is, sends the file to the judge. The judge considers the papers and requests such further information as he or she may desire. If the judge is satisfied that the order sought is appropriate, the order will be made and sent to the claimant.

4. The judge may, if necessary, direct service of notices under CPR 19.8A. Rule 19.8A contains power to make a judgment binding on a non-party. The court may direct that a notice be served on a person

who is not a party but who will or may be affected by any judgment made in the claim. If, following service of a notice under rule 19.8A the party served files an acknowledgement of service he becomes a party; if he does not he will be bound by any judgment in the claim as if he were a party.

5. On a paper application, if a judge directs service of notice of proceedings and an acknowledgement of service is received, the claimant must apply to the Master on notice to the party who has so acknowledged service for directions. If the claimant is asked to pursue the application to the court, in the ordinary case the Master will direct the case proceeds as a Part 8 claim. If on hearing the claim the judge is of the opinion that any party who entered an acknowledgement of service has no reasonably tenable argument contrary to the qualified person's opinion, in the exercise of his or her discretion, he or she may order that such party pay any costs thrown away, or part thereof.

By thus spelling out the risk of an adverse costs order, the Guide discourages an unnecessary intervention by a person served with notice under rule 19.8A.

Charities

21.9 The Charity Commissioners have concurrent jurisdiction with the High Court in respect of charity matters.

The *Charities Act 1993, s 26* gives the Charity Commissioners power to authorise dealings with charity property. Where it appears to the Commissioners that any action proposed or contemplated in the administration of a charity is expedient in the interests of the charity, they may by order sanction that action, whether or not it would otherwise be within the powers exercisable by the charity trustees in the administration of the charity; and anything done under the authority of such an order shall be deemed to be properly done in the exercise of those powers.

An order under *section 26* may be made so as to authorise a particular transaction, compromise or the like, or a particular application of property, or so as to give a more general authority. It may authorise a charity to use common premises, or employ common staff, or otherwise combine for any purpose of administration, with any other charity.

An order under *section 26* may give directions as to the manner in which any expenditure is to be borne and to other matters connected with or arising out of the action thereby authorised; and where anything is done in pursuance of an authority given by such an order, any directions given in connection therewith shall be binding on the charity trustees for the time being as if contained in the trusts of the charity; but such directions may, on the application of the charity, be modified or superseded by a further order.

The directions which may be given by an order under *section 26* shall, in particular, include directions for meeting any expenditure out of a specified fund, for charging any expenditure to capital or to income, for requiring expenditure charged to capital to be recouped out of income within a specified period, for restricting the costs to be incurred at the expense of the charity, or for the investment of monies arising from any transaction.

The provisions of *section 26(5)–(7)* enable an order under *section 26* to override a prohibition in certain disabling Acts relating to ecclesiastical leases but not to confer any authority in relation to a building which has been consecrated and of which the use or disposal is regulated and can be further regulated by a scheme having effect under the *Union of Benefices Measures 1923–1952*, the *Reorganisation Areas Measures 1944* and *1954*, the *Pastoral Measure 1968*, or the *Pastoral Measure 1983*.

Power to authorise ex-gratia payments etc

21.10 Under the *Charities Act 1993, s 27* the Commissioners may by order exercise the same power as is exercisable by the Attorney-General to authorise the charity trustees of a charity:

(*a*) to make any application of property of the charity; or

(*b*) to waive to any extent, on behalf of the charity, its entitlement to receive any property in a case where the charity trustees:

  (i) otherwise have no power to do so; but

  (ii) in all the circumstances regard themselves as being under a moral obligation to do so.

The power conferred on the Commissioners is exercisable by them under the supervision of and in accordance with such directions as may be given by the Attorney-General and any such directions may, in particular, require the Commissioners in such circumstances as are specified in the directions:

- to refrain from exercising that power; or
- to consult the Attorney-General before exercising it.

The Commissioners can, in any event, refer an application to the Attorney-General if they consider it would be desirable for the application to be entertained by the Attorney-General rather than by the Commissioners. If the Commissioners determine an application by refusing to authorise charity trustees to take any action, that refusal shall not preclude the Attorney-General on an application subsequently made to him by the trustees, from authorising the trustees to take that action.

Dormant bank accounts of charities

21.11 The *Charities Act 1993, s 28* gives the Commissioners powers to give directions to the Bank of England and certain other specified institutions, including banks and building societies, in respect of dormant bank accounts where the institution is unable, after making reasonable enquiries, to locate the charity or any of its trustees.

Power to advise

21.12 The Commissioners may on the written application of any charity trustee give him their opinion or advice on any matter affecting the performance of his duties as such. A charity trustee acting in accordance with the opinion or advice of the Commissioners given under the *Charities Act 1993, s 29(1)* with respect to the charity shall be deemed, as regards his responsibility for so acting, to have acted in accordance with his trust unless when he does so either:

- he knows or has reasonable cause to suspect that the opinion or advice was given in ignorance of material facts, or
- the decision of the court has been obtained on the matter or proceedings are pending to obtain one.

The Commissioners have power to order a solicitor's bill of costs for business done for a charity or for charity trustees or trustees for a charity to be subject to detailed assessment by a costs judge of the High Court (*Charities Act 1993, s 31*). No order under that section shall be made after payment of the bill unless the Commissioners are of the opinion that it contains exorbitant charges. No order shall be made in a case where the solicitor's costs are not subject to assessment on an order of the High Court by reason either of an agreement as to the solicitor's remuneration or the lapse of time since payment of the bill.

Schemes

21.13 Under the *Charities Act 1993, s 16* the court has concurrent jurisdiction with the High Court for certain purposes. Included in those purposes is the establishment of a scheme for the administration of a charity. Furthermore, where the court directs a scheme for the administration of a charity to be established, the court may by order refer the matter to the Commissioners for them to prepare or settle a scheme in accordance with such directions (if any) as the court sees fit to give, and any such order may provide for the scheme to be put into effect by order of the Commissioners without further order of the court. The Commissioners do not have jurisdiction under *section 16* to try or determine the title at law or in equity to any property as between the charity or a trustee for a charity and a person holding or claiming the property or an interest in it adversely to the charity, or to try or determine any question as to the existence or extent of any charge or trust. *Section 16* sets out who may make an application for a scheme and includes provisions for appeal.

Section 17 of the Act applies where it is necessary or desirable for a scheme to alter the provisions made by Act of Parliament establishing or regulating the charity, or that it is for any reason proper for the scheme to be subject to parliamentary review. Reference may be made to the section for the detail of those provisions.

Payment of trust monies into court

21.14 The *Trustee Act 1925, s 63* enables trustees, or the majority of trustees, to pay trust monies or securities into court. However, payment into court is now rarely justified as there is usually a better way to deal with the problem. In particular, where there is a real doubt as to the person entitled or conflicting claims (both situations where old authority can be found where payment into court was permitted) the better course would be to issue an application for determination of the issue. Other examples from old authorities are where the trustee could not obtain a discharge from an infant beneficiary or from a beneficiary who was deaf, dumb and blind but in either case the appointment of new trustees for the beneficiary would be preferable. In *Re Elliot's Trusts (1873) LR 15 Eq 194* the beneficiary was abroad and the trustees were uncertain whether he was alive or dead, but in a proper case the court could give leave to distribute on the footing that the missing beneficiary was dead (a Benjamin order) which would protect the trustee but preserve the missing beneficiary's right to follow the trust property in the event that he was alive. Similarly, a distribution on the footing that a woman is no longer able to conceive or a man no longer able to father a child may be authorised, but (save as to the statutory presumption for the purpose of perpetuities) the court proceeds on the basis that every individual remains capable of having a child until the end of his or her life (*Figg v Clarke (Inspector of Taxes) [1997] 1 WLR 603*). For Benjamin orders see further CHAPTER 29: POWER TO APPLY TO THE COURT – THE SURRENDER OF DISCRETION TO THE COURT.

One situation where payment into court might well be ordered would be in the case of litigation between competing beneficiaries over a cash fund, where the trustees had no role to play and had otherwise completed their duties as trustees. Payment into court would enable the trustees to be discharged from their trusteeship and from the litigation.

If money or securities are paid into court the receipt or certificate of the proper officer is a sufficient discharge to the trustee. If there is disagreement between the trustees as to whether money or securities should be paid into court and the majority wish to pay in, then the court may order the payment in without the concurrence of the others and order third parties holding the money or securities to deliver the same to the majority for that purpose (*section 63*).

On payment into court the trustee retires from the trust in respect of the monies paid in and retains no right to deal with it. The trustees should not, therefore, originate an application to deal with the money in court even though the court may order the trustee to be served with notice of the proceedings in order that he can give the court information respecting it (*Re Poplar and Blackwell Free School (1878) 8 Ch D 543 at 546*).

Surrender and release of administrative powers

21.15 In the case of administrative powers which a trustee can decide whether or not to exercise, it would be unusual for the question to arise whether or not an administrative power could be surrendered or released, for the trustee can simply refrain from exercising it. If the matter arises at all, it normally arises in connection with dispositive powers (as to which see CHAPTER 28: DISPOSITIVE POWERS: THEIR DURATION AND RELEASE).

Settled land

21.16 In the case of settled land, it is expressly provided by *section 104* that the powers under the *Settled Land Act 1925* are not capable of assignment or release. A contract by a tenant for life not to exercise his powers under the Act or any of them is void (*section 104(2)*).

Section 104 does not prevent a tenant for life assigning his interest under the settlement but in the case of such assignment the powers of the tenant for life do not pass to the assignee. However, *section 104* makes a number of provisions to protect the position of the assignee, in particular by requiring the consent of the assignee to the investment or application of capital money, if the assignment so provides, or, in the case of an assignment by operation of law (e.g. in the case of bankruptcy) and for notice of transactions to be given to the assignee. The section also contains a number of detailed provisions relating to assignment and consents; reference should be made to the section for these provisions.

Under the *Settled Land Act, s 24*, if it is shown to the satisfaction of the court that a tenant for life, who by reason of bankruptcy, assignment, encumbrance, or otherwise, ceased in the opinion of the court to have a substantial interest in his estate or interest in the settled land, or any part thereof, has unreasonably refused to exercise any of the powers conferred on him by the *Settled Land Act*, or consents to an order under *section 24*, the court may, on the application of any person interested in the settled land or the part thereof affected, make an order authorising the trustees of the settlement to exercise, in the name and on behalf of the tenant for life, any of the powers of the tenant for life under the Act in relation to the settled land or the part thereof affected, either generally and in such manner and for such period as the court may think fit, or in the particular instance, and the court may by the order direct that any documents of title in the possession of the tenant for life relating to the settled land be delivered to the trustees of the settlement. Whilst any such order is in force, the tenant for life shall not, in relation to the settled land or the part thereof affected, exercise any of the powers thereby authorised to be exercised in his name and on his behalf, but no person dealing with the tenant for life shall be affected by any such order, unless the order is for the time being registered as an order affecting land. Such an order is registrable under the *Land Charges Act 1972, s 6*. To exercise power under this Act, a mere failure or neglect on the part of the tenant for life to exercise his powers is not enough. An unreasonable refusal to do so must be proved (see *Re Thornhill Settlement [1941] Ch 24*).

Where the estate or interest of the tenant for life has been surrendered, transferred or conveyed with intent to extinguish the same to the next remainderman, then the statutory powers cease to be exercisable by him, notwithstanding the provisions of *section 104*, and thenceforth become exercisable as if he were dead (*section 105*). That provision applies without prejudice to any encumbrance affecting the estate or interest assured and the rights to which any encumbrancer would have been entitled if those powers had remained exercisable by the tenant for life. The subsection applies whether or not any term of years or charge intervenes, or the estate of the remainderman or reversioner is liable to be defeated, and whether or not the estate or interest of the tenant for life under the settlement was in possession at the date of the assurance. It applies also where the interest has been transferred not by the tenant for life himself but by a person in whom the life estate has vested, e.g. a trustee in bankruptcy (see *Re Shawdon Estates Settlement [1930] 2 Ch 1*).

Perhaps the most important section in the *Settled Land Act* is *section 106*. This provides that, if in a settlement, will, assurance or other instrument a provision is inserted:

(*a*) purporting or attempting, by way of direction, declaration or otherwise, to forbid a tenant for life or statutory owner to exercise any power under the *Settled Land Act*, or his right to require the settled land to be vested in him; or

(*b*) attempting, or intending, or intended, by a limitation, gift or disposition over of settled land, or by limitation, gift or disposition of other real or any personal property, or by the imposition of any condition, or by forfeiture, or in any other manner whatever, to prohibit or prevent him from exercising, or to induce him to abstain from exercising, or to put him in a position inconsistent with his exercising any power under the *Settled Land Act*, or his right to require the settled land to be vested in him, that provision, so far as it purports, or attempts, or tends, or is intended to have, or would or might have, the operation aforesaid, shall be deemed to be void.

The very broad terms in which *section 106* is drawn is intended to entrench the powers of the tenant for life. By *section 106(2)*, an estate or interest limited to continue so long only as a person abstains from exercising any such power or right as aforesaid, shall be and take effect as an estate or interest to continue for the period for which it would continue if that person were to abstain from exercising the power or right, discharged from liability to determination of cesser by or on his exercising the same. *Section 106(3)* also provides that, notwithstanding anything in the settlement, the exercise by the tenant for life or statutory owner of any power under the *Settled Land Act* shall not occasion a forfeiture. An example of this is that, if a property is settled on condition that the tenant for life lives in the property and residence is abandoned on the occasion of and in consequence of the exercise of the statutory power, then the life interest continues – the provision for termination being void under this section (*Re Paget's Settled Estates (1885) 30 Ch D 161*). If a person is given an option to reside in premises and he exercises that option, he becomes tenant for life and can let the premises (*Re Gibbons [1920] 1 Ch 372*).

Chapter 22

Trust Powers and Duties Distinguished

Introduction

22.1 This chapter looks at the differences between *powers* and *duties* in relation to the distribution of an estate or trust fund. A *power* confers the capacity to do something; a *duty* imposes an obligation to do it. A trustee having a power to appoint income has a discretion whether or not to exercise that power, whereas a trustee holding a trust fund on trust for A for life and then for B absolutely is under a duty to A and to B to administer the trusts accordingly. A mere power on the one hand and a fixed trust on the other may be seen as the opposite ends of the spectrum. In the middle lie *trust powers* having aspects of both powers and duties. The gradations between a power and a duty may become very fine indeed, especially when the donee of a power is a fiduciary and the power is conferred on him in his fiduciary capacity.

The distinction is not merely semantic; it is important for a number of practical reasons. To take just three examples:

- if the identity of the objects of a trust cannot be defined with sufficient certainty the trust will fail – however, the test for certainty for the objects of a power or trust power is less stringent;
- the beneficiaries under a trust may call the trustees to account and have access to trust documents – the objects of a discretionary power may not (see CHAPTER 8: PROVISION OF INFORMATION AND DISCLOSURE OF TRUST DOCUMENTS);
- a beneficiary under a trust has a right of action if a trustee does not carry out his duties – the object of a power (save possibly in the case of bad faith) does not have a cause of action either against a trustee in respect of the management of the trust or against the donee of the power (if different from the trustee); the beneficiary entitled in default of the exercise of the power is the person competent to object to the wrongful exercise of the power by the donee (see per Lord Hodson in *McPhail v Doulton [1971] AC 424 at 441*).

Powers – classification

22.2 There are two basic species of dispositive power:

- mere powers; and
- trust powers.

A donee of a mere power has a discretion whether or not to make an appointment and, in the event that the discretion is exercised, a further discretion as to whom and in what shares an appointment will be made. A donee of a trust power has a duty to distribute but a power to select the recipient and the amount. Again, the correct classification of a power may have important consequences. A mere power falling to be exercised from time to time must be exercised within a reasonable time or it will be lost. For example, if a trustee has power to appoint income arising from time to time, that power must be exercised within a reasonable time of the income arising or it will cease to be exercisable in respect of that income (*Re Allen-Meyrick's Will Trusts [1966] 1 WLR 499*). By contrast, a trust power is not lost and may be exercised belatedly, although only in favour of a person who would have been an object at the time it should have been exercised, not in favour of a person who has since become a member of the class of objects (*Re Lockyer's Settlement Trusts [1978] 1 All ER 216*).

Mere powers fall to be further subdivided into fiduciary and non-fiduciary powers depending whether the power is conferred on a person in his personal capacity (non-fiduciary power) or fiduciary capacity (fiduciary power). Although the essence of a mere power is that there is no duty on the donee to exercise the power, a fiduciary power does carry certain duties with it (see 22.4 below). A power (whether fiduciary power or non-fiduciary) can also be classified according to the description of the class of objects into a general power where there is a power to appoint to anyone, including the donee, a special power where the objects are a defined class and hybrid or intermediate powers where there is a power to appoint to anyone except a specified class.

For an example of an hybrid power see *Re Hay's Settlement Trusts [1982] 1 WLR 202* in which it was decided that a hybrid power conferred on trustees in their capacity as trustees was valid; however, the trustee could not on a purported appointment on new trusts delegate the power to the trustees of the new trusts.

Mere powers

22.3 Where it is clear from the trust instrument that the donee of a power of appointment is under no obligation to exercise it, the power is a mere power. Whether the power is or is not a mere power is a matter of construction in order to ascertain the intention of the settlor. Where there is a gift over in default of the exercise of the power, and the default beneficiaries are not the same as the objects of the power, it will generally be a mere power because a trust in default in favour of persons other than the class of objects is inconsistent with a duty to distribute to those objects or an intention to make an ultimate gift to them (see *Re Mills [1930] 1 Ch 654*). A common example of a mere power is where the life tenant, say, the widow of the deceased, is given power to appoint the capital of the trust fund, by deed or will, to one or more of the class of remaindermen with a gift over in default to all the remaindermen equally.

The fact that there is no duty to exercise a mere power has the following consequences:

- if the donee of the power does not exercise the power, the court cannot compel its exercise;
- the objects of the power cannot join together and compel the donee to distribute (*Re Gestetner Settlement [1953] Ch 672 at 688*);
- the donee can release the power even if the release would benefit the donee (*Re Mills*).

If the donee does exercise a mere power, he must exercise it for the purposes intended, otherwise the exercise will be a fraud on the power and, to that extent, the court can intervene at least at the suit of a beneficiary entitled in default of exercise (see per Lord Hodson in *McPhail v Doulton [1971] AC 424 at 441*).

Fiduciary mere powers

22.4 Where a power is conferred on a person in his fiduciary capacity (e.g. as a trustee) then fiduciary duties attach to the power. However, it does not necessarily follow from the fact that a person is a trustee that a power conferred on him is conferred on him in that fiduciary capacity and is, therefore, a fiduciary as opposed to a non-fiduciary power. For example, in *Re Mills*, the testator conferred a power of appointment on his brother who was both one of the two trustees and the person entitled in default of appointment. It was held that the power was a mere power not a power coupled with a trust and could be validly released. Conversely, a power may be conferred on a person who is not a trustee but on a true construction may be held to be a fiduciary power. For example, in *IRC v Schroder [1983] STC 480*, the settlor had power to appoint to the committee of protectors who in turn had power to remove and appoint trustees. The Inland Revenue sought to argue that the settlor, by retaining the power to control the identity of the trustees was, in practice, able to control the application of income of the settlements and was, therefore, liable to tax under the *Income and Corporation Taxes Act 1970, s 478(5)(e)*. However, the court held that the power of appointment was a fiduciary power which could not properly be used to 'pack the committee' to ensure that the majority followed the settlor's wishes and the Inland Revenue's argument failed.

Where a power does carry fiduciary duties, those duties are threefold:

- first, to consider periodically whether or not he should exercise the power;
- second, to consider the range of objects of the power; and
- third, consider the appropriateness of the individual appointments (see per Megarry V-C in *Re Hay's Settlement Trusts [1982] 1 WLR 202*).

In considering the range of objects it is not necessary to compile a list of every object – it is sufficient to find out the permissible area of selection and then consider responsibly in individual cases whether a contemplated beneficiary is within the power and whether in relation to other possible claimants a particular grant is appropriate.

A trustee must use his own judgement as to whether to exercise the discretion from time to time and not, for example, simply follow the wishes of the settlor. In the event that the trustees cannot arrive at a satisfactory answer, they can apply to the court for directions giving the court the necessary information as to the circumstances then prevailing but the court will not generally accept a surrender of a discretion in respect of future income (*Re Allen-Meyrick's Will Trusts [1966] 1 WLR 499*).

A non-fiduciary mere power can be released by the donee of the power. However, a fiduciary power cannot be released unless the trust instrument specifically so provides (see *Mettoy Pensions Trustees Ltd v Evans [1991] 2 All ER 513 at 545*).

The control of the court in relation to mere powers is limited to cases where there has been a fraud on the power or, in relation to a fiduciary mere power, where the trustees have failed to carry out their fiduciary duties (see observations in *Re Gulbenkian's Settlements [1970] AC 508 at 518 and 525*).

Trust powers

22.5 The essential difference between a mere power and a trust power is that in the case of the latter the trustees are under a duty to exercise their discretion whereas in the case of a mere power, they are under no such duty (subject in the case of a fiduciary mere power to the carrying out of their fiduciary duties). In the event of default by the trustee of a trust power the court will execute the trust in the manner best calculated to give effect to the settlor's intentions.

As mentioned at 22.1 above, a trust power lies between a trust on one hand and a power on the other. This hybrid nature gave rise to the question whether the test for certainty of the class of objects was the same as the strict test applied to a class of beneficiaries under a trust, or the more liberal test applied to the class of objects of a mere power. In the case of the former, the trust is void unless the whole class is ascertained or capable of ascertainment; in the case of the latter, it is sufficient if one can say of any given person whether or not he or she is, or is not, a member of the given class. In *IRC v Broadway Cottages Trust [1955] Ch 20*, the trust test had been applied, but this was overruled in *McPhail v Doulton [1971] AC 424* in favour of the application of the powers test.

Given that, in the case of a trust power, the trustee is under a duty to exercise his discretion, his fiduciary duty to consider the range of possible objects is a matter of considerable importance. The practical approach to this was considered in *Re Baden's Deed Trusts (No 2) [1973] Ch 9*. A distinction was drawn between conceptual uncertainty (which would lead to the trust power failing) and evidential uncertainty (which would not). In that case the settlor had established a trust fund for the benefit of the staff of his company, their relatives and dependants, and directed his trustees:

> 'to apply the net income of the fund in making at their absolute discretion grants to or for the benefit of any of the officers and employees or ex-officers or ex-employees of the company or any relatives or dependants of such persons ...'.

It was held that there was no conceptual difficulty in respect of either 'relatives' or 'dependants' and that if a candidate could not, on proper enquiry, establish that he was a member of the class, he must be held not to be a member. In *Re Leek [1969] 1 Ch 563*, Harman LJ thought that a class of persons having a 'moral claim' would be too uncertain if the trust were for persons who 'have a moral claim' but not if the trustees were made the arbiters and objects were such persons as 'they [i.e. the trustees] may consider to have a moral claim' given that, in the latter case, the trustees could make up their minds and arrive at a decision.

It was made clear in *Re Baden (No 2)* that the survey that falls to be conducted by the trustees of the range of objects or possible beneficiaries of a mere power or a trust power, is not a list of individuals or an accurate enumeration of the numbers in the class. What is needed is an assessment of the width of the field from which the beneficiaries may be drawn and which the trustees should have in mind so they can adapt to it their methods of discretionary selection assessing 'in a businesslike way' the 'size of the problem' (see per Sachs LJ at *page 20*).

However, if the range of objects is so large as not to form anything like a class, so that the trust is administratively unworkable in practice, it will fail; the example given by Lord Wilberforce in *McPhail v Doulton [1971]*

AC 424 at 457 is a trust for 'all the residents of Greater London'. In *R v District Auditor No 3 Audit District of West Yorkshire Metropolitan County Council, ex p West Yorkshire Metropolitan County Council [1986] RVR 24*, the council purported to create a trust of unexpended funds, the purpose of which was 'to apply and expend the Trust Fund for the benefit of any or all or some of the inhabitants of West Yorkshire'. There were 2.5 million potential beneficiaries and Lloyd LJ thought that this was far too large a number to form anything like a class. It was not a valid charitable trust and could not take effect as a private trust because there was no certainty as to the persons intended to benefit, and a trust with so many potential beneficiaries was administratively unworkable.

In the event of default by the trustee, the court will execute a discretionary trust in the manner best calculated to give effect to the settlor's intentions. It may do so by appointing new trustees, or by authorising or directing representative persons of the classes of beneficiaries to prepare a scheme of distribution. Where the proper basis for distribution is apparent from the instrument creating the power, the court may even direct the trustees to distribute (Lord Wilberforce in *McPhail at 457*). It is no longer accepted that the court can only execute a trust on the basis of equal division. The court may even execute a discretionary trust where distribution is expressed to be at the sole and absolute discretion of the trustees (*Re Locker's Settlement Trust [1977] 1 WLR 1323*).

Trustees must act unanimously in the exercise of a power. If they are unable to agree, they may apply for directions. However, trustees can collectively ratify an exercise of discretion, and if a matter is properly and fully reported to them and they take no action, then that may indicate concurrence in what has happened (see *Libby v Kennedy [1999] PLR 143*).

The question of certainty

22.6 Where the settlor creates a trust for a class of beneficiaries the trust will fail unless the whole class is either ascertained or capable of ascertainment. The question of certainty must be determinable and determined at the date of the instrument that creates the power (in the case of a will, at the date of death of the testator) – per Lord Upjohn in *Re Gulbenkian's Settlements [1970] AC 508 at 524*. The class need not be closed, e.g. a gift 'to the children of X living at the death of the life tenant' is not uncertain even though one cannot say whether there will be any such children or who they will be.

Care must be taken to consider whether or not one is dealing with a class gift at all. In *Re Barlow's Will Trusts [1979] 1 WLR 278*, the testatrix directed that her executor was to allow members of her family and friends to purchase any of her pictures not specifically disposed of at probate valuation. The testatrix had thereby imposed on her executor a duty, not a power, and had given him no express discretion in the matter. Browne-Wilkinson J held that the term 'friends' was too uncertain to be able to draw up a complete list. However, he held that the direction was not in the nature of a class gift but a series of individual options and that it was for each person coming forward to exercise the option to prove by a reasonable test that he or she was a friend. He suggested some guidelines and indicated that in the case of doubt the executors could apply to the court to determine the matter. He went on to give a similarly wide construction to the deceased's reference to members of her family.

Issues of uncertainty sometimes arise because the class of beneficiaries includes, in addition to precise categories of persons about which no difficulty could arise, other more uncertain relationships. However, there is no equivalent of the 'blue pencil' doctrine and the court has no jurisdiction simply to excise the offending words (*Re Leek [1969] 1 Ch 563*). If a donor defines his intended class too widely the court cannot give effect to it by dividing the fund only between a smaller class than he has attempted to define (Lord Reid – *Re Gulbenkian's Settlements [1970] AC 508 at 524*).

Chapter 23

Construction of Dispositive Powers

Introduction

23.1 This chapter considers in more detail the principles affecting the construction of trust documents, in particular, in respect of their dispositive provisions. Difficulties of construction most commonly (though by no means exclusively) arise in connection with will trusts and reference should be made to the standard works for a more comprehensive treatment of the topic. The object here is to summarise the more important general principles; issues of construction respecting powers of appointment are dealt with in more detail.

The avowed object of any court of construction is to arrive at the intention expressed by the trust document, however direct evidence of the motive or intention of the draftsman is generally not admissible. If a trust deed contains a provision which is clear and unequivocal, but not what the settlor intended, then any remedy must lie in rectification not in construction. The court cannot ignore clear words even if they do not achieve the desired result. That having been said, much can be achieved by construction where the drafting has been clumsy or defective.

Construction – the general approach

23.2 The modern approach has been to move from literal to purposive construction. Words may be given the popular, rather than dictionary, meaning; see for example *Perrin v Morgan [1943] AC 399* where the term 'money' was held to include not just cash but all the net personalty. A striking example of the unhappy consequences of a literal approach to construction is in *Re Rowland [1963] Ch 1*. A married couple made wills before setting sail for the South Pacific to which the husband had been appointed a medical officer. They knew the appointment would lead to hazardous circumstances, in particular, frequent journeys in small vessels travelling between the islands. By his will the husband left his estate to his wife and provided that 'In the event of the decease of [my wife] preceding or coinciding with my own decease I give and bequeath …', he then set out provisions in favour of his own family. His wife made a will in similar terms benefiting a relative of hers in the event that her husband's death 'preceded or coincided' with her own. They died in a shipwreck and no one knew whether one had died before the other. The majority of the Court of Appeal held (as had the first instance judge) that it had not been shown that their deaths had 'coincided'. It therefore applied the statutory rule (*Law of Property Act 1925, s 184*) that the younger (the wife) must be presumed to have survived the elder. The result was that her relative took both estates. The dissenting judgment by Lord Denning pointed out that the calamity which had occurred was precisely the type of event which the couple must have had in mind when making their wills. As he observed (*at page 10*):

> 'the whole object of construction is to find out the testator's intentions and to see that his property is disposed of in the way he wished, and that whilst one must discover that intention from the words he used, one must put upon those words the meaning they had to him'.

It is difficult to conceive of any modern court differing from that approach.

The purposive approach has been given a further substantial boost by the House of Lords decision in *Mannai Investment Co Ltd v Eagle Star Life Assurance Co Ltd [1997] AC 749*. That case concerned the true construction of notices to determine two leases in accordance with break clauses. Because of a misconstruction of the terms of the leases, the notices were one day out. However, the intention of the tenant to bring the leases to an end in accordance with the break clauses was perfectly clear and a reasonable recipient with knowledge of the leases would have understood that the intention was to terminate the leases on the correct day. The House of Lords held that the notices were effective. Lord Hoffmann, in particular, made the point that making sense of what is said involves considering how it will be reasonably understood and adjusting for obvious errors or for unconventional use of language (*page 774D–H*). Therefore, although the court may not be concerned with the speaker's subjective meaning, it is concerned with what the speaker would, objectively, be understood to have meant (*page 775E*); that is not necessarily achieved by a literal construction. Although the case involved a commercial document, the observations of the House seem equally applicable to trust documents, and indeed in the course of his reasoning Lord Hoffmann considered the application of the existing rules as to admissibility of evidence in the construction of wills (*page 778 et seq*). The approach of the House strongly echoes the tenor of the dissenting judgment of Lord Denning in *Re Rowland*.

Document to be construed as a whole

23.3 One of the most basic canons of construction is that a document falls to be construed as a whole; it is wrong to try to construe a clause in isolation. As a general rule, it should be assumed that a testator or settlor intended every word or phrase to play its part and for words or phrases to have a consistent meaning. Some draftsmen, however, manage to defeat every effort to give meaning to what they write, or to achieve consistency, and the general rule has to give way and words be ignored or given different meanings according to the context.

Settlor may provide his own dictionary

23.4 As a general rule words should be given their normal meaning. In the older cases that meant a literal or dictionary definition but since *Perrin v Morgan [1943] AC 399* it includes also the popular or common usage. However, it may be clear that a testator or settlor has used a word in his own particular sense; if so that is the meaning it should be given. Thus a will (described by the judge as the shortest ever known) which simply read 'all for mother' was construed as benefiting the testator's widow (*Thorn v Dickens [1906] WN 54*). Where a testator, at the date of his will, had illegitimate children only and was to his own knowledge incapable of having further children, provisions in his will in favour of his children were to be construed as taking effect in favour of the illegitimate children (*Re Wohlgemuth [1949] Ch 12*). As the law then stood the term 'children' in a will *prima facie* meant legitimate children only.

Extrinsic evidence

23.5 It is well established that extrinsic evidence is admissible in the following circumstances:

- to put the court '... so to speak in his [i.e. the testator's] armchair, and consider the circumstances by which he was surrounded when he made his will to assist in arriving at his intention' (*Boyes v Cook (1880) 14 Ch D 53 at 56*);
- to show that the testator habitually used particular words in a particular way, although not that a draftsman has used words that had a special sense in a particular document (*Re Atkinson's Will Trusts [1978] 1 WLR 586*);
- to resolve a latent ambiguity (e.g. where there is a reference in a will to 'my nephew Arthur Murphy' when he had three nephews of that name – *Re Jackson [1933] Ch 237*). A latent ambiguity may arise even if a body is accurately named in the will if there is some other body of a similar name who might have been the intended recipient although in such case there will be a strong presumption that the body correctly named is the body intended to take (*National Society for the Prevention of Cruelty to Children v Scottish National Society for the Prevention of Cruelty to Children [1915] AC 207*). A patent ambiguity (i.e. one apparent on the face of the document) generally falls to be resolved by construction;

- to identify the subject matter of a gift (*Re Glassington [1906] 2 Ch 305*).

By the *Administration of Justice Act 1982, s 21*, extrinsic evidence (including evidence of the testator's intention) is also admissible in the case of a will in so far as:

(*a*) any part of it is meaningless;

(*b*) the language used in any part of it is ambiguous on the face of it; or

(*c*) evidence, other than evidence of the testator's intention, shows that the language used in any part of it is ambiguous in the light of surrounding circumstances.

Section 21 is applicable only to will trusts and not *inter vivos* trusts. Further, it does not permit the court to give a word or phrase a meaning which it cannot bear (*Re Williams [1985] 1 WLR 905*) or fill the gap when the testator left out the amount left to various pecuniary legatees (*Gibbs v Davies* (1992) unreported, CA). Where a testatrix left her estate to her son, with a gift to her nephews if he predeceased her, the nephews did not take under that provision on the son forfeiting his interest as a result of having killed her; the will simply did not deal with that situation (*Re Jones, Jones v Midland Bank [1998] 1 FLR 246*).

Supplying missing words

23.6 Where it is clear that words have been omitted, and the substance of the omission is clear, then the court can read in the missing words as a matter of construction (not rectification), although it does so with caution (*Re Whitrick [1957] 1 WLR 884 at 887*). In that case the testatrix had survived her husband. Her will made provision in the event of them both dying at the same time; that direction did not cover the event which in fact occurred. The Court of Appeal held that the testatrix had imperfectly provided for the contingency of her husband not surviving her and construed the terms of the will as relating also to the situation of the husband predeceasing his wife. Similarly, where property was given in trust for all the children of a named person 'who being a son or sons shall live to attain the age of 21 years or being a daughter or daughters shall marry under that age' it was held that a gift to an unmarried daughter also vested on her attaining the age of 21 (*Re Hunt (1890) 62 LT 753*). However, if the substance of the omission is not clear then the implication will not be made. So, where a power of appointment in a will obviously omitted words indicating the class of objects, which would have made it a special power, but it was not sufficiently clear what had been left out, the clause was left as drawn and took effect as a general power (*Re Follett [1955] 1 WLR 429*).

The principle is not confined to wills but applies equally to an *inter vivos* trust. In *Re Hargreaves' Trusts [1937] 2 All ER 545* an error similar to that made in *Re Hunt* was similarly construed.

Misdescriptions

23.7 Where a beneficiary is wrongly described, but it is clear who is to take, then the intended beneficiary can take. In *Re Ofner [1909] 1 Ch 60* the deceased named a beneficiary as 'my grandnephew Robert Ofner'; there was no such person and instructions for the will were admitted to show that the deceased intended to benefit the brother of one of his executors whose correct name was 'Richard Ofner'.

Children/issue

23.8 The usual meaning of 'children' is children of the first generation but the context may show that it is intended to apply to grandchildren (see e.g. *Re Smith (1887) 35 Ch D 558*). A similar approach is brought to questions whether 'grandchildren' includes great-grandchildren and nephews and nieces include great-nephews and great-nieces (*Re Cozens [1903] 1 Ch 138*). Stepchildren are not included in 'children' unless the context indicates otherwise.

Gifts by will to children or issue saved from lapse

23.9 Where a will contains a devise or bequest to a child or remoter issue of the testator and the intended beneficiary dies before the testator leaving issue who are living at the testator's death, then unless the contrary intention appears by the will, the devise or bequest takes effect as a devise or bequest to the issue living at the testator's death. Similarly the issue will be substituted for a predeceasing child or issue in a class of person consisting of children or remoter issue. [*Wills Act 1837, s 33*]. *Section 33* provides that issue take under the section through all degrees according to their stock (in equal shares if more than one) the share or shares that their parent would have taken. For the purpose of the section the illegitimacy of any person is to be disregarded and a person conceived before the testator's death, and born living thereafter, is taken to have been living at the testator's death.

Adopted children

23.10 A reference to a 'child' or 'children' in a disposition of property taking effect after 1 January 1976 includes an adopted child and, if the disposition depends on the date of birth of the child or children, the disposition will take effect (save in the case of an illegitimate child adopted by one of its natural parents) as if the adopted child was born on the date of adoption and, if two or more children had been adopted on the same date, as if the elder had been born first (see now *Adoption Act 1976, ss 42, 43*).

A disposition of property includes the conferring of a power of appointment and any other disposition of an interest in or right over property (*section 46*). A will or codicil is regarded as having been made on the date of death of the testator (*section 46(3)*) (contrast the position with regard to illegitimate children – see 23.11 below). For the position prior to 1976, reference should be made to specialist works.

Section 42 gives way to any contrary indication in the trust instrument. It does not apply to the descent of any peerage or dignity or to any property limited (expressly or not) to devolve (as nearly as the law permits) along with any peerage or dignity or title of honour (*section 44*). A trustee is not under any duty to enquire before conveying or distributing any property whether any adoption has been effected, or revoked, if that fact could affect entitlement to the property and is not liable in respect of a conveyance or distribution made without notice that an adoption has been effected or revoked; however, a person affected can follow the property or any property representing it into the hands of another person other than a purchaser who has received it (*section 45*).

Illegitimacy

23.11 In the case of a disposition *inter vivos* or a will and codicil made on or after 4 April 1988, a reference to any relationship between two persons shall, unless the contrary intention appears, be construed without regard to whether or not the father and mother of either of them, or the father or mother of any person through whom the relationship is deduced, have or had been married to each other at any time. [*Family Law Reform Act 1987, ss 1* and *19*]. In other words, unless the contrary intention appears, no distinction is now drawn between legitimate, illegitimate or legitimated persons. For the position in respect of instruments taking effect prior to 4 April 1988, reference should be made to specialist works.

It should be noted that in the case of a will or codicil, it is the date of the document that is relevant, not the date of death. A will or codicil is not treated as made after the relevant date simply because it is confirmed by a codicil made thereafter (*section 19(7)*). (Contrast the position with regard to adopted children – see 23.10 above.) The section gives way to a contrary intention expressed in the document, but the use of the word 'heir' or 'heirs' or any expression used to create an entailed interest in real or personal property does not show a contrary intention for this purpose (*section 19(2)*). The section does not operate to sever property or an interest in property from a dignity or title with which it is limited to devolve (*section 19(4)*).

It should also be noted that the legislation no longer gives trustees express protection from liability if they distribute without notice of an illegitimate child. Formerly, similar protection was given as is given in respect of an adopted child (see 23.10 above and see the *Legitimacy Act 1976, s 7(3)*). However, a trustee may protect himself by advertising under the *Trustee Act 1925, s 27*.

Artificial insemination

23.12 Where, on or after 4 April 1988, a child is born as a result of the artificial insemination of a woman who was at the time of the insemination a party to a marriage (not dissolved or annulled) and was artificially inseminated by the semen of some person other than her husband, then unless it is proved to the satisfaction of the court that the husband did not consent to the insemination, the child shall be treated as the child of the parties to the marriage and not any other person. [*Family Law Reform Act 1987, s 27(1)*]. Reference to marriage includes a reference to a void marriage if at the time of the marriage either or both of the parties reasonably believed that the marriage was valid (*section 27(2)*). The section does not affect the succession to any dignity or title of honour (*section 27(3)*).

Whereas the *Family Law Reform Act 1987* made provision in respect of a child born to a married couple as a result of artificial insemination, the *Human Fertilisation and Embryology Act 1990, ss 27–30* makes comprehensive provision for the determination of who is to be treated as the mother and father respectively of a child so conceived. It applies in relation to a child carried by a woman as a result of treatment carried out on or after 1 August 1991 (*section 49(3)*). In summary, the woman who carries a child, and no other woman, is to be treated as the mother; the husband of a subsisting marriage is to be treated as the father unless it is shown that he did not consent to the insemination, otherwise a man for whom (with the woman) treatment services were provided by a licensed person shall be treated as the father of the child; in neither case is any other man to be treated as the father. Where by virtue of *section 27* or *28* of the Act, a person is to be treated as the mother or father of a child, that person is to be treated in law as the mother or, as the case may be, father of the child for all purposes. Where by virtue of the sections a person is not to be treated as the mother or father of the child then that person is not to be so treated for any purpose. References to any relationship between two people in any enactment, deed or other instrument or document (whenever passed or made) are to be read accordingly. However, the section does not affect the succession to any dignity or title of honour or the devolution of property limited to devolve with any dignity or title of honour (*section 29*).

Powers of appointment

23.13 If, following a power of appointment, there is an express gift over in default of appointment, the power is to be construed as a mere power.

If there is no gift over, the question arises whether the trust fund is undisposed of (so passing on partial intestacy or on resulting trust to the settlor) or whether it is right to imply a gift in favour of the class as a whole (*Burrough v Philcox (1840) 5 My & Cr 72* per Lord Cottenham *at 92*). In *Lambert v Thwaites (1866) LR 2 Eq 151*, Kindersley V-C thought that there were two kinds of case where a gift in default might be implied:

- where, on the instrument itself, there was a gift in favour of a class, subject to exercise of a power of selection; and
- where there was no class gift but a power to A to bestow the property as he thought fit among members of a class. The objects of the gift in default would be different as between the two kinds of case.

For the court to imply a gift to the class of objects as a whole there must be a clear indication in the will that the settlor intended that the class of objects should take in any event (*Re Weekes' Settlement [1897] 1 Ch 289*). This must be a matter of construction of the particular document, but where the class is small (as in *Re Llewelyn's Settlement [1921] 2 Ch 281* –'children and grandchildren') rather than large or indefinite (as in *Re Perowne [1951] Ch 785* – 'my family') the implication that there is a gift to the class as a whole is more easily made. As Harman J pointed out in *Re Perowne*, a power of appointment among a large and indefinite class of people is one thing; a trust is quite another. A gift to 'relations' might be saved from failing by construing it as a gift to the statutory next of kin as joint tenants, i.e. importing from the rules of intestacy those provisions which identify the individuals who take on intestacy but not the provisions which determine the amount and interest that they take (*Re Gansloser's Will Trusts [1952] Ch 30*). In *Re Perowne*, Harman J found that the word 'family' in the will he was considering was not confined to nearest kin or statutory next of kin and, the power of appointment not having been exercised, the fund was treated as undisposed of by the will.

A division between all the objects of a power raises the further question when the class of objects falls to be determined (i.e. when the power comes into being or when the donee dies without having exercised it) and whether the objects take as joint tenants or tenants in common. When the matter falls within the first class mentioned by Kindersley V-C in *Lambert v Thwaites* (see above), i.e. where there was a gift in favour of a class, subject to exercise of a power of selection, then *prima facie* a distribution in default of appointment will be equally between all the members of the class determined as at the date of the deed (or, in the case of a will, the date of death) and the members of the class take as joint tenants (*Re Kilvert [1957] Ch 388*). Where, however, the matter is within the second class mentioned, i.e. there was no class gift as such, but a power to A to bestow the property as he thought fit among members of a class, the distribution will be between the possible objects of the power per capita not as joint tenants (*Re Arnold [1947] Ch 131*). In that case, a declaration of trust provided that the trustees should stand possessed of the trust fund to pay the income to the settlor's daughter during her life with power for her to appoint that after her death the whole or any part of the income should be paid to any husband of hers who might survive her and in default of such appointment 'in trust for the children of [the daughter] or any of her issue in such shares (if more than one) and in such manner as she shall by any deed or deeds or by her will appoint'. Wynn-Parry J thought it was impossible to hold that there was a gift to a class. Rather, he held that the case came within the second category in *Lambert v Thwaites* and on the death of the daughter the trust funds became divisible between all the children and remoter issue of the daughter born in her lifetime, whether or not they survived her, in equal shares.

The court will only imply an intention to give to those who might have taken under an exercise of the power (*Lambert v Thwaites*). Thus, if the power can only be exercised by will, the default beneficiaries will be only those in being at the death of the donee. If the gift is properly construed as conferring on the members of the class of objects a vested interest, liable to be divested by the exercise of the power of appointment, then on default of exercise the fund will fall to be divided between all the members of the class whether or not they have survived the donee of the power (*Re Jackson's Will (1879) 13 Ch D 189*).

Trust powers – default of exercise

23.14 In the case of a trust power, the trustees are under an obligation not only to consider whether to exercise their discretion but actually to exercise the discretion itself. The objects only obtain an interest in the trust fund through the exercise of the power. The court, if called upon to execute such a trust, is not confined to equal distribution among the beneficiaries (*McPhail v Doulton [1971] AC 424*). The court can deal with a failure by the trustees to carry out their duty either by appointing new trustees who can then exercise the power or by drawing up a scheme of distribution.

Resolving issues of construction

23.15 Issues of construction, which cannot be resolved by consent, should (unless within the county court jurisdiction) be referred to the Chancery Division of the High Court for determination. Application is under the Part 8 procedure and the matter may proceed to an oral hearing in the usual way. However, the *Administration of Justice Act 1985, s 48* provides that where any question of construction arises on the terms of a will or trust and an opinion in writing has been obtained from a person who has a ten-year High Court qualification on that question by the personal representatives or trustees under the will or trust, the High Court may, on the application of the personal representatives or trustees and without hearing argument, make an order authorising those persons to take such steps in reliance on the said opinion as are specified in the order. The application proceeds as a purely paper application. The reference to a person who has a ten-year High Court qualification means a person who has a right of audience in relation to all proceedings in the High Court and has had that right for at least ten (not necessarily continuous) years (see 21.8).

Chapter 24

Powers of Maintenance

Introduction

24.1 When a fund is held for an infant, the income may be required for that infant's maintenance, education or benefit. Trustees may be given an express power for this purpose; if so, then the extent of the power is determined by the construction of the relevant clause. More commonly a trust instrument will incorporate the statutory provision made by *section 31* of the *Trustee Act 1925* (*TA 1925*), either as it stands or in a modified form. If the trust instrument is silent, then the statutory power applies unless it is expressly or impliedly excluded by other provisions of the deed.

Statutory power

24.2 The *Trustee Act 1925, s 31* provides a comprehensive code dealing with the application of income for the maintenance of an infant beneficiary, the accumulation of any income not so applied, the entitlement to such accumulations and the right of the infant to receive income as it arises after attaining his or her majority. The section applies to personal representatives where the context admits. It is excluded by a contrary intention expressed in the document (*section 69(2)*) and may be, and commonly is, modified.

Interest must carry the intermediate income

24.3 *TA 1925, s 31* can only apply if the interest in question carries the intermediate income (see 24.13 below).

Maintenance during infancy

24.4 *TA 1925, s 31(1)(i)* provides that where any property is held by trustees on trust for any person for any interest whatsoever, whether vested or contingent, then, subject to any prior interests or charges affecting that property:

'during the infancy of any such person, if his interest so long continues, the trustees may, at their sole discretion, pay to his parent or guardian, if any, or otherwise apply for or towards his maintenance, education or benefit, the whole or such part, if any, of the income of that property as may, in all the circumstances, be reasonable, whether or not there is—

(*a*) any other fund applicable to the same purpose; or

(*b*) any person bound by law to provide for his maintenance or education'.

Infancy

24.5 The *Family Law Reform Act 1969, s 1* reduced the age of majority from 21 to 18 when it came into force on 1 January 1970 but not in respect of an interest under an instrument made before that date. However, where a special power of appointment created under a pre-1970 deed was exercised after that date, then the reduced age of majority applied (*Begg-McBrearty (HM Inspector of Taxes) v Stilwell [1996] 1 WLR 951*).

Income of property held by trustees

24.6 Where trustees in the exercise of a discretionary power to distribute income resolved that a portion of income should be held for the minor beneficiaries in specified shares (so as to give those infants a vested interest in that income) *TA 1925, s 31* applied only to income earned by the appointed funds, not to the appointed funds themselves (*Re Baron Vestey's Settlement [1951] Ch 209*). The trustees could have (but expressly had not) appointed the income for the maintenance, education or benefit of the children.

To pay or otherwise apply

24.7 The trustees may apply the income either by paying it to the infant's parent or guardian or otherwise. In certain circumstances, it may be appropriate to make a payment direct to the infant, e.g. making a modest allowance to the child direct. A married infant has power to give a valid receipt for all income including statutory accumulations of income made during the minority. [*Law of Property Act 1925, s 21*].

Maintenance, education and benefit

24.8 The inclusion of the word 'benefit' makes the phrase of the widest application. However, the application must be such as is in all the circumstances reasonable and the trustees must have regard to the age of the infant and to his requirements and generally to the circumstances of the case.

Alternative sources of maintenance

24.9 One of the circumstances to which the trustee must have particular regard is what income (if any) is available for the purpose of maintenance, education and benefit of the infant. Where the trustees have notice that income of more than one fund is available for the purpose, then, so far as practicable, unless the entire income of the funds is paid or applied or the court otherwise directs, a proportionate part only of the fund should be so applied.

Notwithstanding that last requirement, the fact that an exercise of the power of maintenance will relieve another person of the burden of maintaining the infant is not a bar to the exercise of the power of maintenance if the trustees reach the conclusion that it is in the best interests of the beneficiary. Thus, in *Fuller v Evans [2000] 1 All ER 636* it was held that the trustees were entitled to pay the school fees of the children, notwithstanding that this had the effect of relieving *pro tanto* an obligation to make those payments imposed on the children's father by an order made in divorce proceedings. That decision concerned an express power of maintenance but it would apply equally to an exercise of a discretion under *TA 1925, s 31*.

The requirement to have regard to other available funds is frequently excluded by a modification of *section 31* in the trust instrument.

Accumulation of income during minority

24.10 *TA 1925, s 31(2),* as amended by the *Trustee Act 2000* (*TA 2000*), provides that during the infancy of any person for whom property is held in trust, if his interest so long continues, the trustees shall accumulate all the residue of that income by investing it, and any profits from so investing it, from time to time in authorised investments.

The trustees may, at any time during the infancy of such person, apply accumulated income (or any part thereof) as if it were income arising in the then current year. Subject to that, the right to income so accumulated is as follows.

If the infant attains his majority or marries under that age and his interest in income was a vested interest, then he is entitled to the accumulations absolutely. Similarly, if the infant attains his majority or marries and thereby becomes entitled to the capital of the fund in fee simple, absolute or determinable, or absolutely, or for an entailed interest, he is entitled to the accumulations absolutely. In either case the receipt of the infant if married is a good discharge.

In any other case, the trustees hold the accumulations as an accretion to the capital of the property from which such accumulations arose, and as one fund with such capital for all purposes. This is so even if the infant had a vested interest in income. Therefore, if an infant entitled to a *life interest* in a fund dies before attaining the age of 18 or marrying under that age, his or her estate is not entitled to income accumulated prior to the infant's death. Where, however, income was to be held for an infant, his right to accumulated income was indefeasible (*Re Delamere's Settlement Trusts [1984] 1 WLR 813*).

Right to income from age of 18

24.11 If a beneficiary on attaining his majority has an interest in a fund which falls short of a vested interest, then *TA 1925, s 31(1)(ii)* directs the trustees to pay the income of that fund to that beneficiary until he either attains a vested interest therein or dies, or until failure of his interest. However, in the case of a future gift of a fund which is vested subject to being divested, then income should be accumulated until the gift is indefeasible and *section 31(1)(ii)* does not apply (*Re McGeorge [1963] Ch 544*).

Contrary intention

24.12 *TA 1925, s 69(2)* provides that the powers conferred on trustees by the 1925 Act apply only if and so far as a contrary intention is not expressed in the instrument creating the trust. Accordingly *section 31* can be excluded by contrary provision. A contrary intention need not expressly refer to *section 31*.

Section 31 will not apply if, on a fair reading of the instrument in question, the application of the section would be inconsistent with the purport of the instrument (see *Re Delamere's Settlement Trusts [1984] 1 WLR 813 at 818*). An express power for trustees to make payments of capital and income to certain beneficiaries on account of their expectant shares of the trust fund was held sufficient to exclude *section 31(1)(ii)* (*Re Geering [1964] Ch 136*).

Similarly, an express trust for accumulation will prevail over *section 31(1)(ii)* which would otherwise have entitled the beneficiary to receive the income (*Re Reade-Revell [1930] 1 Ch 52*; *Re Turner's Will Trusts [1937] Ch 15*). Even a direction to accumulate income which, to the extent that it infringed the rule against perpetuities, failed was sufficient to exclude the provisions of *section 31* (see *Re Ransome [1957] Ch 348*).

However, where there is no express direction to accumulate, the mere fact that under the general law the surplus intermediate income would otherwise be accumulated and added to the corpus will not be sufficient to exclude *section 31(1)* (*Re Leng [1938] Ch 821*).

A gift to A not to take effect until a stated time after the death of B indicates that the testator did not want A to have the intermediate income and, therefore, *section 31* cannot apply (see *Re McGeorge [1963] Ch 544*).

Gifts that carry the intermediate income

24.13 As stated above, the power of maintenance only applies if the interest of the beneficiary carries the intermediate income.

In the case of an *inter vivos* settlement, it will normally be clear from the instrument whether or not the intervening income is carried by the interest.

In respect of a testamentary gift or trust, the position as to which gifts carry income or interest and from what date, is complex and reference should be made to the specialist textbooks. However, so far as necessary for considering the power or maintenance, the position may be summarised below.

A *vested* pecuniary or general legacy carries interest from the first anniversary of the testator's death unless the will provides otherwise. A direction to pay a legacy 'immediately after my death for her immediate requirements' carries interest from the date of death (*Re Pollock [1943] Ch 338*).

A *future or contingent* pecuniary or general legacy (e.g. a legacy to A on the death of B) generally does not carry interest until the time for payment arrives. An exception is a legacy by the parent of, or a person standing *in loco parentis* to, the legatee where there is no other provision for the maintenance of the legatee or the testator has directed that the legacy be appropriated and invested for the benefit of the legatee (*Re Raine [1929] 1 Ch 716*). *TA 1925, s 31(3)* expressly provides that if the legacy carries interest under the general law, the rate of interest shall (if the income is sufficient, and subject to any rules of the court to the contrary) be 5% per annum. The Rules of the Supreme Court, rule 44.10 provides for a rate of 6% per annum.

An immediate gift of residue or an immediate vested specific devise or bequest carries income from the date of death of the testator. However, if a gift of residue is specifically deferred to a future date then, whether vested, vested subject to being divested or contingent, *prima facie* it does not carry the intermediate income (*Re Geering [1964] Ch 136*).

In the case of a contingent residuary bequest of personalty, the income should be accumulated (so far as the law permits) until the contingency occurs (*Re Geering*).

By virtue of the *Law of Property Act 1925, s 175* the following gifts carry the intermediate income from the date of death unless the income is otherwise expressly disposed of:

- a contingent or future specific devise or bequest of property, whether real or personal;
- a contingent residuary devise of freehold land;
- a specific or residuary devise of freehold land to trustees on trust for persons whose interests are contingent or executory.

In the case of a residuary trust fund established by a will in which the testator's children on attaining their majority took a life interest only in their respective shares of the trust fund but where there was no express direction to accumulate the income during the minority of the beneficiaries, the fund carried the intermediate income and *TA 1925, s 31* applied (*Re Leng [1938] Ch 821*).

Vested annuities

24.14 By *TA 1925, s 31(4)*, *section 31* treats a vested annuity as if it were the income of property held on trust to pay the income to the annuitant for a period of time equal to the duration of the annuity with the exception being that accumulations made during the minority of the annuitant will, in all cases, be held for the annuitant or his personal representatives absolutely.

Class gifts

24.15 In the case of a gift to a class of beneficiaries where the members of the class have contingent interests and the class is not yet closed, the precise share of each member of the class is uncertain. Thus in *Re Joel's Will Trusts [1967] Ch 14* the beneficiaries were grandchildren of the testator who were living 21 years after the death of the testator's son, or who attained 21, or married under that age, before that date. Goff J set out how the trustees should apply the income as required by *TA 1925, s 31*.

The trustees had to first ascertain the amount of the income and the amount to which each grandchild was contingently entitled by apportioning the amount of the income and outgoings according to the state of the class as it exists when the income arises. A grandchild had no right or interest in income (*qua* income) arising before he was born, only to income arising thereafter. A separate account should be kept of the income of the contingent share of each grandchild.

In the event of the death of a grandchild before obtaining a vested interest, the accumulated income of his presumptive share should be added to and dealt with as part of the general capital of the fund to be divided between all those grandchildren who took a vested share whether or not born at the time the accumulation was made.

Vesting order

24.16 Where an infant is beneficially entitled to any property the court may, with a view to the application of capital or income thereof for the maintenance, education or benefit of the infant, make an order appointing a person to convey such property or a vesting order to enable it to be dealt with. An example of the type of situation where this power might be required is *Re Heyworth's Contingent Reversionary Interest [1956] Ch 364*. In that case, a class of grandchildren was entitled under a fund subject to a life interest. The life tenant (mother of the grandchildren) proposed to purchase the grandchildren's reversionary interest. One such grandchild was an infant and so not able to make an effective sale and the court was asked to use the jurisdiction under *TA 1925, s 53*, or the inherent jurisdiction, to enable the sale to proceed.

In the event, the court held that the proposal was not being made with a view to the application of capital or income for the maintenance, education or benefit of the infant (the incentive was to save estate duty) and so declined to make the order. A different decision on the facts might be reached today.

Chapter 25

Power of Advancement

Introduction

25.1 The purpose of a power of advancement is to empower a trustee to apply all or part of capital to, or for the benefit of, a person with a present or prospective interest in that capital whether his interest is absolute or contingent, or subject to a gift over on his death (or some other event) and whether that interest is in possession, in remainder or in reversion.

A power of advancement differs from the exercise of a discretionary power of appointment, in that an appointment confers the beneficial interest and thereby determines the nature of the beneficial interest, whereas in the case of a power of advancement the nature of the beneficial interest is already established and the enjoyment of that interest is accelerated to the extent of the advance. The exercise of a power of advancement can, however, impact on the beneficial interests created by the trust, given that the exercise of the power anticipates the vesting in possession of an interest which, had the power not been exercised, might not have happened. If, for example, one takes a common example of a gift to 'A' contingent upon his attaining the age of 25 and in default to 'B', the exercise of the power of advancement in A's favour will effectively accelerate A's interest in the funds advanced to the detriment of B in the event that A subsequently dies under the specified age.

A power of advancement may be conferred on the trustees by express words or by incorporating the statutory power given by *section 32* of the *Trustee Act 1925* (*TA 1925*) either as it stands, or in a modified form. If the trust instrument is silent then *section 32* will apply unless it is expressly or impliedly excluded by other provisions in the deed (*section 69(2)*).

The power of advancement in respect of a beneficiary's share necessarily ends when the interest vests absolutely (*Re Wills' Will Trusts [1959] Ch 1*) although in the case of an infant, from whom a good receipt cannot be taken until he attains his majority (or marries under that age), the power of advancement remains exercisable during infancy notwithstanding that his interest may have vested.

Although a power of advancement applies to a wide range of interests, including interests which, being contingent, may never fall into possession, it does not apply to the interest of a person which is dependent on the failure of a prior interest in the capital (see *Re Winch's Settlement [1917] 1 Ch 633*).

The statutory power

25.2 *TA 1925, s 32* provides that trustees may at any time or times, pay or apply any capital money subject to a trust, for the advancement or benefit of any person entitled to the capital of the trust property or of any share thereof, in such manner as they may in their absolute discretion think fit, up to one half of his presumptive or vested share.

An advance may be made under *section 32*, whether the person is entitled to capital absolutely or contingently on his attaining any specified age or on the occurrence of any other event, or subject to a gift over on his death under any specified age or on the occurrence of any other event, and whether in possession or in remainder or reversion. An advance may be made notwithstanding that the interest of such person is liable to be defeated by the exercise of a power of appointment or revocation, or to be diminished by the increase of the class to which he belongs.

Person entitled to a prior interest must consent

25.3 No advance may be made so as to prejudice any person entitled to any prior life or other interest, whether vested or contingent, in the money paid or applied unless such person is in existence and of full age and consents in writing to such payment or application. [*TA 1925, s 32(1)(c)*].

In the case of a protective trust, consent to an exercise of the power of advancement by a life tenant with a protected life interest will not cause a forfeiture of the life interest (*Re Rees' Will Trusts [1954] 1 All ER 7*).

A bankrupt life tenant may consent to an exercise of the power of advancement but must have the sanction of the trustee in bankruptcy (*Re Cooper (1884) 27 Ch D 565*).

In the case of a patient within the meaning of the *Mental Health Act 1983*, the judge may give the necessary consent pursuant to the *Mental Health Act 1983, s 96*.

Limited to one half of the fund

25.4 Although *TA 1925, s 32* expressly provides that the trustees can exercise the power in favour of a beneficiary at any time and more than once, it also limits the amount of the fund that can be advanced to one half of the presumptive or vested share of that person in the trust property. Once a beneficiary has received one half of his share, no further exercise of the power is possible even if the residue of the share thereafter significantly increases in value (*Re Marquess of Abergavenny's Estate Trusts [1981] 1 WLR 843*). In that case, the power was an express power but the principle would seem to be equally applicable to the statutory power. Goulding J thought it was plain that, where there is a power to make successive payments to a beneficiary up to a limit of a certain fraction of a fund and, at a certain date, the beneficiary has received assets then fully reaching the prescribed limit, thereafter no further exercise of the power is possible; all that the settlor had authorised had been done.

A common modification to *section 32* is to remove the reference to one half of the beneficiary's presumptive or vested share so that the power of advancement extends to the whole share.

The duty of a trustee in respect of the power of advancement

25.5 The power of advancement is a fiduciary power. The trustees must weigh the benefit to the proposed advancee against the interests of those who are or might become interested under the settlement and whose interest would be adversely affected by the advance. If the circumstances warrant an advance for a particular purpose specified by the trustees then it is the duty of the trustees to see that the advance is so applied and the trustees should not leave the advancee free to spend the advance in whatever way he chooses. In *Re Pauling's Settlement Trusts [1964] Ch 303*, the trustee (a trust corporation) made a number of advances on behalf of children whilst they were infants or, having come of age, still under the undue influence of their parents. In the event, the advances were used to finance the living expenses of the family who lived beyond their means and were continually in financial difficulties. The advances were held to be in breach of trust and the trustee was liable for the sums advanced, although the children had to give credit for property which they had actually received and the children were not entitled to recover in respect of those advances to which they had assented as adults once emancipated from parental control.

Advancement not restricted to money

25.6 Although the statutory power refers to the payment or application of capital *money*, trustees may make an advance by the transfer of investments to a beneficiary and even a conveyance of land. In *Re Collard's Will Trusts [1961] Ch 293*, the court held that trustees in the exercise of their statutory power of advancement could legitimately convey a farm to a beneficiary. Buckley J, whilst noting that the section authorised the trustees to make payments or apply capital moneys in certain ways and that primarily the power under *section 32* is a power to deal with cash, observed that the trustees, having made an advance of cash, could equally sell part of the trust property to the beneficiary. A court of equity would not insist on circuity of action if the same legitimate result could be achieved by direct action.

What is meant by advancement or benefit

25.7 *TA 1925, s 32* refers to a payment or application of capital money 'for the advancement or benefit' of the beneficiary. The term 'advancement' in this context means the advancement in life of a beneficiary such as, for example, helping him to establish himself in a profession; it carries the idea of some step in life of permanent significance. However, 'benefit' is a far more general concept. Taken as a whole, the phrase authorises any use of the money which will improve the material situation of the beneficiary (*Pilkington v IRC [1964] AC 612*).

In *Re Hampden's Settlement Trusts [2001] WTLR 195*, dealing with an express power of advancement, the court accepted the proposition that under a wide power of advancement the trustees can deal with capital in any way which, viewed objectively, can fairly be regarded as being to the benefit of the object of the power, and subjectively they believe to be so.

Section 32, in terms, gives trustees an absolute discretion as to the manner of the advance. The power of advancement can be exercised by way of a direct payment of capital to a beneficiary, provided the trustees are satisfied that it is a proper case for such a payment (*Re Moxon's Will Trusts [1958] 1 WLR 165*), by resettlement of the beneficiary's share (*Pilkington v IRC*), or by the conveyance to him of land or investments held as part of his share (*Re Collard's Will Trusts [1961] Ch 293*). Payment of a beneficiary's debts, the interest on which absorbed nearly the whole of his income, and the principal of which he was unable to pay out of his own resources, was a proper exercise of a power of advancement (*Lowther v Bentinck (1874) LR 19 Eq 166*).

The exercise of a power of advancement is not confined to provision of a direct financial advantage to a beneficiary. A wealthy person, who recognised a moral obligation to make appropriate donations to charity, was materially benefited by having such obligation discharged out of the trust fund rather than his own pocket (*Re Clore's Settlement Trusts [1966] 1 WLR 955*). However, in that case, Pennycuick J emphasised that it was essential that the beneficiary himself should recognise a moral obligation; it was not for the trustees to decide independently of the beneficiary to pay money in discharge of what they considered to be his moral obligations.

Accordingly, an advance of that nature can only be made with the approval of the beneficiary. Pennycuick J also observed that the advance proposed was 'not excessive' indicating that the quantum of a proposed advance is a relevant consideration for the trustees.

The importance of the beneficiary himself recognising a moral obligation was emphasized in *Re Esteem Settlement, Grupo Torras AS v Al-Sabah [2001] WTLR 641*. In that case Sheikh Fahad Mohammed Al-Sabah owed the claimant a sum of US$687million as a consequence of a fraud by him. He had two discretionary trusts in Jersey, which between them held assets worth US$18million and of which he and his family were beneficiaries. The trustees surrendered their discretion to the Jersey court that considered whether or not it should order a distribution of all or most of the trust fund for the Sheikh's benefit by paying the sums to the claimant in reduction of the debt. The Sheikh objected to the payment being made. The court held that it should not make any such payment. The level of indebtedness was such that reduction of the debt would make no difference to the ability of the Sheikh to support himself and his family. Furthermore, it was not for a trustee to determine what were the beneficiary's moral obligations, or to impose the trustee's sense of morality on an adult beneficiary. The court also indicated that, had it reached a different view on the principle of a payment, it would not, in any event, have exercised its discretion to pay out all or most of the trust funds to the claimant, for to have done so would have been to have conferred a very intangible benefit on the Sheikh and caused a material disadvantage to other beneficiaries under the trust. The decision of the Jersey Royal Court was affirmed on appeal (*Re Esteem Settlement, Grupo Torras AS v Al-Sabah [2002] WTLR 337*).

In reality, such a payment would have been for the benefit of the creditor rather than for the benefit of the beneficiary. The Court of Appeal did, however, indicate that in some circumstances a trustee might properly conclude that the discharge of a moral obligation might be for an objecting beneficiary's benefit, although in the instant case there was no sufficient benefit to justify the distribution.

Fiscal planning

25.8 A direct payment of capital to a beneficiary which the beneficiary does not presently require, but which will reduce the amount of tax that would otherwise be payable may be for the beneficiary's benefit (see *Re Moxon's Will Trusts [1958] 1 WLR 165*). Similarly a resettlement of the share of a beneficiary for the purpose of minimising or avoiding tax which would otherwise be payable from that share comes within the statutory power as being for the benefit of that beneficiary (*Pilkington v IRC [1964] AC 612*).

Incidental benefits to third parties

25.9 Although the power of advancement must be exercised for the benefit of a beneficiary, if the provision made is for the benefit of that beneficiary, it is no objection to the exercise of the power that other persons benefit incidentally as a result of the exercise (per Viscount Radcliffe in *Pilkington v IRC [1964] AC 612 at 636*). The provision being contemplated in *Pilkington* was a resettlement of the contingent share of a beneficiary on trusts under which children of hers might benefit, although such children were not beneficiaries under the main trust. See also *Re Halsted's Will Trusts [1937] 2 All ER 570*, where, in the context of an express power of advancement with similar wording to the statutory power, Farwell J thought that a settlement made for the benefit of the wife and child of a beneficiary would be for the benefit of the beneficiary since it enabled him to make provision for his family in the event of his death and therefore it would relieve the beneficiary 'from what would be a very anxious position'. However, Farwell J thought that the power would only permit the inclusion of the spouse and children of the beneficiary and any ultimate trust would have to be for the benefit of the estate.

If a beneficiary himself had only very limited means, it is doubtful whether the settlement of an extremely large sum of money on his children could be regarded as conferring a benefit upon him (see *Re Hampden Settlement Trusts [2001] WTLR 195*).

It is not a requirement for a valid exercise of the power that the beneficiary should ask for the money to be advanced or even that he should consent to the exercise of the power (*Pilkington v IRC [1964] AC 612*). The power of advancement is frequently exercised in respect of the interests of infants who cannot give an effective consent. A not uncommon form of advance is the resettlement of capital to which an infant will become absolutely entitled on terms that postpone possession until the infant has reached more mature years. Although, in the short term, the infant is financially worse off than he or she would have been, in the long term such a resettlement will operate to his or her benefit. Another common incentive for an advance by way of resettlement is the avoidance or reduction of possible capital tax liabilities.

In appropriate circumstances trustees may conclude that an advance is for the benefit of a beneficiary even though the beneficiary objects to the advance proposed to be made (*Re Esteem Settlement, Grupo Torras AS v Al-Sabah (No 6) [2001] WTLR 641*).

Resettlement must be confined to the perpetuity period

25.10 When a power of advancement is exercised so as to resettle the share of a beneficiary, the relevant perpetuity period is that applicable to the trust under which the power of advancement arose (*Pilkington v IRC [1964] AC 612*).

For the purpose of identifying the perpetuity period, the power of advancement is treated as if it was a special power of appointment, but the analogy is not a perfect one. Whereas a special power gives power to allocate property among a class of beneficiaries, a power of advancement has only one object. Therefore, if the power of advancement is exercised by way of resettlement and some of the limitations are void for perpetuity, then (unless those limitations are of a minor nature) it may not be possible to sever the invalid parts of the settlement from the valid parts and the whole appointment may be bad. Cross J in *Re Abraham's Will Trusts [1969] 1 Ch 463 at 485* explained the reasoning as follows:

> 'It is one thing to say that if a trustee has power to appoint a fund to all or any of a class of objects and he appoints a life interest to one object which is not void for perpetuity and remainders to other objects which are not void, then the life interest survives the invalidity of the remainders; but it is another thing to say that if a trustee has power to benefit A in a number of different ways and he chooses to benefit him by making a settlement on him for life with remainders to his issue, which remainders are void for perpetuity, then A can claim to obtain that part of the benefit intended for him which is represented by the life interest. The interests given to separate objects of an ordinary special power are separate interests, but all the interests created in [A's] fund were intended as part and parcel of a single benefit to her'.

Section 32 subject to contrary intention

25.11 Like the power of maintenance, a power of advancement applies only if and so far as a contrary intention is not expressed in the instrument creating the trust and has effect subject to the terms of that instrument. [*TA 1925, s 69(2)*].

Thus, if, on a fair reading of the instrument, applying *TA 1925, s 32* would be inconsistent with the purport of the trust it will not apply. However, an express protective trust does not amount to a contrary intention for these purposes (*Re Rees' Will Trusts [1954] 1 All ER 7*).

A settlor may exclude the statutory power expressly or by implication, for example by including an express power of advancement in a settlement. Alternatively, he may choose to modify the statutory power. A very common modification is to remove the limit on advancement and so permit up to the whole of a beneficiary's presumptive share to be advanced. A far less common modification was made in *Re Collard's Will Trusts [1961] Ch 293* where the testator prohibited an advance 'for any purpose connected with business'.

Class gifts

25.12 *TA 1925, s 32*, in terms, permits an advance to be made to a person notwithstanding that his interest is liable to be defeated by the exercise of a power of appointment or revocation or to be diminished by the increase of the class to which he belongs. However, the strength of the possibility that a person's presumptive share will be reduced is clearly a relevant consideration for the trustees when contemplating whether or not to make an advance, and if so, how much.

If a person to whom or for whose benefit an advance has been made is or becomes absolutely and indefeasibly entitled to a share in the trust property, the advance must be brought into account as part of that person's share (*section 32(1)(b)*). If the advance was in money, then it is the sum advanced rather than the proportion of the fund which is brought into account; if the advance was in the form of property then it is brought into account at its value as at the date of the advance not the date of distribution (*Re Gollin's Declaration of Trust [1969] 1 WLR 1858*). This may work to the advantage of the beneficiary advanced in times of inflation. However, if a trustee is empowered to and does advance the whole of a beneficiary's presumptive share, then it is anticipated that such beneficiary does not take any further benefit even if the value of the remaining trust fund increases, for he has already received all he was entitled to.

Settled land

25.13 *TA 1925, s 32* does not apply to capital money arising under the *Settled Land Act 1925*.

Chapter 26

Power to Appoint

Duty to consider

26.1 When a trustee is considering the exercise of a dispositive power (whether in the nature of a mere power or a trust power or a hybrid power) he must do so in a responsible manner and not capriciously. Obviously, the trustee must obey the trust instrument and make no appointment that is not authorised by it. In *Re Hay's Settlement Trusts [1982] 1 WLR 202 at 210*, Megarry V-C laid down three further duties which he regarded not necessarily as exhaustive but containing the essentials. The trustee must consider:

- periodically whether or not he should exercise the power;
- the range of objects of the power;
- the appropriateness of individual appointments.

Periodic consideration

26.2 How frequently a trustee must consider the exercise of a dispositive power depends on all the circumstances of the case. Clearly, a discretion to appoint income will usually fall to be considered more frequently than a discretion to appoint capital. In a proper case it may be sufficient for a trustee to await a relevant event either in the trust (such as the death of the life tenant, or the attaining of majority of an infant, or a birth which increases the size of the class) or an extrinsic event (such as a serious change of financial or personal circumstances of a member of the class, or an application to the trustee for consideration).

The range of objects

26.3 As has been pointed out (see CHAPTER 22: TRUST POWERS AND DUTIES DISTINGUISHED), the requirement for certainty of objects differs between a trust and a power, and the class of objects of a mere power can be very wide indeed without the power being invalid. When faced with a wide class of objects, the trustee must not simply proceed to exercise the power in favour of such of the objects as happen to be at hand or claim attention. The trustee must first consider what persons or classes of persons are objects of the power within the definition in the settlement or will. In doing this, there is no need to compile a complete list of the objects, or even to make an accurate assessment of the number of them: what is needed is an appreciation of the width of the field (*Re Hay's Settlement Trust [1982] 1 WLR 202 at 209*). That being said, in the case of a very wide class of objects the duty does not require the trustees to consider every member of the class. As was observed in *Re Gestetner Settlement [1953] Ch 672*, trustees need not 'worry their heads to survey the world from China to Peru, when there are perfectly good objects of the class in England'.

The appropriateness of individual appointments

26.4 Where trustees have an absolute and uncontrolled discretion, then provided they act bona fide the court will not interfere with that discretion even if the court would have exercised it differently. So, for example, in *Gisborne v Gisborne (1877) 2 App Cas 300*, trustees exercised their discretion by declining to appoint income to the widow of the deceased who, since her husband's death, had been of unsound mind so that she was being maintained out of her own property. The practice at the time, had the matter been in the discretion of the court, would have been to have thrown the cost of her upkeep on the fund rather than her own property, but the court refused to interfere with the trustees' discretion.

Fraud on the power

26.5 An improper exercise of a power of appointment is usually referred to as a fraud on the power although it does not necessarily involve fraud in the sense of deceit: 'it indicates a sense of doing something which is not right … at least a deliberate defeating of what the donor of the power authorised and intended' (per Evershed MR in *Re Dick [1953] Ch 343 at 360*).

In the context of special powers (e.g. a power to appoint among a specified class of objects) reference has been made to a trustee acting 'capriciously, that is to say [acting] for reasons which … could be said to be irrational, perverse or irrelevant to any sensible expectation of the settlor' (per Templeman J in *Re Manisty's Settlement [1973] 2 All ER 1203 at 1210*). A wide or general power of appointment, however, will not evince any such expectation; if a donee has power to appoint a fund to himself, there is no basis for impeaching his exercise of the power if he chooses to divert it to another.

Improper or excessive appointment

26.6 Obviously an appointment made to a person who is outside the class of objects is bad, as is an appointment of more than a permitted sum. Appointments transgressing rules of law or the scope of the power are said to be 'excessive' in their execution.

An appointment may be bad even though made to a proper appointee if it is made for a purpose foreign to the object of the power. So, for example, where an appointor with power to appoint to his wife and children, purported to appoint an annuity to his wife on condition that she should expend a certain sum in payment of his debts, that execution of the power was void, it having been made for the purpose of benefiting the appointor rather than the appointee (*Re Cohen [1911] 1 Ch 37*).

Similarly, an appointment accompanied by a non-binding obligation to apply all or part of the funds appointed to a non-object may be a fraud on the power and held bad – see *Re Dick [1953] Ch 343 at 360*, where a letter of wishes written by the appointor demonstrated that the exercise of the power was for the purpose of benefiting a non-object.

Where in family proceedings an order had been made against a husband (who was an object of a power) in favour of his ex-wife (who was not) it was not a fraud on the power to exercise the discretion to restore the husband's depleted assets even though the family court might have reviewed the order had the trustees declined (*Netherton v Netherton [2000] WTLR 1171*).

In connection with a power of advancement, the court held that a payment direct to a creditor to reduce the indebtedness of the beneficiary to the creditor, such payment being opposed by the beneficiary, would not have been for his benefit and should not be made; it was not for the trustee to determine what the beneficiary's moral obligations were (*Re Esteem Settlement, Grupo Torras SA v Al-Sabbah (No 6) [2001] WTLR 641*).

Where a variation of trust, to which the approval of the court under the *Variation of Trusts Act 1958* was required, had been preceded by an exercise of a power of appointment and there was a fair case for investigation whether a fraud on the power was involved, approval to the arrangement was withheld until such investigation had been made and the question satisfactorily resolved (*Re Wallace's Settlement [1968] 1 WLR 711*). In that case, the tenant for life had a power to appoint capital and income of her share to her children or remoter issue; there were trusts in default of appointment. In order to mitigate the burden of estate duty on her death, the tenant for life proposed a variation whereby the fund was split between herself and her two children in accordance with an actuarial valuation. The variation was preceded by the exercise of the power of appointment in favour of the two children. The court found that the power of appointment had been exercised bona fide for the purpose for which it was intended and not for any ulterior purpose.

In *Re Crawshay [1948] Ch 123*, the Court of Appeal accepted six propositions of law relating to improper exercise of a power of appointment. They were:

- One case for fraud on a power is where the donee of a special power of appointment makes an appointment intended to benefit some person not an object of the power.
- To establish a fraud on the power, it is not necessary to prove a bargain between the donee of the power and the appointee.
- What the court looks to is the intention or purpose of the appointor in making the appointment.
- It is not necessary that:
  - (*a*) the appointee should be a party to or know of the corrupt intention or purpose; or
  - (*b*) that the purpose should in fact take effect.
- The relevant date at which the intention of the appointor has to be ascertained is the date of the exercise of the power.
- Evidence is admissible as to the state of mind of the appointor, including statements by the appointor which go to show his or her state of mind at the material date. Such statements may be material although they are not contemporaneous with the date of exercise of the power.

It was also stated that if a corrupt purpose is shown ever to have been entertained but it is said to have been abandoned prior to the execution of the power, then the court reaches a conclusion as to the propriety of the exercise on the basis of the evidence as a whole; there is not necessarily an onus of proof on those who support the appointment to show that the corrupt intention has been abandoned.

Those six propositions listed above were dictated by the facts of that case and *Re Dick* and were stated not to be an exhaustive formulation of frauds on a power or the methods of establishing allegations of frauds on a power. However, subject to that caveat, they provide a useful guide.

The more general rule (stated in *Re Dick* at *page 360* as the rule which should guide the court) is:

> 'It is enough that the appointor's purpose and intention is to secure a benefit for himself or some other person not an object of the power'.

However, this must itself be treated with care as was demonstrated in *Re Dick* by an immediate qualification that not every intention 'however secreted in the bosom of the appointor' to benefit some non-object in some measure made the appointment bad. There is a distinction between the motive and purpose and it is the latter that counts (see per Knox J in *Hillsdown Holdings plc v Pensions Ombudsman [1996] PLR 427 at 442*).

Benefit not per se objectionable

26.7 The fact that the appointor, or another stranger, might obtain some benefit as a consequence of the appointment is not of itself enough to make bad an appointment otherwise bona fide; the purpose of the appointment must be to benefit the appointor or some person other than the appointee (*Vatcher v Paull [1915] AC 372*).

A recent example of this principle is *Fuller v Evans [2000] 1 All ER 636*, where the trustees had power during the accumulation period to pay or apply income for the maintenance, education or benefit of the children of the marriage and the settlor and his wife. On a divorce, the settlor was ordered to pay maintenance in respect of the children together with a further amount sufficient to defray their school fees. The trustees took the view that it would be for the benefit of the children for their school fees to be paid from the income of the trust fund pursuant to the power so to do. The court held that they were entitled to exercise that power notwithstanding that a consequence would be that the settlor was relieved of his obligation under the divorce order to pay those school fees. The judge made clear that the trustees must have regard to the obligation of the settlor to provide for the beneficiaries' maintenance and education when undertaking the decision-making process, but the existence of the settlor's obligation was no more than a consideration to which due weight must be given. That was a reflection of the *Trustee Act 1925, s 31(1)(i)(b)* which provides that payment of income for the maintenance, education or benefit of an infant may be reasonable whether or not there is any person bound by law to provide for his maintenance or education. The settlor had been a trustee but retired as a trustee to avoid any conflict of interest and duty. The settlement contained an express provision (included, no doubt, for fiscal purposes) excluding any benefit to the settlor or any spouse of the settlor. The court held that the provision did little (if anything) more than 'vigorously reaffirm' the duty of the trustees to have regard exclusively to the best interests of the beneficiaries and ignore those of the settlor.

Appointment subject to a condition

26.8 An appointor may attach a condition to the exercise of a power of appointment, providing that the real purpose and object of the appointment is to benefit the object of the power. So an appointment made on condition that the appointed funds be settled by the appointee for the benefit of the appointee and her children was held to be a good appointment (*Re Burton's Settlement [1955] Ch 82*). The case was quite unlike *Re Cohen [1911] 1 Ch 37* (see 26.6 above) where the purpose of the condition had been to procure a benefit from the appointment to the appointor.

Power to appoint to one object only

26.9 A striking case is *Re Nicholson's Settlement [1939] Ch 11*. In that case, Miss Nicholson, a spinster, was entitled to the income from a fund. She was living with a family in Oregon in the United States of America and wished to make some provision for them. Under the settlement she had the power to appoint income to be paid to her husband after her death. She began correspondence with solicitors acting for the trustees and family generally, endeavouring to negotiate a release of that power in return for a share of capital, representing that, if that were not agreed, she would marry and exercise her power of appointment. She was then aged over 80 years of age. They refused. She then proceeded to marry a man who was a near relation of the friends that she wanted to assist and exercised the power of appointment in his favour. They never lived together as man and wife. The court found that there was no arrangement between the lady and her husband as to how he would deal with the income and declined to interfere with the appointment. The court held that there was a distinction between the cases where someone had a right to appoint to an individual as opposed to the power of selection amongst a class.

The closing words of the judgment suggest that it really turned on the difference between the purpose of the appointment (which was to procure the payment of the income to the man she had married) and the motives which had led to that purpose which was a hope that the husband would use that income for the benefit of the relations whose welfare was a matter of concern to her. If there had been some bargain arrangement or understanding requiring the husband to use the income for that purpose, different considerations would have applied.

Failure to give proper consideration

26.10 The court will interfere if an appointor fails to give proper consideration to the exercise of a power of appointment. An example is *Klug v Klug [1918] 2 Ch 67*. In that case, trustees had a power of advancement in favour of the testator's daughter. The trustees comprised the Public Trustee and the widow of the testator. The Public Trustee wished to exercise the power but the widow would not agree. Her refusal was because her daughter had married without her consent and she declined to consider whether or not it would be for her daughter's welfare that an advance should be made. The court held that the widow was not exercising her discretion at all and in those circumstances it was the duty of the court to interfere and in the exercise of its control over the discretion given to the trustees to direct that an advance be made. In *Turner v Turner [1984] Ch 100*, a solicitor acting on the instructions of the settlor prepared documents for the trustees (all members of the family) to sign which purported to be, and to effect, an exercise of their power of appointment. The court found that the trustees were unaware of their discretion and had not read or understood the documents they were asked to sign. It followed that they had not applied their minds to the exercise of the power of appointment which had not been validly exercised. The appointments were therefore set aside.

Duty to take account of tax consequences of an appointment

26.11 An appointor must take account of the fiscal consequences of an appointment – see *Green v Cobham [2000] WTLR 1101*, where a purported appointment was a material event which would have led to a huge liability to capital gains tax. The appointment was held to be bad. The trustees had not considered, as they should have considered, the possible risks with regard to capital gains tax that the appointment would have involved. The case is of particular interest in that the appointment would not, in itself, have triggered the capital gains tax liability but set up a situation where the capital gains tax liability could be triggered by a change of trustees of a deed, the composition of which trustees was outside the control of the trustees of the will trust. The judge found on the evidence that, had the trustees of the will trust had regard to the possible capital gains tax consequences of the proposed appointment, they would not have gone ahead with it. Their failure to direct their minds to considerations of capital gains tax was sufficient to make the purported appointment an invalid exercise of the trustees' power of appointment and consequently void in its entirety.

The Hastings-Bass principle

26.12 Not every invalid exercise of a power of appointment is a consequence of deliberate intention on the part of the appointor. Where contrary to Counsel's advice, an appointment was effected immediately before, rather than immediately after, the end of the financial year (with adverse tax consequences), the appointment was invalidated and set aside (*Abacus Trust Company v National Society for the Prevention of Cruelty to Children [2001] WTLR 953*). The trustees had failed to take into account the adverse tax consequences of their actions which they were under a duty to take into account.

The court applied the principle set out in *Re Hastings-Bass [1975] Ch 25* expressed thus:

'... where by the terms of a trust ... a trustee is given a discretion as to some matter under which he acts in good faith, the court should not interfere with his action notwithstanding that it does not have the full effect which he intended, unless:

(1) what he has achieved is unauthorised by the power conferred on him; or

(2) it is clear that he would not have acted as he did:

   (*a*) had he not taken into account considerations which he should not have taken into account; or

   (*b*) had he not failed to take into account considerations which he ought to have taken into account'.

The *Hasting-Bass* principle, which was expressed in the negative, was transposed into the positive by Warner J in *Mettoy Pension Trustees v Evans [1990] 1 WLR 1587 at page 1621* thus:

> 'Where a trustee acts under a discretion given to him by the clear terms of the trust, the court will interfere with his action if it is clear that he would not have acted as he did had he not failed to take into account considerations which he ought to have taken into account'.

The *Hasting-Bass* principle may also apply not only where the trustees *would* not have acted as they did had they appreciated the true position but *might not* have so acted – see *Stannard v Fisons Pension Trust Ltd [1991] PLR 225*, where the current value of the fund was a material fact for the trustees to consider. They were not properly informed of the value of the fund and their decision was therefore bad.

Not every error will demonstrate a failure on the part of the trustees to act properly, such as to make the appointment bad. In *Re Hastings-Bass* itself the test was not satisfied as the principal object of the exercise (to create a life interest) was achieved. It was only the ulterior trusts which failed as they infringed the rule against perpetuity. The appointment was held good. The principle, as now established, does not operate in an 'all or nothing' way (*Mettoy Pension Trustees v Evans [1990] 1 WLR 1587 at pp 1624–25*). Nevertheless, if the power of appointment is a mere power and has expired no doctrine of equity can revive it (*Breadner v Granville-Grossman [2000] WTLR 829*).

Giving or withholding of reasons

26.13 Trustees are not obliged to disclose to the beneficiaries the reasons for their decision (*Re Beloved Wilkes Charity (1851) 3 Mac & G 440*). Accordingly, in principle they are not bound to disclose to their beneficiaries the agenda or minutes of their meetings or document prepared for those meetings, or letters between an individual beneficiary and the trustee or appointor (*Re Londonderry's Settlement [1965] Ch 918*).

The court does, however, retain a discretion to direct disclosure, e.g. of a settlor's letter of wishes, if there are good grounds for doing so (*Re Rabaiotti 1989 Settlement (1999–2000) 2 ITELR 763*).

Remedies

26.14 If trustees wrongly refuse to exercise a trust power the court may exercise it and will do so in a manner best calculated to give effect to the settlor's or the testator's wishes. It may do so by appointing new trustees, or by authorising or directing representative persons of classes of beneficiaries to prepare a scheme of distribution, or should the proper basis of distribution appear by itself directing the trustees so to distribute (*McPhail v Doulton [1971] AC 424 at 457*). If the trustees who have failed to exercise a discretion wish to repair that omission and are not disentitled from doing so, the court may in the exercise of its discretion permit them to do so but only in favour of those persons who would have been objects had the discretion been exercised at the appropriate time (*Re Locker's Settlement [1977] 1 WLR 1323*).

In the case of an appointment improperly made, the court will declare the appointment to be void. A trustee who has transferred assets or paid away money pursuant to the defective exercise will be liable to reinstate the trust fund if the assets or money cannot be recovered.

Release of a power of appointment

26.15 In the case of a power of appointment which can be released (as to which see CHAPTER 21: TAKING ADDITIONAL ADMINISTRATIVE POWERS OR SURRENDERING OR RELEASING POWERS) the doctrine of fraud on the power does not apply to a release, even if the release is intended to benefit the appointor (*Re Somes [1896] 1 Ch 250*; *Re Radcliffe [1892] 1 Ch 227*; *Re Greaves [1954] Ch 434*). It is important to note that this applies only to a power of appointment not coupled with a duty, i.e. a power which the appointor is under no duty to exercise.

Pension funds

26.16 Beneficiaries under a pension scheme are not volunteers. Their rights derive from contractual and commercial origins. They have purchased their rights as part of their employment. The trustees, therefore, do not have an uncontrolled discretion in respect of a claim for benefit. The duty of the trustee is to give properly informed consideration to the application (*Kerr v British Leyland (Staff) Trustee Ltd* (26 March 1986) unreported, but referred to in *Stannard v Fisons Pension Trust Ltd [1991] PLR 225*).

Even though beneficiaries under a pension scheme are not volunteers, the principles applicable to private trusts, as a matter of trust law, apply equally to pension schemes (*Wilson v Law Debenture Trust Corporation [1995] 2 All ER 337*; *Cowan v Scargill [1985] Ch 270*). Accordingly, a trustee of a pension fund is not required to give reasons for the exercise of a discretion and in the absence of evidence that the trustee has acted improperly, whether from an improper motive or by taking account of factors which the trustee should not have taken into account, or not taking into account factors which the trustee should have taken into account, the court will not interfere with the exercise of the trustee's discretion or compel disclosure of trust documents which indicate or might indicate the reason for the trustee's determination (*Wilson v Law Debenture Trust Corporation*).

A trustee of a pension fund is under a duty to act impartially, that being no more than the ordinary duty which the law imposes on a person entrusted with the exercise of a discretionary power, namely the duty to exercise the power for its proper purpose, giving proper consideration to relevant matters and excluding from consideration irrelevant matters. Providing that pension fund trustees so act, they cannot be criticised if they reach a decision which appears to prefer the claims of one interest over others. On the contrary, such a preference would be the result of a proper exercise of the discretionary power (*Edge v Pensions Ombudsman [2000] Ch 602*).

Chapter 27

The Rule Against Perpetuities

Introduction

27.1 All future estates must vest within the relevant perpetuity period. A trustee will, of course, consider whether or not the trust he is administering does or does not comply with the perpetuity rule, but given the nature and scope of this work this chapter will concentrate principally on the rule as it affects new or subsidiary settlements created by the exercise of the power of appointment or the power of advancement.

The common law rule was modified by the *Perpetuities and Accumulations Act 1964*. *Section 15* provides that those modifications (save in one respect) apply only to interests arising under an instrument taking effect after the commencement of the 1964 Act (16 July 1964) so care must always be taken when dealing with an older trust to consider whether the 1964 Act applies at all. The Act provides retrospectively that the rule against perpetuities should not operate to invalidate a power conferred on trustees (or any other person) to sell, lease, exchange or otherwise dispose of any property for full consideration or do any other act of administration (as opposed to the distribution) of any property and shall not prevent the payment to trustees or other person of reasonable remuneration for their services.

In the case of the exercise of a special power of appointment, the provisions of the 1964 Act apply only if the instrument creating the power of appointment took effect after commencement of the Act. Where a disposition takes effect without an instrument, the Act applies as if the disposition had been contained in an instrument on that date.

In some cases it may not be immediately obvious whether the trust does or does not post-date the commencement of the Act. In *Re Thomas Meadows & Co Ltd and Subsidiary Companies (1960) Staff Pension Scheme Rules [1971] 1 All ER 239* a company established a staff pension scheme which an employee would join by having his name entered on the register. If he or she was promoted (and so became entitled to a higher pension) that would be noted on the register. It was held that there was a 'disposition' when the employee was first entered on the register and a fresh 'disposition' if he or she was promoted and so the provisions of the 1964 Act applied to any member who was registered after the date it came into force and to increments for those who were then already on the register but subsequently promoted.

The rule

27.2 At common law the perpetuity period was a life in being plus 21 years. A future interest was void if it was not certain to vest within the perpetuity period. The reference to vesting meant vesting in interest, not necessarily in possession. The 21-year period was added as a matter of course and did not have to relate to a period of minority. A further period of gestation could be added if, but only if, the beneficiary was conceived but unborn (*en ventre sa mère*).

The 1964 Act made the following important modifications to the rule in respect of dispositions taking effect after the commencement of the Act:

- it permitted the instrument by which a disposition was made to specify a number of years not exceeding 80 to be the perpetuity period;
- it introduced certain presumptions and permitted evidence to be led as to whether a living person could or could not have a child;
- it introduced the concept of 'wait and see'.

General and special powers of appointment

27.3 For the purpose of the rule against perpetuities, a general power of appointment is one which is exercisable by one person only and which he could at any time (when of full age and capacity) exercise so as immediately to transfer to himself the whole of the interest governed by the power, without the consent of any other person or compliance with any other condition, not being a formal condition relating only to the mode of exercise of the power. Any other power is a special power. [*Perpetuities and Accumulations Act 1964, s 7*].

If a special power of appointment is exercised by appointing all or part of the trust property to be held on new trusts, then the interests under the new trust must vest within the existing perpetuity period, i.e. the perpetuity period applicable to the instrument creating the special power of appointment (*Re Earl of Coventry's Indentures [1974] Ch 77*).

If a settlement is created by the exercise of a general power of appointment then it creates its own perpetuity period. This is perfectly logical as, given the definition of a general power of appointment, the appointee is, for all practical purposes, disposing of the property as if it were his own.

Power of advancement

27.4 A power of advancement is treated by analogy with a special power of appointment and the relevant perpetuity period is the period applicable to the settlement under which the power was created (*Pilkington v IRC [1964] AC 612*).

However, the analogy between a power of advancement and a special power of appointment is not a perfect one. Whereas a special power gives power to allocate property among a class of beneficiaries, a power of advancement has only one object. Therefore, if the power of advancement is exercised by way of resettlement, the whole resettlement is intended to be for the benefit of the beneficiary for whom the advance is being made. If some of the limitations are void for perpetuity, then (unless those limitations are of a minor nature) it may not be possible to sever the invalid parts of the settlement from the valid parts and the whole appointment may be bad (*Re Abrahams' Will Trusts [1969] 1 Ch 463*). If the advance has been worded as an absolute gift with trusts engrafted thereon, then if the trusts are void for remoteness the absolute gift may take effect (see *Hancock v Watson [1902] AC 14*, a case on a testamentary gift).

Variation of trusts

27.5 If a trust is varied by agreement of the beneficiaries and, if necessary, the approval of the court under the *Variation of Trusts Act 1958* (see CHAPTER 30: POWER TO VARY TRUSTS), the arrangement can take advantage of a new perpetuity period. This is because the arrangement owes its authority to the consent rather than to anything in the original settlement (*Re Holt's Settlement [1969] 1 Ch 100 at 120*).

'Wait and see'

27.6 In respect of instruments to which the *Perpetuities and Accumulations Act 1964* applies, 'wait and see' is available. Wait and see operates as follows. If, at the outset, it is uncertain whether a future interest will or will not vest within the relevant perpetuity period, the interest is treated as valid until such time (if any) as it becomes established that the vesting must occur, if at all, after the end of the perpetuity period. Once it becomes established that the interest will not vest within the perpetuity period it will be void, but this does not affect the validity of anything previously done in relation to the interest disposed of by way of advancement, application of intermediate income or otherwise. [*Perpetuities and Accumulations Act 1964, s 3(1)*].

The 'wait and see' approach is applied to a disposition conferring a general power of appointment where it would be void on the ground that the power might not become exercisable until too remote a time (*Perpetuities and Accumulations Act 1964, s 3(2)*). It also applies to dispositions conferring powers, options or other rights that would otherwise be void because they might be exercised at too remote a time. Where it is established that the right will contravene the rule against perpetuities in this way, it will only be treated as void to the extent that it is not fully exercised within the perpetuity period (*section 3(3)*).

Section 3(4) and *(5)* lay down who, for the purpose of the 'wait and see' provisions, are to be regarded as lives in being. The lives are specified in *section 3(5)*. Where there are no such lives, the perpetuity period is 21 years. *Section 3(5)* provides as follows:

'The said persons are as follows:

(*a*) the person by whom the disposition was made;

(*b*) a person to whom or in whose favour the disposition was made, that is to say—

(i) in the case of a disposition to a class of persons, any member or potential member of the class;

(ii) in the case of an individual disposition to a person taking only on certain conditions being satisfied, any person as to whom some of the conditions are satisfied and the remainder may in time be satisfied;

(iii) in the case of a special power of appointment exercisable in favour of members of a class, any member or potential member of the class;

(iv) in the case of a special power of appointment exercisable in favour of one person only, that person or, where the object of the power is ascertainable only on certain conditions being satisfied, any person as to whom some of the conditions are satisfied and the remainder may in time be satisfied;

(v) in the case of any power, option or other right, the person on whom the right is conferred;

(*c*) a person having a child or grandchild within sub-paragraphs (i) to (iv) of paragraph (*b*) above, or any of whose children or grandchildren, if subsequently born, would by virtue of his or her descent fall within those sub-paragraphs;

(*d*) any person on the failure or determination of whose prior interest the disposition is limited to take effect.'

Where the number of persons within *section 3(5)(b)* or *(c)* is such as to render it impracticable to ascertain the date of death of the survivor, their lives shall be disregarded (*section 3(4)(a)*). By *section 15(2)* a person 'in being' is expressly defined so as to include a child *en ventre sa mère*, in conformity with the rule at common law.

Vesting

27.7 In order to comply with the rule against perpetuities, it is only necessary for a gift to vest in interest within the perpetuity period (vesting in possession is not required). However, in order for an interest to vest within the perpetuity period, the beneficiary must be ascertained and the interest ready to take effect in possession subject only to the prior interest; if there remains to be satisfied any other contingency, then the interest does not vest unless and until that contingency has occurred.

Provisions to avoid remoteness

27.8 The *Perpetuities and Accumulations Act 1964, s 4* provides for the reduction of age and exclusion of class members to save a disposition being void for remoteness. Where a disposition is limited by reference to the attaining of an age exceeding 21 years and as a consequence is void, whereas it would not have been void had it specified 21 years, the age is reduced so far as is necessary to save it from being void. It is not necessarily reduced to 21 years if a lesser reduction (e.g. to 24 years) would suffice. If different ages are specified in relation to different persons, each age is reduced so far as necessary. This provision replaced a similar (although not identical) provision in the *Law of Property Act 1925, s 163*.

The operation of *section 4* to a disposition to which wait and see applies, does not affect the validity of anything previously done in relation to the interest disposed of by way of advancement, application of intermediate income or otherwise.

The unborn widow

27.9 The *Perpetuities and Accumulations Act 1964, s 5* deals in part with the 'trap of the unborn widow'. A disposition by reference to the death of the spouse of A offended the common law rule against perpetuities as A might marry a woman not in being at the date of the instrument. *Section 5* operates, in the case of a limitation by reference to the time of death of the survivor of a person in being and any spouse of that person, to substitute a limitation by reference to the time immediately before the end of the perpetuity period.

'Wait and see' to be operated first

27.10 The *Perpetuities and Accumulations Act 1964, ss 4* and *5* only come into play if, operating 'wait and see', it has become clear that the disposition would otherwise be void for remoteness.

Saving future interests

27.11 At common law, a trust which did not itself contravene the rule against perpetuities could yet be void if it was intended to take effect upon the determination of a prior interest which was void for perpetuity. *Section 6* of the 1964 Act removes this possibility for dispositions to which the Act applies and provides for the interest to be accelerated.

Class gifts

27.12 For a gift to a class, e.g. 'all my grandchildren' to be valid at common law, it had to be clear that each member of the class would obtain a vested interest within the perpetuity period and the gift to the class was void if the interests of any possible member might vest outside the period. The gift could be saved by the class closing rule known as the rule in *Andrews v Partington (1791) 3 Bro CC 401* by which a class of beneficiaries normally closes when the first member of the class becomes entitled to be paid his share. The rule is, however, a rule of construction only and can be excluded expressly or by necessary implication.

Where, under a disposition taking effect after 16 July 1964, a class gift would be void at common law and it is not saved by the 'wait and see' provisions and the inclusion of persons, being potential members of a class or unborn persons who at birth would become members or potential members of the class, would either prevent the age reduction provision from saving a disposition, or cause the disposition to be void for perpetuity, then, (save where, in the latter case, the exclusion of those persons would exhaust the class) those persons are thenceforth to be deemed for all purposes of the disposition to be excluded from the class. [*Perpetuities and Accumulations Act 1964, s 4(3), (4)*].

By *section 15(3)* a person is treated as a member of the class if in his case all the conditions identifying him as a member are satisfied; where only some of those conditions are satisfied in relation to a person, but there is a possibility that the remainder will in time be satisfied, that person is treated as a potential member of the class.

By *section 4(5)*, the reduction of age or exclusion of class members where 'wait and see' has applied, does not affect the validity of anything previously done by way of advancement, application of intermediate income or otherwise in relation to the interest disposed of. If, for example, during the period of 'wait and see', income has been applied for the maintenance of a potential member of a class who is subsequently excluded from membership under *section 4(3)*, that application of income is unaffected by the subsequent exclusion of that individual from membership of the class.

Future parenthood

27.13 At common law, in the context of the rule against perpetuities, evidence of incapacity of a particular beneficiary to bear a child was inadmissible and the court will regard any living person, however old, as capable of bearing a child (see the summary of the case law in *Figg v Clarke [1997] 1 WLR 603*).

For instruments taking effect on or after 16 July 1964, and for the purpose of the rule against perpetuities, the *Perpetuities and Accumulations Act 1964, s 2(1)(a)* lays down a presumption that a male can have a child at 14 or over and that a female can have a child between the ages of 12 and 55. A presumption is rebuttable and by *section 2(1)(b)*, in the case of a living person, evidence may be given to show that he or she will or will not be able to have a child at the time in question.

Where, for the purpose of perpetuities, a person has been treated as unable to have a child at a particular time, and in the event that person does have a child, the High Court is given power to make such order as it thinks fit for placing persons interested in the property so far as may be just in the position in which they would have been, had the question of the ability of the person to have a child not been so decided (*section 2(2)*). Where a question turning on the ability of a person to have a child at some future time has been decided, then he or she is to be so treated for the purpose of any question which may arise on the rule against perpetuities in relation to the same disposition in any subsequent proceedings (*section 2(3)*).

References to having a child apply to begetting or giving birth to a child and also to having a child by adoption, legitimation or other means (*section 2(4)*). The *Family Law Reform Act 1987* and the *Human Fertilisation and Embryology Act 1990* make comprehensive provision for the determination of who is to be treated as the mother and the father respectively of a child conceived as a result of artificial insemination.

Chapter 28

Dispositive Powers: Their Duration and Release

Introduction

28.1 A power may be expressly or impliedly limited in time and, if so, the exercise of the power outside those limits will be bad. It may be important to decide whether a power given to a trustee or another can or cannot be released by the donee of the power, and if it can what is the effect of the release. It is also pertinent to consider whether an object of the power can release the donee from further consideration of him as an object of the power, i.e. exclude himself as an object of the discretion.

Duration

28.2 A power to appoint may be limited in time. If the limit is expressly defined then an early or late appointment will be bad. In *Breadner v Granville Grossman [2000] 4 All ER 705*, the trustees were one day late in exercising a power of appointment and it was held that the appointment was bad. The power was a mere power which the trustees had a discretion whether or not to exercise, not a trust power which they were under duty to exercise – therefore equity would not intervene to save the defective appointment. A power which falls to be exercised 'before' a specified date is not available to be exercised *on* the specified date: it has by then expired (*Breadner v Granville Grossman*).

A limit in time may be implied. For example, in the case of a discretion in respect of income arising from time to time, the trustees may be under a duty to exercise their discretion within a reasonable time of the income arising and, if they do not, the discretion is taken to have expired in respect of that income (*Re Gulbenkian's Settlement Trusts (No 2) [1970] Ch 408*). That may be the result even though the reason why the discretion has not been exercised is because the trustees cannot reach agreement how their discretion should be exercised (*Re Allen-Meyrick's Will Trusts [1966] 1 WLR 499*).

What constitutes a reasonable time depends on the circumstances in each case. There may be special circumstances which justify the postponement of the exercise of discretion for longer than would otherwise be reasonable (*Re Gulbenkian's Settlement Trusts*). In that case, the trustees held off exercising their discretion pending the resolution of a doubt caused by a decision in another case. It was held that the trustees had not lost the right to exercise their discretion.

No implied limit on a fiduciary duty

28.3 If the trustees are under a duty to apply income and their discretion extends only to the identity of the object or the amount, then the discretion is not lost by the lapse of a reasonable time with no exercise of the discretion and the trustees may exercise their discretion belatedly. In this event, however, the trustees' discretion should be exercised only in favour of such beneficiaries as would have been objects of the trustees' discretion had it been exercised within a reasonable time after receipt of the relevant income (*Re Locker's Settlement [1978] 1 All ER 216*).

Future exercise of discretion may not be fettered

28.4 A donee of a power or discretion exercisable from time to time may not (in the absence of express provision to the contrary) bind himself either:

- to exercise it in a particular way; or
- not to exercise it in the future (*Re Gibson's Settlement [1981] Ch 179*).

There is, however, no objection to a statement of policy provided that this is open to review and possible alteration (*Re Vestey's Settlement [1951] Ch 209*).

Disclaimer

28.5 The *Law of Property Act 1925, s 156* provides for a person to disclaim a power. Unlike a release, a disclaimer does not put an end to a power and, unless the contrary is expressed in the instrument, the power may be exercised by the other person or persons to whom the power is given. If a power is vested in a person as trustee that person cannot disclaim and remain a trustee (*Re Eyre (1883) 49 LT 259*). Nor can a trustee make a partial disclaimer, e.g. *Re Lord and Fullerton's Contract [1896] 1 Ch 228* – where a testator died leaving property in England and America; one of the persons named as executor and trustee (being in America) purported to disclaim in respect of the English property only and it was held that the disclaimer was of no effect. The problem would not have arisen if the testator had appointed distinct bodies of trustees, one for the English estate and one for the American, even if the same persons had been appointed to each body of trustees.

The question whether or not a power can be released turns on the nature of the power in question. In *Mettoy Pensions Trustees Ltd v Evans [1991] 2 All ER 513 at 545* Warner J classified powers into four categories as follows:

(*a*) any power given to a person to determine the destination of trust property without that person being under any obligation to exercise the power or to preserve it. Typical of powers in this category is a special power of appointment given to an individual where there is a trust in default of appointment. The donee owes a duty to the beneficiaries under that trust not to misuse it but owes no duty to the objects of the power;

(*b*) any power conferred on the trustees of property or any other person as a trustee of the power itself, i.e. a fiduciary power;

(*c*) any discretion which is really a duty to form a judgement as to the existence or otherwise of particular circumstances giving rise to particular consequences, e.g. where a legacy was payable to a hospital only if the trustees were in their sole and absolute discretion satisfied that at the death of the deceased the hospital had not been taken over by the state or local authority (as in *Dundee General Hospitals v Walker [1952] 1 All ER 896*);

(*d*) discretionary trusts where the trustee or some other person is under a duty to select from among a class of beneficiaries those who are to receive and the proportions in which they are to receive income or capital of the trust property.

A power in category (*a*) above can be released by the donee; for an example see *Re Mills [1930] 1 Ch 654*. A power in any of the other three categories cannot be released.

Release

Express power

28.6 If the trust instrument contains an express provision entitling a donee of a power to release it, then the power is capable of release by virtue of that express provision.

Statutory power

28.7 The *Law of Property Act 1925, s 155* provides that a person to whom any power, whether coupled with an interest or not, is given may by deed release, or contract not to exercise, the power. The side note refers to 'release of powers simply collateral'. A power 'simply collateral' is a power given to a person who has no interest in the property over which the power is given, although the section in terms applies whether or not the power is coupled with an interest. However, despite its wide wording, it appears that the section does not apply to a power coupled with a duty (*Re Eyre (1883) 49 LT 259*).

Effecting a release

28.8 A release may be effected in a number of ways. An express release may be by a deed of release or by a contract not to exercise the power. An implied release may be by any dealing with the property by the donee of the power which is inconsistent with its further exercise (see *Re Courtauld's Settlement [1965] 2 All ER 544n* where a variation would have the effect of extinguishing a power of appointment). In the case of a variation, if any doubt might arise, the fact of release should be recited in the deed or in the order (as in *Re Christie Miller's Settlement Trusts [1961] 1 WLR 462*).

Unless the trust instrument otherwise provides, a release may be effected in respect of one or some only of a class or in respect of part only of the trust property (*Re Evered [1910] 2 Ch 147*; *Re Brown's Settlement [1939] Ch 944*).

Release by variation

28.9 If trustees have power to vary a settlement and do so in a way which is inconsistent with the continuation of a power of appointment, then the same is impliedly released (*Muir v IRC [1966] 1 WLR 1269*). Similarly, where trustees had power to appoint capital upon trust and did so on identical trusts to those in the settlement, save that, for fiscal reasons, they excluded the wife or widow of the settlor from the class of objects, the appointment was effective to exclude the wife or widow from the specified class (*Blausten v IRC [1972] Ch 256*).

Release by the object of a discretion

28.10 A person who is an object of a discretion may by release for valuable consideration or under seal exclude himself as an object of the discretion (*Re Gulbenkian's Settlement Trusts (No 2) [1970] Ch 408*). In that case, the court was considering a release for valuable consideration and reserved the position on whether a different result might have followed if the release had been a voluntary release not under seal.

Care must be taken in drafting any document intended to effect a release of a power of appointment. In *IRC v Cookson [1977] 2 All ER 331*, the settlor had settled certain property on himself for life and thereafter on successive interests. By a deed of release the settlor surrendered his life interest:

> '... to the intent that the said life interest shall forthwith be merged and extinguished in the capital of the trust fund and that the trustees shall

> stand possessed of the released property upon the trusts declared by the trust instrument as if the [settlor] were dead'.

The trust instrument also contained a provision entitling the trustees during the lifetime of the settlor to appoint all or part of the trust property to him. If that discretion remained alive, then the settlor was liable for income tax on the trust income. It was held that although the deed of release of the life interest accelerated the subsequent interests, it did not operate to extinguish the trustees' discretion to apply property for the taxpayer's benefit.

Chapter 29

Power to Apply to the Court – the Surrender of Discretion to the Court

Introduction

29.1 A trustee is not obliged to run any risks in connection with the conduct of his trusteeship. Where there is conflict with some or all of the beneficiaries, or a real doubt over whether a course of action is authorised or (being authorised) a proper course of action for the trustees to take, the trustee is entitled to apply to the court for guidance or for directions. The matter is considered in connection with administrative powers (see CHAPTER 21: TAKING ADDITIONAL ADMINISTRATIVE POWERS OR SURRENDERING OR RELEASING POWERS) and precisely the same considerations apply with regard to issues of doubt or conflict arising over dispositive powers.

Apart from situations where there is uncertainty or a dispute over the trustee's powers, a trustee may wish to have the court's approval of a decision or a course of action, which the trustee has made or wishes to pursue, i.e. to have the court's blessing on the trustee's own judgement.

Categories of application

29.2 In *Marley v Mutual Security Merchant Bank and Trust Co Ltd [1991] 3 All ER 198* (a judgment of the Privy Council), it appeared to be suggested that a trustee who seeks the approval of the court to the exercise of his discretion about the propriety of any contemplated course of action in the exercise of his fiduciary duties necessarily surrenders his discretion to the court. However, in *Public Trustee v Cooper [2001] WTLR 901* the differing nature of applications to the court was set out in more detail and, citing from an unreported case heard in chambers, four categories of application were identified. The distinction between the different categories is important both in respect of the substantive question whether the trustees have surrendered their discretion (see 29.8 below) and as to whether a matter should be heard in open court or in private.

The four categories

29.3 The four categories of application identified in *Public Trustee v Cooper [2001] WTLR 901* are:

1. to determine whether some proposed cause of action is within the trustees' powers;
2. to determine whether the proposed course of action is a proper exercise of the trustees' powers, where there is no real doubt as to the nature of the trustees' powers and the trustees have decided how they want to exercise them but, because the decision is particularly momentous, the trustees wish to obtain the blessing of the court for the action on which they have resolved and which is within their powers;
3. the surrender of discretion properly so called;
4. where the trustees have taken action and that action is attacked as being either outside their powers or an improper exercise of their powers.

The court made clear the paradigm nature of the classification; there might be variations within each category and an application might straddle more than one category. There was no 'bright line distinction' between the case in which the trustees surrender their discretion and the case where they do not. Even where the discretion was surrendered it was important to be clear about the extent to which it was surrendered. For example, trustees might be agreed that special circumstances justified a sale of private company shares but the trustees were divided whether in fact a sale was desirable; the court would not necessarily revisit the question whether special circumstances did in fact exist.

Category 1 applications

29.4 Where there is doubt as to the extent of a trustee's powers, it is ultimately a matter of construction of the trust instrument or statute (or both). The matter then falls to be determined like any other point of construction in open court after hearing argument from both sides. Examples are *Pilkington v IRC [1964] AC 612*; *Re Hampden's Settlement Trusts [2001] WTLR 195*.

Category 2 applications

29.5 In making the categorisation in *Public Trustee v Cooper [2001] WTLR 901*, examples given were a decision to sell the family estate or a controlling interest in a family company. In such circumstances there is no doubt at all of the trustees' powers or what they want to do but they think it prudent to have the court's blessing on such a momentous decision. In that case, there is no question of surrendering the discretion and it was observed that it would be most unlikely that, in the absence of special circumstances, the court would accept a surrender of discretion on a question of that sort, where the trustees are *prima facie* in a much better position than the court to know what is in the best interests of the beneficiaries. The application would be heard in private. In this sort of case the court must be satisfied of three matters:

- that the trustees had in fact formed an opinion on the issue;
- that the opinion formed was one at which a reasonable body of trustees properly instructed as to the relevant clause could properly have arrived;
- that opinion was not vitiated by any conflict of interest which had or might have had an effect on the decision which they took.

Category 3 applications

29.6 A surrender of discretion, properly so called, will be accepted for good reason. Examples given were: the trustees are deadlocked (i.e. honestly deadlocked where the matter could not be resolved by removing one trustee rather than another) or the trustees are disabled by a conflict of interest. The application would be heard in private and might or might not (depending on the circumstances) involve adversarial argument. For example, see *Abacus (CI) Ltd v Hirshfield (2002) 4 ITELR 686.*

Category 4 applications

29.7 By their nature these involve hostile litigation which is heard and decided in open court. An example is *Re Pauling's Settlement Trusts [1964] Ch 303.*

Surrender of discretion

29.8 In any matter where a trustee has a discretion, the trustee may in a proper case go further than simply ask for directions: he may surrender his discretion to the court. The court is not obliged to accept the surrender. If it does so, then the court exercises its independent judgment. An example of the court declining to accept a surrender of discretion is *Re Allen-Meyrick's Will Trusts [1966] 1 WLR 499*. In that case, the trustees had a discretion to apply income of the trust fund for the maintenance of the testatrix's husband and the trustees were unable to agree on the extent to which they ought to exercise that discretion, the husband being an undischarged bankrupt. The court held that the discretion was of a kind which essentially depended on circumstances that would or might change from year to year or from period to period. The discretion was, therefore, not one which could be exercised in advance and not one that the trustees could surrender to the court in advance. If the trustees found themselves in difficulty on any particular occasion, then they could come to the court to resolve that difficulty.

Procedure

Generally

29.9 An application is made by a claim form issued under Part 8 of the Civil Procedure Rules. The provisions of RSC Ord 85 still apply but will be replaced by CPR Part 64 and a new Practice Direction from 2 December 2002.

Proceedings are in the first instance listed in private so that the order made and other documents among the court records (apart from the claim form) will not be open to inspection by third parties without the court's permission. If confidentiality of the direction sought is important (for example, the directions relate to actual proposed litigation with a third party who could find out what directions the trustees are seeking through access to the claim form under CPR r 5.4) the statement of the remedy sought, for the purposes of CPR r 8.2(b), may be expressed in general terms. In that case, the trustees must state specifically in the evidence (which will not be open for inspection without the court's permission) what it is that they seek to be allowed to do.

RSC Ord 85 r 3 specifically provides that all persons who have or might have a beneficial interest or claim against the estate or trust need not be parties to the proceedings and the Practice Direction deals with the need to consider at an early directions hearing what beneficiaries need to be joined or given notice of the proceedings (see CPR r 19.8A). In the case of a trust with numerous beneficiaries, it may be possible to have a representative defendant for each class of beneficiary appointed under CPR r 19.7. After 2 December 2002 a claim may be brought by or against trustees, executors or administrators in that capacity without adding as parties any persons who have a beneficial interest in the trust or estate; a judgment or order given or made in the claim will bind the beneficiaries unless the court orders otherwise in the same or other proceedings (CPR r 19.7A).

The court will always consider whether it is possible to deal with the application on paper without a hearing.

Paragraph 7.1 of the Practice Direction states that the trustees' evidence should be given by witness statement and that in order to ensure that, if directions are given, the trustees are properly protected by the order, they must ensure full disclosure of all relevant matters, even if the case is to proceed with the participation of beneficiaries as defendants. As it was put by Templeman J in *Midland Bank Trust Co Ltd v Green [1980] Ch 590 at 606*:

> '... it is necessary for the trustees to open their hearts to the judge and tell him exactly what the action looks like. The judge is acting in some respects as though he were the adviser and trustee giving guidance'.

Where an application has arisen out of a dispute between beneficiaries, it is not for the trustees to take sides in that dispute and whilst ensuring full disclosure of all relevant matters the trustees should take care to couch that disclosure in neutral terms. A partisan intervention which is unsuccessful is likely to be penalised in costs (*Alsop Wilkinson v Neary [1996] 1 WLR 1220 at 1225*).

Paragraph 7.7 of the Practice Direction requires the evidence to explain what, if any, consultation there has been with beneficiaries, and with what result. In respect of preparation for an application for directions in respect of litigation, there is specific guidance, which is dealt with in CHAPTER 16: POWER TO COMPROMISE AND POWER TO LITIGATE.

Prospective costs orders

29.10 The current Practice Direction incorporates a Practice Statement issued in May 2001 relating to prospective costs orders in respect of the costs of applications by trustees or beneficiaries or other persons concerned in relation to the administration of a trust, including questions of construction, questions relating to the exercise of powers conferred by the trust, or questions as to the validity of the trust.

Where trustees have power to agree to pay such costs and exercise that power, an order is not required and the trustees are entitled to recover out of the trust fund any costs which they pay pursuant to the agreement they have made in exercise of such power. However, where trustees do not have, or decide not to exercise, a power to make such an agreement, the trustees or the party concerned may apply to the court at any stage of the proceedings for an order that the costs of any party to the application should be paid out of the fund. This is called a 'prospective costs order'. The Practice Direction includes a model form of order.

The Practice Statement states that the court will always consider whether it is possible to deal with such an application for a prospective costs order on paper without a hearing and in an ordinary case would expect to be able to do so. If the trustees consider that a hearing is needed for any reason, they should say so and explain why in their evidence. If any party to the application or any other person interested in the trust fund considers a hearing necessary (for instance, because he wishes to oppose the making of a prospective costs order) this should be stated and the reasons explained in that person's evidence or a letter to the court. If a court is minded to refuse the application on a consideration of the papers alone, the parties will be notified and given the opportunity within a stated time to ask for a hearing.

The Practice Statement makes clear that evidence in support of an application for a prospective costs order should be given by witness statement. The trustees and the applicant (if different) must ensure full disclosure of the relevant matters to show that the case is one which falls within the category of case where a prospective costs order can properly be made. The model form of order is designed for straightforward cases and may be adapted when necessary.

Construction issues

Paper applications to the court

29.11 If the trustees face a difficulty arising out of an issue of construction only and the trustees wish to clarify the extent of their powers (i.e. a Category 1 application – see 29.4 above), it may be possible to make use of the procedure for a paper application to the court. The procedure is set out in the Chancery Guide paragraphs 26.36 to 26.41 and is described in CHAPTER 21: TAKING ADDITIONAL ADMINISTRATIVE POWERS OR SURRENDERING OR RELEASING POWERS. In brief, if an opinion in writing has been obtained from a person who has a ten-year High Court qualification on that question by the personal representatives or trustees under the will or trust, the High Court may, on the application of the personal representatives or trustees and without hearing argument, make an order authorising those persons to take such steps in reliance on the said opinion as are specified in the order. [*Administration of Justice Act 1985, s 48*]. The section provides that the court shall not make an order it if appears that a dispute exists which would make it inappropriate for the court to make an order without hearing argument.

Benjamin orders

29.12 If a fund is otherwise ready for distribution but there is difficulty in determining whether a beneficiary is alive or dead, or whether all the members of a class have been traced, a trustee or personal representative may apply for a Benjamin order (*Re Benjamin [1902] 1 Ch 723*). On such an application the court is asked to sanction distribution on the footing that a particular state of affairs is correct, e.g. that 'A' is dead or that the known members of a class represent all the members entitled. If, following a distribution, it subsequently transpires that the assumed footing was wrong, and the missing beneficiary appears, the trustee or personal representative is protected by the order from an action for breach of trust; however, the beneficiary may follow his or her share into the hands of the beneficiaries who have been overpaid.

Another example would be an order of the court that the trustees proceed on the footing that a given person could have no, or no further, children.

Such an order avoids the inconvenience of the rule of construction that (perpetuity questions apart) the court proceeds on the basis that every individual remained capable of having a child until the end of his or her life (*Figg v Clarke [1997] 1 WLR 603*). Such an order would only be made if there were no beneficiaries living who might be prejudiced thereby.

If the sum involved is small, then it may be more economic to cover the risk of a missing beneficiary by insurance (*Re Evans [1999] 2 All ER 777*).

Charities

Concurrent jurisdiction

29.13 The Charity Commissioners have concurrent jurisdiction with the High Court in respect of charity matters. In particular, the Commissioners may, on the written application of any charity trustee, give him their opinion or advice on any matter affecting the performance of his duties as such. [*Charities Act 1993, s 29*].

A charity trustee acting in accordance with the opinion or advice of the Commissioners given under *section 29(1)* with respect to the charity shall be deemed, as regards his responsibility for so acting, to have acted in accordance with his trust unless when he does so either:

- he knows or has reasonable cause to suspect that the opinion or advice was given in ignorance of material facts; or
- the decision of the court has been obtained on the matter or proceedings are pending to obtain one.

Ex-gratia payments and schemes

29.14 Other important powers vested in the Commissioners are the power under the *Charities Act 1993, s 27* to authorise ex-gratia payments and the power under *section 16* to authorise schemes. Either power may provide a practical solution to a difficulty or dilemma facing a charity trustee.

Under *section 27*, the Commissioners may by order exercise the same power as is exercisable by the Attorney-General to authorise the charity trustees of a charity:

(*a*) to make any application of property of the charity; or

(*b*) to waive to any extent, on behalf of the charity, its entitlement to receive any property in a case where the charity trustees:

  (i) otherwise have no power to do so; but

  (ii) in all the circumstances regard themselves as being under a moral obligation to do so.

The power conferred on the Commissioners is exercisable by them under the supervision of and in accordance with such directions as may be given by the Attorney-General and any such directions may, in particular, require the Commissioners in such circumstances as are specified in the directions to:

- refrain from exercising that power; or
- consult the Attorney-General before exercising it.

The Commissioners can, in any event, refer an application to the Attorney-General if they consider it would be desirable for the application to be entertained by the Attorney-General rather than by the Commissioners. If the Commissioners determine an application by refusing to authorise charity trustees to take any action, that refusal shall not preclude the Attorney-General on an application subsequently made to him by the trustees, from authorising the trustees to take that action.

Under the *Charities Act 1993, s 16*, the Commissioners have concurrent jurisdiction with the High Court for certain purposes. Included in those purposes is the establishment of a scheme for the administration of a charity. Furthermore, where the court directs a scheme for the administration of a charity to be established, the court may by order refer the matter to the Commissioners for them to prepare or settle a scheme in accordance with such directions (if any) as the court sees fit to give, and any such order may provide for the scheme to be put into effect by order of the Commissioners without further order of the court. The Commissioners do not have jurisdiction under *section 16* to try or determine the title at law or in equity to any property as between the charity or a trustee for a charity and a person holding or claiming the property or an interest in it adversely to the charity, or to try or determine any question as to the existence or extent of any charge or trust. *Section 16* sets out who may make an application for a scheme and includes provisions for appeal.

Chapter 30

Power to Vary Trusts

Introduction

30.1 Prior to the *Variation of Trusts Act 1958*, there was a very limited jurisdiction to vary a trust. If all the beneficiaries were adult and of full capacity they could agree to bring a trust to an end or, with the consent of the trustees, to vary the terms of the trust (*Saunders v Vautier (1841) 4 Beav 115*). The court had an inherent jurisdiction but this was limited to four situations (see *Chapman v Chapman [1954] AC 429 at 445*, per Lord Simonds LC):

- to change the nature of an infant's property from real to personal estate and vice versa;
- to provide maintenance for an infant, and, more rarely, for an adult beneficiary;
- to direct, as a means of 'salvaging' the trust, the carrying out of some transaction unauthorised by the trust instrument; and
- to sanction a compromise by an infant in a suit to which he was a party.

Beyond this, however, the courts had no common law jurisdiction to effect or permit a variation in the terms of a trust. In particular, they had no common law power to alter a trust merely because the alteration was thought to be advantageous to an infant beneficiary. The lacuna was highlighted by the decision of the House of Lords in *Chapman v Chapman [1954] AC 429*, following which the *Variation of Trusts Act 1958* was enacted, giving the courts a wide statutory power to approve proposals for the variation of terms of trusts.

Variation of Trusts Act 1958

Key provisions

30.2 The key provision of the 1958 Act is *section 1(1)*:

> 'Where property, whether real or personal, is held on trusts arising, whether before or after the passing of this Act, under any will,

settlement or other disposition, the court may if it thinks fit by order approve on behalf of—

(*a*) any person having, directly or indirectly, an interest, whether vested or contingent, under the trusts who by reason of infancy or other incapacity is incapable of assenting, or

(*b*) any person (whether ascertained or not) who may become entitled, directly or indirectly, to an interest under the trusts as being at a future date or on the happening of a future event a person of any specified description or a member of any specified class of persons, so however that this paragraph shall not include any person who would be of that description, or a member of that class, as the case may be, if the said date had fallen or the said event had happened at the date of the application to the court, or

(*c*) any person unborn, or

(*d*) any person in respect of any discretionary interest of his under protective trusts where the interest of the principal beneficiary has not failed or determined,

any arrangement (by whomsoever proposed, and whether or not there is any other person beneficially interested who is capable of assenting thereto) varying or revoking all or any of the trusts, or enlarging the powers of the trustees of managing or administering any of the property subject to the trusts:

Provided that except by virtue of paragraph (*d*) of this subsection the court shall not approve an arrangement on behalf of any person unless the carrying out thereof would be for the benefit of that person'.

The function of the court

30.3 Where an application is made to the court under the *Variation of Trusts Act 1958*, the function of the court is not to vary the trust but to approve the variation on behalf of those beneficiaries, or possible beneficiaries, who are unable to give a valid consent themselves. The court has no jurisdiction under the Act to approve a variation on behalf of an adult of full capacity – it is for that beneficiary to give his own consent. The matter was explained thus by Lord Reid in *IRC v Holmden [1968] AC 685 at 701*:

'Under the *Variation of Trusts Act* the court does not itself amend or vary the trusts of the original settlement. The beneficiaries are not bound by variations because the court has made the variation. Each beneficiary is bound because he has consented to the variation. If he was not of full age when the arrangement was made he is bound because the court was authorised by the Act to approve of it on his behalf and did so by making an order. If he was of full age and did not in fact consent he is not affected by the order of the court and he is not bound. So the arrangement must be regarded as an arrangement made by the beneficiaries themselves. The court merely acted on behalf of or as representing those beneficiaries who were not in a position to give their own consent and approval'.

How the variation is effected

30.4 It would logically follow from the statement of Lord Reid as to the function of the court, that the variation was effected not by the order of the court but by the agreement to which the adults had consented and which the court had approved on behalf of those unable to consent and that the agreement should be in a form that satisfied *section 53(1)(c)* (which regulates a disposition of an equitable interest or trust). This was the view of Megarry J in *Re Holt's Settlement [1969] 1 Ch 100*. However, since *Re Hambleden's Will Trusts [1960] 1 WLR 82*, it had been assumed that the court order itself effected the variation and that no signed writing was, therefore, required from the adult beneficiaries. Although Megarry J did not find compelling the arguments of counsel in support of that assumption, as a matter of practical convenience and given the practice which had been established, he ruled that an arrangement approved by the court under the *Variation of Trusts Act 1958, s 1* was effective, without more, to vary or revoke the terms of the trust.

Jurisdiction

30.5 Subject to one qualification in the case of patients, the jurisdiction under the *Variation of Trusts Act 1958* is exercisable by the High Court (*section 1(3)*). The county court has jurisdiction up to the amount of the county court limit (presently £30,000) (*County Courts Act 1984, s 23*). A wider jurisdiction cannot be conferred by agreement (*section 24(3)*).

Persons who are infants or are otherwise incapacitated

30.6 Under the *Variation of Trusts Act 1958, s 1(1)(a)*, the court may consent on behalf of anyone with a direct or indirect interest under the trust, vested or contingent, who is incapable of assenting by reason of infancy or other incapacity. In the case of a person who is a patient within the meaning of *Part VII* of the *Mental Health Act 1983*, the Act requires the Court of Protection to determine whether or not the arrangement would be for the benefit of the patient, not the court before which the arrangement comes for approval; 'benefit' for a patient has the same meaning in the context of a variation as it has in the context of an advancement and it is not always necessary that there must be some element of financial advantage to the patient (*Re CL [1969] 1 Ch 587*). The court approving the arrangement can deal with the costs incurred in the Court of Protection as well as the costs in the High Court (*Re Sanderson's Settlement Trusts [1961] 1 WLR 36*).

Persons (whether or not ascertained) who may in the future become entitled to an interest under the trusts

30.7 An example of a person on whose behalf the court can consent under the *Variation of Trusts Act 1958, s 1(1)(b)* is a potential widow of a life tenant (other than a current wife) for it is possible that the life tenant might in future remarry (*Re Lister's Will Trusts [1962] 1 WLR 1441*).

The potentially very wide ambit of this class is substantially narrowed by the qualification. This excludes from the ambit of the court's jurisdiction any person of a specified description, or a member of a specified class, who may become entitled on the happening of a future event, if that person would be of that description or of that class if the future event had happened at the date of the application to the court. So, for example, where a class comprised the persons entitled to the life tenant's estate if she died intestate, two cousins who would have taken had the life tenant died on the date of the application to the court, and who were *sui juris*, were excluded from *section 1(1)(b)*; it was for those cousins themselves to give or withhold their consent (*Re Suffert's Settlement [1961] Ch 1*). In the case of Re *Lister*, a *current* wife of the life tenant would not have been *within section 1(1)(b)* because, if the life tenant died on the date of the application, she would have satisfied the description as his widow. The court has no jurisdiction to approve an arrangement on behalf of persons who satisfy the qualification simply because it is impracticable to obtain their consent or because their interests are remote (*Knocker v Youle [1986] 1 WLR 934* – where there were numerous cousins in Australia, whose interests were dependent on a contingency, or, if they were under 21, a double contingency, and were in any event capable of being defeated by the exercise of a power of appointment).

In *Re Suffert's Settlement [1961] Ch 1*, Buckley J held that, for the purposes of the proviso, 'the date of the application to the court' means the date on which the application to vary was issued.

Persons who are as yet unborn

30.8 Although, for the purpose of construction, every individual is treated as remaining capable of having a child until the end of his or her life, the *Variation of Trusts Act 1958, s 1(1)(c)* is concerned with events which would or might happen. It was thus not appropriate to use the Act to cover the contingency of a woman aged over 70 having a child; the trustees could perfectly properly distribute the fund on the footing that a woman of that age would not have another child (*Re Pettifor's Will Trusts [1966] Ch 257*).

Persons with discretionary interests under protective trusts, where the interest of the principal beneficiary has not yet failed or determined

30.9 *Section 1(2)* of the *Variation of Trusts Act 1958* defines 'protective trusts' as those trusts specified in the *Trustee Act 1925, s 33(1)(i) and (ii)* 'or any like trusts'. In *Re Wallace's Settlements [1968] 1 WLR 711 at 716*, Megarry J held that 'like' for these purposes meant similarity in substance without any need for similarity in form or detail or wording. The terms 'principal beneficiary' and 'discretionary interest' have corresponding meanings. Although not expressly stated, the words 'any person' in *section 1(1)(d)* include an unascertained or an unborn person (*Re Turner's Will Trusts, Bridgman v Turner [1960] Ch 122*).

In short, a protective trust is one under which the principal beneficiary enjoys the income during the trust period or until he or she does anything, or suffers anything to be done, or an event occurs other than an advance under any statutory or express power, whereby he or she would be deprived of the right to receive the income or any part thereof; thereafter, the income is held during the trust period on a discretionary trust for the maintenance, support or benefit of a class of beneficiaries, including the principal beneficiary.

Persons in this category are treated differently to persons in any other category in that the court may approve an arrangement on behalf of any person in respect of any discretionary interest of his under the protective trust notwithstanding that it would not be for his benefit. However, if an event causing the interest to fail or determine has occurred, then *section 1(1)(d)* ceases to have effect and the matter will fall within one or other of *subsections (a)–(c)*, and benefit must be shown.

What 'arrangement' may the court approve?

30.10 It is clear from the wording of the *Variation of Trusts Act 1958* that 'arrangement' is to be given a wide meaning – the court can, in effect, be asked to approve any proposal for varying or revoking the trusts, or adding to (although not reducing or restricting) the trustees' administrative powers. Thus, as Lord Evershed MR observed in *Re Steed's Will Trusts [1960] Ch 407 at 419*:

> 'I think that the word "arrangement" is deliberately used in the widest possible sense so as to cover any proposal which any person may put forward for varying or revoking the trusts'.

However, the words are not without limit, and the court has no jurisdiction to approve a complete resettlement. In *Re T's Settlement Trusts [1964] Ch 158 at 162*, the infant beneficiary was due to receive her share in possession on attaining the age of 21, but it was said that she was irresponsible and immature and that the immediate possession of a large sum of money would be detrimental to her. The court was initially asked to approve an arrangement under which the infant's share would be transferred to new trustees to hold on protective trusts for her life with remainder to her issue and a further gift over in default. The court took the view that this arrangement went too far. It did, however, approve a revised arrangement under which the infant's entitlement was deferred for a period, with her having a protected life interest meanwhile.

The dividing line between a variation on the one hand and a wholesale resettlement on the other must be drawn by looking at the substance of the arrangement rather than the form in which it is presented (*Re Holt's Settlement [1969] 1 Ch 100 at 117*). In *Re Ball's Settlement Trusts [1968] 1 WLR 899 at 905*, Megarry J articulated the test for identifying a permissible variation in a borderline case as follows:

> 'If an arrangement changes the whole substratum of the trust, then it may well be that it cannot be regarded merely as varying that trust. But if an arrangement, while leaving the substratum, effectuates the purpose of the original trust by other means, it may still be possible to regard that arrangement as merely varying the original trusts, even though the means employed are wholly different and even though the form is completely changed'.

In that case, the settlor had a life interest in a trust fund and a testamentary power to appoint (among others) to each of his two named sons, the fund to go to the two sons absolutely in default of appointment (with a proviso in respect of their issue). The settlor sought a variation whereby his life interest, the testamentary power of appointment and the provisions for those entitled in default of appointment were all swept away, to be replaced by life interests for the two sons (each in one half of the trust fund) with remainder to their children absolutely, in certain events. Other objects of the power were excluded from the arrangement and they were not made parties to the proceedings (this difficulty was removed by the settlor expressly releasing his power of appointment, so that the court no longer had to consider the interests of possible appointees under the power). Megarry J accepted that the proposal involved new provisions very different from the old saying that:

> '... all that remains of the old trusts are what I may call the general drift or purport, namely, that a moiety of the trust fund is to be held on certain trusts for each son and certain of his issue'.

However, he was satisfied that the differences between the old and new provisions were differences of detail rather than substance, and the arrangement was approved by him.

Parliamentary trusts

30.11 By virtue of *Variation of Trusts Act 1958, s 1(5)*, 'trusts affecting property settled by Act of Parliament' cannot be varied under the Act.

However, in *Hambro v Duke of Marlborough [1994] Ch 158* a variation of a parliamentary settlement was, in effect, achieved by a conveyance approved by the court under the *Settled Land Act 1925, s 64* (the powers conferred by that section not having been affected by the 1958 Act, as made clear in *section 1(6)*).

The enlargement of trustees' administrative powers under the Act

30.12 *Section 1(1)* of the Act expressly permits the making of an application thereunder for the approval of a scheme for 'enlarging the powers of the trustees of managing or administering any of the property subject to the trusts', although *section 1(6)* states that:

> '... nothing in this section shall be taken to limit the powers conferred by *section 64* of the *Settled Land Act 1925* [or] *section 57* of the *Trustee Act 1925*'.

Where an arrangement will alter both the beneficial interest and the administrative powers, an application under the 1958 Act is appropriate, but if no alteration of the beneficial interests is proposed, then it is more convenient to use the *Trustee Act 1925, s 57* (*Anker-Petersen v Anker-Petersen [2000] WTLR 581*). In the case of settled land, similar considerations would apply in respect of the *Settled Land Act 1925, s 64*.

Perpetuities

30.13 Despite the distinction drawn between a variation and a resettlement, an arrangement may take advantage of a new perpetuity period. In that respect it differs from the position which obtains when a power of advancement or a special power of appointment is exercised by advancing or appointing funds on trust (as to which see CHAPTER 27: THE RULE AGAINST PERPETUITIES). The reason is that an arrangement owes its authority not to anything in the initial settlement but to the statute and to the consents of the adult beneficiaries (*Re Holt's Settlement [1969] 1 Ch 100 at 120*).

Approval of arrangements under the Act

30.14 Many arrangements have been proposed with a view to obviating or palliating the actual or potential tax burden on beneficiaries. Not all proposed arrangements are, however, concerned with tax avoidance. So, for example, in *Re Lister's Will Trusts [1962] 1 WLR 1441* the court approved a proposal to incorporate in the will trusts the statutory power of advancement contained in the *Trustee Act 1925, s 32(1)*, and to remove certain wording from the will which rendered the interest of any widow of the life tenants liable to be defeated by an *inter vivos* direction given by her husband.

In *Re Remnant's Settlement Trusts [1970] Ch 560*, the court approved a proposal involving, *inter alia*, the removal of forfeiture provisions in a will aimed at disinheriting beneficiaries who practised Roman Catholicism or married or cohabited with a Roman Catholic.

In *Re T's Settlement Trusts [1964] Ch 158*, the court approved a (modified) proposal to postpone the date of absolute vesting of the interest of a beneficiary who was about to attain her majority but who had shown herself to be particularly immature and irresponsible.

Applicants

30.15 The Act itself makes no stipulation as to the identity of the proposer of an arrangement. Usually it will be made by a beneficiary but this is not inevitable. In *Re Weston's Settlements [1969] 1 Ch 223* the application was made by the settlor. In *Re T's Settlement Trusts [1964] Ch 158* the application was made by the parent of an infant beneficiary, although the parent had no interest under the particular fund the trusts of which were sought to be varied.

It is not normally proper for the trustees to propose a variation for their duty is to act as the watchdog for the interests of all potential beneficiaries. Trustees should not be the applicants in a variation application, unless they are satisfied:

- that the proposals are beneficial to the persons interested;
- that the proposals have a good prospect of being approved by the court; and
- that if they (the trustees) do not make the application, no one else will (*Re Druce's Settlement Trusts [1962] 1 WLR 363*).

The settlor may propose a variation even though he is not a beneficiary under the trust. Where the settlor and any other person who provided property for the purposes of the trusts to which the application relates, is still alive and not the claimant, he should be made a defendant unless the court for some special reason otherwise directs. [*RSC Ord 93 r 6* applied by *CPR Pt 50 and Sch 1* – to be replaced from 2 December 2002 by *CPR r 64.4*].

The questions to be asked by the court

30.16 When presented with a proposed arrangement, the court must ask:

(i) is the carrying out of the arrangement for the benefit of every person on whose behalf the court is concerned to approve the arrangement; and

(ii) having been satisfied as to question (i), is the court further satisfied that the arrangement is in its nature a fair and proper one (see *Re Remnant's Settlement Trusts [1970] Ch 560 at 565*).

The requirement of benefit

30.17 The proviso to *Variation of Trusts Act 1958, s 1(1)* expressly states that, except by virtue of paragraph (*d*), the court shall not approve an arrangement on behalf of any person unless the carrying out thereof would be for the benefit of that person. For these purposes 'benefit' is not confined to purely financial benefit, but can include benefit of any kind, such as educational, social and moral benefit (see *Re Weston's Settlement [1969] 1 Ch 223 at 245*). The court can approve an arrangement notwithstanding that it involves some aspects which are disadvantageous provided that the advantages outweigh the disadvantages (*Re Holt's Settlement [1969] 1 Ch 100* – where the arrangement included the postponement of the vesting of the right to capital until each child attained the age of 30 years but that financial detriment was outweighed by an acceleration of their interests in a moiety of the trust fund and anticipated savings of estate duty).

More strikingly, in *Re Remnant's Settlement Trusts [1970] Ch 560*, one group of beneficiaries (the Hooper children) had a 'real and substantial chance' of acquiring their cousins' share under the forfeiture provisions of the will trusts relating to Roman Catholicism, yet the removal of those forfeiture provisions was still held to redound to their (as well as to their cousins') benefit. Among the matters taken into account by Pennycuick J in assessing benefit to the Hooper children were the fact that the forfeiture provisions could operate to deter them from marrying someone in the future if he were a Roman Catholic, and the fact that the provisions 'represent a source of possible family dissension'.

Similarly, in *Re CL [1969] 1 Ch 587*, Cross J held that a variation which resulted in the satisfaction of a 'strong moral obligation' owed by a beneficiary could be said to be for his benefit, even if it were detrimental in purely financial terms.

Benefit to all beneficiaries on whose behalf the court is acting

30.18 The court must be satisfied (other than in a *section 1(1)(d)* case) that a proposed arrangement will redound to the benefit of *every* person on whose behalf the court is concerned to approve the arrangement. This includes unborn or otherwise non-existent beneficiaries who, in reality, are very unlikely to materialise or to take any interest under the trusts sought to be varied. However small their prospect of benefit, the court cannot ignore their interests. See *Re Ball's Settlement Trusts [1968] 1 WLR 899 at 902* where Megarry J observed:

> 'I cannot see how it could be said that it is for the benefit of a person to destroy even the smallest hope of receiving a beneficial interest if nothing is put in its place'.

However, the likelihood or otherwise of a contingency being satisfied is by no means irrelevant. A common way of dealing with a contingent interest is to determine the actuarial value of the contingent interest and to provide, in the arrangement, a vested interest in a fund which is equal to, or exceeds, that actuarial valuation. The less the likelihood of the contingency being satisfied, the smaller the actuarial valuation of that interest and the smaller the size of the substitute fund that must be provided.

In deciding whether or not the proposed arrangement is fair and proper, and suitable for approval, the court will undertake a practical and businesslike consideration of the arrangement, including the total amount of the advantages which the various parties obtain, and their bargaining strength. Taking this broad overview of the nature and effects of the proposal, the court will then ask whether, if the beneficiaries on whose behalf the court is acting had the capacities of a reasonable person, they would enter into this arrangement now, and as it at present stands (*Re Van Gruisen's Will Trusts [1964] 1 WLR 449 at 450*).

In assessing whether an arrangement is or is not for the benefit of a beneficiary, the court must look at the scheme as a whole. The consideration is not whether the arrangement is bound to confer a benefit in every event but whether, in the probable events, it is calculated to confer a benefit (*Re Michelham's Will Trusts [1964] Ch 550 at 557*). The fact that in improbable circumstances no benefit or even some loss is possible will not necessarily deprive the arrangement of that quality (*Re Druce's Settlement Trusts [1962] 1 WLR 363*).

Interests of other beneficiaries are not the court's concern

30.19 The court, in deciding whether to approve a proposed arrangement, is not concerned with the interests of beneficiaries other than those on whose behalf it is asked to approve the proposal. In *Re Berry's Settlement [1966] 3 All ER 431n* the court, when approving an arrangement on behalf of infants and unborns made clear that it was not approving the arrangement as representing a fair bargain between the tenant for life (who was to receive a sum in excess of the value of her life interest) and her adult children.

Intentions of the settlor

30.20 The fact that an arrangement, which is for the benefit of the persons on whose behalf the court is being asked to consent, would be contrary to the wishes of the settlor (or, in the case of a will trust, the testator) is not, *per se*, a ground for refusing to approve a variation. The issue is whether those wishes and intentions are relevant from the point of view of the beneficiary, or class of beneficiaries, on whose behalf the court is being asked to approve the variation.

In *Goulding v James [1997] 2 All ER 239 at 249* a testatrix had by will settled her residuary estate on trust for her daughter for life and remainder to her grandson provided he survived the daughter and attained the age of 40; if he failed to do so, the testatrix's great-grandchildren took by substitution. The arrangement proposed was that 10% of residue should be held for the great-grandchildren absolutely and the daughter and grandson should divide residue between themselves absolutely. There was evidence before the court that the testatrix did not wish her daughter to have access to capital because she did not trust her daughter's husband, and wished to ensure that her grandson did not have access to capital until he was 40, because he had not yet 'settled down'.

At first instance the judge had refused to consent to the arrangement on the basis that it was clearly contrary to the firm intention of the testatrix. The judge took the view that, although not binding, those wishes were a matter which the court could take into account. The Court of Appeal allowed the appeal. It pointed out that the intentions and wishes of the testatrix related to the beneficial interests of the daughter and grandson rather than to the contingent interests of the unborn great-grandchildren whose interests the court was concerned to protect. From the point of view of the great-grandchildren, for whom the provision represented a figure some five times higher than the actuarial value of their contingent interest, the testatrix's intentions and wishes had little, if any, relevance or weight.

A rather different case was in *Re Steed's Will Trusts [1960] Ch 407*. The testator left certain property on protective trusts for the benefit of the plaintiff for life. There was evidence to the effect that the testator was anxious that the plaintiff should not be put in a position in which she might be 'sponged upon' by one of her brothers. The plaintiff applied to vary the trusts so that the property would be held on trust for her absolutely. The court was being asked to approve the variation on behalf of a future husband of the plaintiff (who was then a spinster with no intentions of marriage). Although it seems that the point was not beyond doubt, the matter was dealt with as falling within *Variation of Trusts Act 1958, s 1(1)(d)* so that the arrangement did not have to include any benefit for the 'spectral' spouse (as a future husband was described). However, the court took account of the testator's wishes and intentions in including the spectral spouse when creating his will trusts and concluded that it should not approve the variation on his behalf.

The settlor or any other person who provided property for the purposes of the trusts to which the application relates must, if still alive and not the claimant, be made a defendant to an application under the *Variation of Trusts Act 1958* unless the court for some special reason otherwise directs.

[*RSC Ord 93 r 6* applied by *CPR Pt 50 and Sch 1* – to be replaced from 2 December 2002 by *CPR r 64.4*]. That procedural rule does not, however, imply that the court attaches any overbearing or special significance to the wishes of a settlor (*Goulding v James [1997] 2 All ER 239 at 251*).

The views of the trustees

30.21 If the trustees express a view in respect of the proposed arrangement, then the court will have regard to what they say, but it is not conclusive (*Re Steed's Will Trusts [1960] Ch 407*). The trustees should look after the interest of persons who may be affected but have not been joined as parties (*Re Moncrieff's Settlement [1962] 1 WLR 1344*).

Fraud on a power

30.22 If the arrangement has been facilitated by the exercise of a special power of appointment, then the court may require to be satisfied that the exercise of the power was bona fide. The approval of the court can be withheld on the ground that a fraud on the power is or might be involved (*Re Wallace's Settlement [1968] 1 WLR 711*). In that case the life tenant, who had a life interest on protective trusts, exercised a power of appointment in favour of her two children (thereby defeating the interests of those entitled in default) and proposed an arrangement under which the trust fund would be partitioned between them. However, evidence was filed to the effect that such an appointment had long been intended, and that the widow would receive no more than the actuarial value of her life interest had it not been determinable, and the court determined that there was no fraud on the power and approved the arrangement.

Public policy

30.23 The court, in the exercise of its discretion, will take into consideration any aspect of the trust or the proposed arrangement which may run counter to some aspect of public policy, such as a prohibition or restriction on marriage. So in *Re Remnant's Settlement Trusts [1970] Ch 560*, Pennycuick J found 'real weight' in the fact that, under the trust as created, the forfeiture provisions (under which, *inter alia*, there would be a forfeiture if a beneficiary married a Roman Catholic) would operate as a deterrent to each of the Hooper children (on whose behalf the court was being asked to approve the variation) in the selection of a husband when the time came.

Conversely in *Re Michelham's Will Trusts [1964] Ch 550*, an arrangement which included a proposal to insure against the event of either of two beneficiaries, one a bachelor and one a widower, marrying. The question arose whether such arrangements were in restraint of marriage and contrary to public policy. The court approved the arrangement despite the fact that it involved some obligations which might be said to tend to discourage either of the brothers from marrying.

Charities

30.24 In the case of charitable trusts, variation is dealt with by a cy-près scheme made pursuant to an order of the court or the Charity Commissioners. Cy-près is a substantial topic in its own right and, for fuller treatment, reference should be made to the specialist works. One of the duties of a trustee of a charitable trust is to take steps, when it is necessary for the property or some part thereof to be applied cy-près, to take the necessary steps to apply for a scheme. [*Charities Act 1993, s 13(5)*].

The object of a cy-près application is to secure that the charitable purpose is carried out as nearly as possible in the way intended whether the funds or property are held for a specific charity, for a charitable purpose or for charity generally. The need for a cy-près scheme can arise at the outset, for example where the original gift or trust is inchoate, the terms not having been adequately set out (and which, in the case of a private gift or trust, might result in the gift failing for uncertainty) or where the intended gift or trust is impossible or impracticable; or the need for a cy-près scheme can arise during the currency of a trust where supervening events make the further conduct of the trust impossible or impracticable or the original purpose of the trust could be better realised in some other way.

In the case of a gift which is impossible or impracticable from the outset, it is necessary to show that the testator or settlor had a general charitable intention rather than a specific intention to benefit a particular organisation or achieve a particular purpose in a specific way. Thus if a testator names a charity which has ceased to exist before his death, a cy-près application is possible if, but only if, the testator intended to benefit the charitable purpose rather than the specific charity (see, for example, *Re Fingers Will Trusts [1972] Ch 286*). If the testator's paramount intention is to benefit a particular organisation which in truth did not exist, or which has ceased to exist before his death then cy-près is not applicable and the gift fails: see, for example, *Re Thackrah [1939] 2 All ER 4* (gift to a non-existent 'Oxford Group'); *Re Good's Will Trusts [1950] 2 All ER 653* (gift to establish 'Good's Rest Homes' did not establish a general, as opposed to a particular, charitable intention).

An interesting application of the cy-près doctrine is *Re Lysaght [1966] Ch 191*. The testatrix expressed a wish to found certain medical studentships and for that purpose left a fund to the Royal College of Surgeons. However, she specifically excluded students of Jewish or Roman Catholic faiths. The college declined to accept the gift on those terms.

The court found that the gift was conditional on the college being able and willing to accept the office of trustee so that their disclaimer would cause the trust to fail. The court, however, also found that the direction to discriminate on grounds of faith was not an essential part of the testatrix's paramount intention which was to found the studentships. It therefore ordered a scheme that excluded the offending term. The finding that the gift was dependent on the college acting as trustee was an essential element in the reasoning. The mere fact that a person named as a trustee is not willing to act does not warrant a cy-près application of the funds if the trust is lawful and some other person can be appointed a trustee to carry it out. Also essential to the outcome was the finding that the exclusion of students on the grounds of faith was not an essential part of the testatrix's scheme; had it been otherwise, it would have defeated the paramount intention of the testatrix.

A similar problem arose in *Re Woodhams [1981] 1 WLR 493* where Vinelott J approached the matter by considering whether the modification of the prescribed scheme or project would frustrate the intention of the testator or settlor.

Cy-près is also available when a charitable purpose has subsequently become impossible or impracticable (see e.g. *Re Burton's Charity [1938] 3 All ER 90*, where a trust to augment the stipends of three or more curates was no longer adequate to do so and a scheme was ordered to make the fund available for the augmentation of two stipends only). In the case of a supervening impossibility or impracticability it is not necessary to identify a general charitable intention.

The *Charities Act 1993, s 13(1)* lays down five occasions for application of property cy-près. In summary they are:

(*a*) where the original purposes, in whole or in part:

- (i) have been as far as may be fulfilled; or
- (ii) cannot be carried out, or not according to the directions given and the spirit of the gift; or

(*b*) where the original purposes provide a use for part only of the property available by virtue of the gift; or

(*c*) where the property available by virtue of the gift and other property applicable for similar circumstances can be more effectively used in conjunction, and to that end can suitably, regard being had to the spirit of the gift, be made applicable to common purposes; or

(*d*) where the original purposes were laid down by reference to an area which then was, but has since ceased to be, a unit for some other purpose, or by reference to a class of persons or to an area which has for any reason since ceased to be suitable, regard being had to the spirit of the gift, or to be practical in administering the gift; or (*e*) where the original purposes, in whole or in part, have, since they were laid down:

(i) been adequately provided for by other means; or

(ii) ceased, as being useless or harmful to the community or for other reasons, to be in law charitable; or

(iii) ceased in any other way to provide a suitable and effective method of using the property available by virtue of the gift, regard being had to the spirit of the gift.

Section 13(1) does not affect the conditions which must be satisfied in order that property given for charitable purposes may be applied cy-près, except in so far as those conditions require a failure of the original purposes (*section 13(2)*). Where there has already been a scheme, the reference to the original purposes of the gift refers to the purposes for which the property is for the time being applicable (*section 13(3)*). In the case of purposes laid down by reference to an area, *Schedule 3* to the Act provides a schedule of permissible enlargement.

The High Court and the Charity Commissioners have concurrent jurisdiction with regard to the establishment of a scheme. Where the court directs a scheme for the administration of a charity, it may refer the matter to the Commissioners to prepare or settle a scheme in accordance with such directions (if any) as the court sees fit to give. The Commissioners must not exercise their jurisdiction except on the application of the charity, or on the application of the Attorney-General, although in the case of a charity with an income not exceeding £500 a year the Commissioners may exercise their jurisdiction on the application of any one or more of the charity trustees, any person interested in the charity or any two or more inhabitants of the area of the charity, if it is a local charity (*section 16(1)–(5)*).

Where the Commissioners are satisfied that the charity trustees ought, in the interests of the charity, to apply for a scheme, but have unreasonably refused or neglected to do so and the Charity Commissioners have given the charity trustees an opportunity to make representations to them, the Commissioners may proceed as if an application for a scheme has been made by the charity. The Commissioners may not, however, alter the purposes of a charity unless 40 years have elapsed from its foundation. [*Charities Act 1993, s 16(6)*].

If a charity cannot apply to the Commissioners for a scheme by reason of a vacancy among the charity trustees or the absence or incapacity of any of them, but the application is made by what the Commissioners consider to be an appropriate number of them, the Commissioners may proceed as if the application were an application by the charity. [*Charities Act 1993, s 16(7)*].

Before exercising its jurisdiction, otherwise than on an order of the court, the Commissioners must give notice to each of the charity trustees, except any that cannot be found or has no known address in the United Kingdom, or who is party or privy to an application for the exercise of the jurisdiction. [*Charities Act 1993, s 16(9)*].

There is an unfettered right of appeal by the Attorney-General to the High Court against an order of the Commissioners. Otherwise, an appeal must be brought within three months beginning with the date of publication of the order and with a certificate of the Commissioners that it is a proper case for an appeal, or with the leave of a judge of the Chancery Division of the High Court. [*Charities Act 1993, s 16(11)–(14)*].

A number of the provisions do not apply to an exempt charity and a list of institutions which are exempt charities is set out in *Schedule 2* to the Act. Where a charity has been established or is regulated by Act of Parliament, *section 17* makes specific provisions in respect of a scheme.

Index

para